The Failure of Land Reform i
Twentieth-Century England

CW01022855

Based on a mixture of primary historical research and secondary sources, this book explores the reasons for the failure of the state in England during the twentieth century to regulate, tax, and control the market in land for the common or public good. It is maintained that this created the circumstances in which private property relationships had triumphed by the end of the century. Explaining a complex field of legislation and policy in accessible terms, the book concludes by asking what type of land reform might be relevant in the twenty-first century to address the current housing crisis, which seen in its widest context, has become the new land question of the modern era.

Michael Tichelar is Visiting Fellow in History at the University of the West of England, UK, and author of *The History of Opposition to Blood Sports in Twentieth Century England: Hunting at Bay*.

The Failure of Land Reform in Twentieth-Century England
The Triumph of Private Property

Michael Tichelar

Routledge
Taylor & Francis Group

LONDON AND NEW YORK

First published 2019 by Routledge

2 Park Square, Milton Park, Abingdon, Oxfordshire OX14 4RN
52 Vanderbilt Avenue, New York, NY 10017

Routledge is an imprint of the Taylor & Francis Group, an informa business

First issued in paperback 2019

British Library Cataloguing-in-Publication Data
A catalogue record for this book is available from the British Library

Library of Congress Cataloging-in-Publication Data
Names: Tichelar, Michael, author.
Title: The failure of land reform in twentieth-century England : the triumph of private property / Michael Tichelar.
Description: Abingdon, Oxon ; New York, NY : Routledge, 2019. | Includes bibliographical references and index.
Identifiers: LCCN 2018009402 | ISBN 9780415793346 (hbk) | ISBN 9781315211121 (ebk)
Subjects: LCSH: Land reform–England–History–20th century. | Land use–England–History–20th century. | Land tenure–England–History–20th century.
Classification: LCC HD1333.G72 E5485 2018 | DDC 333.3/1420904–dc23
LC record available at https://lccn.loc.gov/2018009402

ISBN: 978-0-415-79334-6 (hbk)
ISBN: 978-0-367-89738-3 (pbk)

Typeset in Times New Roman
by Out of House Publishing

Contents

Preface

by Kenneth O. Morgan

For close to four centuries, ever since the Civil Wars, radical movements in England have been arguing over reform of the land – its ownership, its use, its profitability, its value as a source of wealth for the community as a whole. Similar conflicts took place in Scotland, Wales and especially southern Ireland, inflamed there by the power of nationalism. It is a central theme in our social and political history, but, unlike conflicts in industrial England, has seldom received the synoptic attention from historians that it deserves. It is, therefore, a pleasure to welcome this lucid and thoroughly researched book by my former student, Michael Tichelar. He initially wrote an excellent doctoral thesis under my supervision covering the Labour Party's policies and ideas on the land question down to the Attlee government after 1945. Here he takes a broader view of radical pressures for land reform in late nineteenth- and twentieth-century Britain, the focus of their campaigns, and the many and complex reasons for their failure to achieve significant results.

He begins with the debates of the late Victorian period, focussing on the political and economic power of aristocratic landlords during the high noon of industrialisation. The problems of the land now had identifiable human causes in the owners of great estates: they had names and addresses. Two broad demands emerged from the left at that time. There was concern over ownership, focussing on pressures for land nationalisation, much stimulated by the writings of the American single landtax advocate, Henry George, which featured in the programme of the Labour Party after the First World War. And there was the alternative demand for the taxation of the rising value of land, the so-called 'unearned increment', created not by parasitic landowners but by the advance and progress of the community as a whole. The Liberals called for the rating of site values. In the Edwardian period this reached a climax in Lloyd George's 'People's Budget' of 1909, rejected at first by a reactionary House of Lords, which included taxes on the growth of the value of especially urban land. The unearned increment was at last being confronted. To Liberals it was a supreme political and moral issue – 'God gave the land to the people' as the land campaign song had it. In fact, the taxes on land produced very little, were condemned for holding back housebuilding, and were abolished in 1920 – ironically when Lloyd George himself was prime minister.

After the First World War, the vastly increased power of the state in controlling and planning land use led to the land question changing its character. The pre-war issue of site value rating went into severe decline, like the Liberal Party, its champion. The large estates of the past were widely sold off and land-holdings transferred. Interest now turned to the role of land use in connection with town and country planning. The land was now of major interest as a public amenity (through the national parks movement) and its efficiency for productive agriculture. The former Liberal Minister Dr Christopher Addison committed Labour to policies for marketing agricultural products and guaranteed farm prices. Meanwhile Labour swung from taxes on land to state ownership to nationalisation as the Chartists had long ago demanded.

The Second World War, even more than the First, saw another thrust towards state intervention in the land market. This was partly due to the social disaster inflicted by the Luftwaffe during the Blitz, which in this one respect had some positive outcome. It also led to fierce arguments within the Churchill Cabinet in 1944 over the Uthwatt Report, which called for the widespread acquisition of land for public purposes and 75% taxes on annual increases in the site value of land. But Uthwatt proved to be more divisive than Beveridge and calls for a betterment levy on land development were set aside. So too was land nationalisation which had featured prominently on Labour's programme in the 1930s but was destined not to follow mines, railways, iron and steel into public ownership. A reason for the failure of these schemes was the opposition of Labour-led local authorities to the control of this vital resource by central government. Here wartime campaigns for radical post-war reconstruction yielded very little.

After the war, Labour remained cautious on land reform. Land nationalisation retreated as a priority for the left, and the party returned again to the issue of the unearned increment through recouping the proceeds via betterment taxation. The party turned now to the productivity of land and the need for stimulating food production and the general efficiency of the farming industry. The main energy of ministers went into town and country planning, including the development of new towns. But the surge of private property in land and housing after 1951, during years of Conservative government, committed ideologically to 'a property-owning democracy' led to a revival in ideas of land reform in the sixties. A Land Commission, set up in 1964, tried to check the profit-making by rampaging property developers (who faced much public ignominy by this time), renewed the attack on the unearned increment and gave some force to older ideas of public ownership or control by seeking to buy all land earmarked for development. But this, too, proved to be ineffective and the Conservatives abandoned the Commission on both efficiency and ideological grounds. The rights of property owners were given priority, attempts by the state to intrude into the ownership of developed land or tax its profits were rebuffed, and a thriving land market, backed by a huge mortgage market, held sway.

From the start of the Thatcher government, after 1979, attempts at land reform made little headway against an ethos which favoured owner-occupation in urban and rural areas alike, a planning system which favoured developers, and a policy of encouraging the 'Right to Buy'. Nor did challenging policies on land and housebuilding re-emerge in any strength when Labour returned to government in 1997, since the party's economic premises were largely those of their Thatcherite opponents. The older issues were still echoed in party contention – not really land nationalisation any more but proposals for taxing the massive unearned increment acquired by private property developers and surviving landowning families. These resurfaced after the collapse of the markets in 2008. But little was achieved. In Michael Thompson's vivid words, the old arguments on land use and land values simply 'dropped out of history'.

The story of land reform, up to 2018 at least, is broadly one of failure. The targets of radical or socialist critics moved on as faceless finance capitalism replaced aristocratic landowners. There were many reasons for this lack of success. Land nationalisation came up against many technical problems, notably the difficulties of land valuation and the absence of a meaningful land register. There were also cries, even on the left and in the Labour Party, that fundamental libertarian values were being attacked in so fundamental an assault on the sacred rights of property. But the story is still well worth telling, especially by so authoritative a scholar as Dr Tichelar for the light it sheds on wider themes in our recent history and the interplay it reveals between ideological arguments over the rights of property and the wider needs of the community, especially perhaps after the economic troubles to come. Britain's withdrawal from the European Union, conflict over efforts to deal with the nationwide housing shortage may see older arguments over the land rekindled. It can safely be forecast that the passionate debates spelt out here are very far from over.

Long Hanborough, West Oxon
Easter 2018

Acknowledgements

I am very grateful for the help provided by the archivists, librarians and staff of the Bodleian Library, Oxford; Churchill College, Cambridge; British Library of Political and Economic Science, London; People's History Museum, Manchester; Modern Records Centre, University of Warwick; University of Birmingham Archives; BBC Written Archives, Caversham; Museum of English Rural Life, Reading; and Nuffield College, Oxford.

I have benefited enormously from the expertise, knowledge and patience of a wide range of friends and colleagues. I owe a special debt of gratitude to Professor Kenneth O. Morgan (Lord Morgan) who supervised my PhD on 'The Labour Party and Land Reform, 1900–1945' while I was a student at the University of the West of England (1997–2000). I would also like to thank Professor Emerita June Hannam, University West of England, Nick Abercrombie and my wife Dr Linda Watts. Professor Peter Weiler, Boston College, very kindly read a whole draft of the book and provided me with very valuable feedback. I would also like to thank the editorial staff who provided sound and timely advice.

I am grateful to Oxford University Press for permission to reproduce some passages from the following articles of mine published in *Twentieth Century British History*, namely 'The Conflict over Property Rights during the Second World War: The Labour Party's Abandonment of Land Nationalisation', 15, 3 (2003); and 'Socialists, Labour and the Land: The Response of the Labour Party to the Land Campaign of Lloyd George before the First World War', 8, 2 (1997). I am grateful to Edinburgh University Press for permission to reproduce some passages from the following article of mine published in *Labour History Review*, namely 'Central-Local Tensions: The Case of the Labour Party, Regional Government and Land-Use Reform during the Second World War', 66, 2 (2001). I am grateful to Cambridge University Press for permission to reproduce some passages from the following articles of mine published in *Rural History*, namely 'The Labour Party and Land Reform in the Inter-War Period', 13, 1 (2002); and 'The Scott Report and the Labour Party: The Protection of the Countryside during the Second World War',

15, 2 (2004). I am grateful to the Agricultural History Society for permission to reproduce some passages from the following article of mine published in *Agricultural History Review*, namely 'The Labour Party, Agricultural Policy and the Retreat from Rural Land Nationalisation during the Second World War', 51, 2 (2003).

Introduction

While the question of English land reform has received a great deal of attention from historians before 1914, there has been a noticeable neglect of the subject during the twentieth century. It remains a topical issue in the academic literature on town and country planning, and for contemporary economists taking a greater interest in land as a factor in economic development. But as a matter of historical controversy it has been largely ignored. This book seeks to redress this gap and to bring the subject up-to-date. It also provides an important context for a historical understanding of the current housing crisis. It will explore the history of the conflict over landed property in England during the twentieth century and the failure to achieve a permanent solution to the question of the taxation of land values. More specifically, the book charts the various political attempts that were made by the Labour Party after 1945 to nationalise the development rights in land and locates this controversy within the wider context of land reform.

The book focuses in particular on the period from the Second World War up to the election of the Thatcher government in 1979. It was during this time that the Labour Party, which inherited from the Liberal Party a tradition of radical agrarianism, made three serious legislative attempts to capture increases in the value of land following the granting of planning permission in order to fund state-led redevelopment, such as new towns and other large-scale public housing programmes. Such attempts to capture these values were consistently repealed by incoming Conservative governments committed to the defence of private property. The book will argue that the ideological conflict over landed property was largely responsible for the failure to successfully tax land values. This generated acute political controversy at key moments after 1943, precipitated in the main by concerns about property speculation and its adverse consequences for housing and redevelopment.

This controversy over land rights has remained one of the major unresolved issues of land reform during the twentieth century. It is commonly referred to as the problem of compensation and betterment. The classic and most up-to-date definition of the issue was provided by the *Report of the Expert Committee on Compensation and Betterment*, better known as the Uthwatt Report, published in 1942 at the height of concern about property speculation in blitzed sites and the price the state would have to pay for land for post-war reconstruction. The contemporary meaning of the issue has been usefully described by one of the few historians to examine the matter in any detail as hinging on two differing and very controversial views about the role of the state in the market for land:

> The first relates to the level at which the state should *compensate* land-owners who lose their right to develop land or whose land is acquired, either by agreement or by compulsion, for essential public or community purposes. The second is whether or not, and at what level, the state should seek to collect increases (*betterment*) in land values whether they are created by the state, the landowner or the natural progression of society.[1]

In other words, how far should landowners be compensated for land acquired by the state for redevelopment and should increases in the value of land arising from general economic activity or the granting of planning permission be taxed to recover some or all of this increase for the state? For the general public and politicians, the issue was defined more in terms of the scandal over rising house and land prices and the evils of property speculation. Who should benefit from or share in the unprecedented increases in the cost of land for development and housing which has increased by nearly 1,000% since 1945 and over 400% since 1995, with the cost rising to over 70% of the price paid for a dwelling in 2016?[2]

Before the Second World War, the policy of taxation of land focused on attempts to introduce the rating of site values, a general tax on all land irrespective of whether it had planning permission for development. But after 1945 the policy became more explicitly linked to the nationalisation of development rights, rather than the nationalisation of the land itself. It was included in the Town and Country Planning Act of 1947 in order to recover increases in the value of land by a Labour government committed to positive planning and the building of a 'New Jerusalem'. During the 1950s the issue died a political death but revived again in the 1960s and 1970s following a series of speculative booms and crashes in the market for landed property, after financial institutions started to invest heavily in land. Again, Labour governments sought to tax development rights in land through a Land Commission in the 1960s and the Community Land Act in the 1970s.

The question of the rights of private landowners has become an equally controversial issue of contemporary concern as a result of the way in which

---

1 Cox, *Adversary Politics and Land*, pp. 25–6; *Report of the Expert Committee on Compensation and Betterment (Uthwatt Report) – Final*, Cmnd. 6386 (1942).
2 Ryan-Collins et al., *Rethinking the Economics of Land and Housing*, p. 8; ONS, *The UK National Balance Sheet: 2017 Estimates* (December 2017).

housing and land has increasingly been used since the 1980s as an investment within a globalised financial market and the extent to which it now underpins the performance of the economy as a whole. The problem of land values has reasserted itself as an important question of land reform to this day, made even more relevant by the soaring cost of land, the financial crash of 2008 and the current housing crisis. It has been recently estimated that 74% of the increase in UK house prices between 1950 and 2012 was the result of land price inflation, with most of this increase having taken place since the mid-1990s, creating in its turn a 'housing affordability crisis' in London and the South East and reversing the historic trend towards home ownership – decreasing from 70% in 2002 to 64% in 2013.[3] This book will explore the reasons for the failure of the state during the twentieth century to control or tax land for the public benefit. It concludes by asking what type of land reform might be relevant in the twenty-first century to address the current housing crisis. Indeed, it questions whether the housing crisis, seen in its widest context, has become the new 'land question' of the modern era?

The scope and outline of the book

By way of essential context and introduction, the book describes the way the 'land question' before 1914 occupied a central place in the political programmes of all parties and formed an important part of debates on political economy. It will identify the intellectual and radical origins of the taxation of land, especially the attempt to recover 'the unearned increment' for the community. Before the First World War, the key demand was for the taxation of land to be achieved by the rating of site values, regarded as a more politically acceptable and practicable alternative to outright land nationalisation. But after 1918, this aspect of land reform no longer attracted the level of political attention or controversy as it had done before 1914.

This book explores the fortunes of the demand for taxation of land values in England and locates it within the wider context of land reform. It will focus on the period after 1945 when it became more closely associated with the new system of town and country planning (development control) introduced in 1947. At this time, the control and price of land for building and housing was seen as a very important part of land reform in general. Where, for example, the state at a local or central level was able to purchase land at existing use value (i.e. at non-inflated prices without having to pay high levels of compensation), it was capable of introducing significant and long-lasting land reforms, such as new towns, the early creation of the green belt around London and the large-scale building of public housing. When it was unable to do this, because large increases in land values accrued to the landowner rather

---

3 Bentley, *The Land Question*; Knoll, Schularick and Steger, 'No Price Like Home: Global House Prices, 1870–2012'; Hilber, 'UK Housing and Planning Policies: The Evidence from Economic Research'.

than the state, the cause of land reform was restricted, if not denied, by the interests and power of landed property.

In the twentieth century there have been a number of political attempts to legislate different schemes of land taxation. By far the most well-known was Lloyd George's 'Peoples Budget' in 1909, when, as part of a wider land campaign, he sought to introduce the rating of site values, a tax on the unimproved value of land. This legislation was repealed in 1921 by the post-war coalition government in the name of austerity and without generating significant controversy. The attempt was repeated during the interwar period when Labour's Chancellor of the Exchequer, Philip Snowden, sought to enact the taxation of land values in his budgets of 1924 and 1931. But again, these failed to be carried out following loss of office and lack of political support. After the Second World War, Labour made three more unsuccessful attempts to recover betterment from building and development land – the Town and Country Planning Act of 1947, the Land Commission of 1967 and the Community Land Act of 1975, all of which involved the collection of a betterment levy or tax. These attempts did not seek to introduce the taxation of land values in the form originally proposed by Lloyd George (the rating of site values), which has remained largely a lost cause during the twentieth century.

However, it should be emphasised that other strands of land reform have had a much better record of success after 1918. To a large extent these reforms eclipsed the cause of taxation of land values as originally advocated by Lloyd George. Before 1914, the land question was much wider than just a matter of taxation, embracing a range of other issues. In terms of rural policy, it included policies to revive a depressed agriculture, including the promotion of peasant proprietorships and smallholdings and better conditions for rural workers; and access to and protection of common land and footpaths. In terms of urban policy, it covered housing reform, the early town and country planning movement, and especially the advocacy of garden cities. All of these policy areas were a continuation of a long-term tradition of land reform reflecting a range of different literary, political or cultural attitudes to town and country. As a result, the state acquired, during the course of the twentieth century, radical powers of access and control over land for specific purposes. This fell short of outright land nationalisation, a policy which the Labour Party supported on occasion as a long-term aim in opposition, but never sought to carry it out in practice when in government. The book will seek to account for the party's retreat from a policy of land nationalisation after 1945.

In contrast to the fortunes of nationalisation or taxation of land values, other permanent and highly successful land reform legislation has been enacted through the strengthening of town and country planning, such as development control by local authorities with powers to compulsorily purchase land for building and housing. Similar and very influential reforms include the enforcement of the 'green belt' to preserve the countryside from urban encroachment; the setting up of national agencies like the Forestry Commission to safeguard woodlands as a natural resource; the requisitioning of land for war purposes, especially during the Second World War; and not least the establishment of new towns and garden cities. Moreover, the creation of national parks and long-distance footpaths to ensure public access to the countryside can be regarded as very successful land reform measures. The National Trust, and other voluntary organisations, have also made an important contribution in protecting the countryside as heritage and have been seen by many reformers as a more acceptable alternative to land nationalisation. The state now intervenes to support agriculture and to preserve the countryside and the environment, and to control urban development, in ways that land reformers before 1914 would have regarded as revolutionary.

But the taxation of land values, which was such a vitally important element of land reform before 1914, has never been successfully enacted as central government legislation or effectively introduced at a local or regional level. The book will explore the reasons why attempts to recover land values through town and country planning failed to meet the objectives of land reformers. It will account for this failure largely in terms of the ideological triumph of landed property rights. But it will also explore in detail some of the more specific reasons put forward by historians as to why different schemes of reform, especially in the period from 1945 to 1979, were so quickly repealed after their enactment. Was it, for example, the complexity or paradoxical nature of the legislation involved, which having rejected the more radical demand of land nationalisation, had the general aim of holding down the price of land 'only to force it up as landowners withheld their property from the market'?[4] Why was town and country planning regarded as a better vehicle for recouping land values than the more traditional land reform policy of site value rating as promoted by Lloyd George and Philip Snowden? Was the failure to introduce a more long-standing system of taxation of land values a result of the adversarial nature of the ideological conflict between Conservative and Labour parties in relation to property rights?[5] Or was the history of land and property policy more tangled than a straightforward 'conflict between a Conservative Party dedicated to the defence of property and opposition parties bent on clipping the wings of property owners'?[6] Or were these attempts possibly theoretically sound but never had a real chance of success because they were so quickly repealed?[7] Did the influence and bureaucratic power of different professional groups, such as solicitors and town planners thwart or undermine attempts at reform? Similarly, did the conflict between central and local government reduce the effectiveness of different schemes to control land use in the public interest?

Chapters 1 and 2 are by way of introduction and context. Chapter 1 discusses the way in which the land question has been interpreted by historians, paying

4 O'Hara, *Governing Post-War Britain*, p. 195.
5 Cox, *Adversary Politics and Land*.
6 Perkin, *The Rise of Professional Society*, p. 383.
7 Ravetz, *Remaking Cities*, p. 67.

particular attention to the twentieth century and how the meaning of landed property changed over time. Chapter 2 traces the way land reform movements developed before 1914. It will identify the intellectual origins of taxation of land values, and in particular the idea of the 'unearned increment', and the way in which this inspired practical attempts at reform in the late Victorian and Edwardian periods, reaching a climax in the 'Peoples Budget' of Lloyd George in 1909. Chapters 3 and 4 look at the declining fortunes of taxation of land values during the interwar period. Chapter 3 discusses the impact of the war and the spread of owner-occupation, while chapter 4 examines in more detail the way other reform measures, such as the growth of town and country planning, and increasing support for land nationalisation as part of a more centralised approach to state planning, had eclipsed the more trad-itional policy of site value rating by 1939.

Chapters 5 to 8 set out the main focus of the book. They explore the con-flict over landed property from 1943 up to the election of Mrs Thatcher in 1979. This conflict resurfaced during the Second World War as a result of the impact of the Blitz on popular attitudes to land and planning and the price that the state should pay for land for post-war reconstruction. This is dealt with in chapter 5. This wartime experience helped give birth to the for-mation of a post-war settlement on land reform. But it also created acute tensions within the wartime coalition government with regard to post-war reconstruction that nearly brought the coalition to a premature end. This lack of consensus continued after the war. The consequences and nature of this conflict are discussed in chapter 6, with particular focus on the way in which the Labour Party retreated from a policy of land nationalisation in favour of seeking to recover the 'unearned increment' by nationalising the development rights in land, rather than the land itself. Chapter 7 reviews the way policy developed after 1945 and how the Labour government laid the foundations of a post-war settlement on land reform in general. But this settlement did not include the financial provisions of the Town and Country Planning Act of 1947, which sought to introduce a charge on development values and which generated an ongoing conflict over the rights of landed property. Chapter 8 describes the way this conflict continued after the election of a Labour gov-ernment in 1964 and up to 1979. It was in this period that successive Labour governments made two more serious attempts to recover the 'unearned incre-ment' from building and development land, but each attempt was repealed by incoming Conservative administrations. Chapter 9 summarises developments after the election of Mrs Thatcher in 1979 and describes the ideological and practical triumph of landed property, in particular the government sale of council housing, the promotion of owner-occupation and the prevention of local authorities from building council accommodation.

This book therefore seeks to fill a gap in our historical understanding of the way in which the land question developed during the twentieth century. It adopts a chronological approach as it is important to emphasise the intellec-tual origins of the idea of the 'unearned increment' and how this influenced policy at particular moments of controversy during the twentieth century. As a unifying issue, it may have suffered a slow lingering death after 1918 with the demise of the Liberal Party, the decline in political influence of the landed aristocracy and the spread of owner-occupation. But it resurfaced during the Second World War in a new and controversial way and expressed itself as part of a long-term conflict over the rights of landed property. The book therefore focuses on the period from 1940 to 1979 when serious legislative attempts were made to resolve the controversy. Such conflicts have been an irregular, and to a large extent, unreported feature of English history. Although such attempts at reform ultimately failed, and that is perhaps one reason why they have been neglected by historians, it is important that they are rescued for posterity as they help provide an explanation for the origins of the current housing crisis.

The book will focus on the English experience as there is insufficient scope to do justice to the radically different traditions of land reform in Scotland, Ireland and Wales, where demands for reform were part of nationalist responses to English domination. The book is based on a mix of primary and secondary sources, especially the records of the two main governing parties, the Country Landowners' Association, which represented the interests of mainly rural landowners and farmers, and the rich collection of published and specialist articles that remain largely inaccessible to the general reader.

Part I
The historical setting

1 The English land question in historical perspective

This chapter discusses the way in which the 'land question' in England has been interpreted by historians and other academics up to the present day. In doing so it seeks to restore a general discussion of land reform to a more central place in English history and contemporary political debate. The chapter will start by reviewing how the meaning of landed property has changed during the course of the twentieth century and how it has become an important aspect of the ideology supporting a property-owning democracy with important implications for land reform. This will be followed by a discussion of how historians have understood the development of land reform in England during the twentieth century, noting how they have tended to neglect the broader question of the role of land in society in the light of the remarkable spread of owner-occupation and the relative decline of the political influence of the landed aristocracy. The chapter will conclude by identifying a number of new approaches being undertaken by historians, economists and town planners, who have started to widen our understanding of land reform in the context of the current housing crisis and the financial crash of 2008.

Changing meanings of landed property during the twentieth century

The meaning of property ownership underwent important changes during the twentieth century. Such changes played a crucial part in the fortunes of different land reform movements. They have also influenced the way historians and others have interpreted developments after 1900. Landed wealth as a source of economic and political power was by far the most important aspect of property ownership before 1914. Rent income from agricultural land guaranteed significant political power for the landed aristocracy. Although large-scale landownership is still a significant part of overall wealth at the end of the twentieth century, (especially rural estates), and a surprisingly large number of aristocratic landowners have survived during the course of the century, other forms of landed property have assumed greater economic importance, especially owner-occupation and ownership of land by financial institutions investing in land as a commodity. The role of land in the economy has changed dramatically, as Thomas Piketty has demonstrated in his book *Capital in the Twenty-First Century*.[1] From being a site for agricultural production before 1900, the value of residential property has now replaced agricultural land as a result of the spread of owner-occupation. A recent economic analysis has concluded that 'the proportion of the total stock of wealth represented by housing has risen rapidly since the mid-twentieth century, while the value of agricultural land has dwindled to almost nothing as a share of GDP', and the family home has become the site of a near-universally entitled consumption good and increasingly the source of speculative investment.[2] Furthermore, the economic power of landed property has been displaced by other more intangible types of ownership such as equity, shares and bank accounts, and intellectual property in the form of patents and ownership of the airways controlling the World Wide Web.

It is no longer possible for radical reformers to identify the landed aristocrat as the sole enemy of democracy and progress, as it was before 1914. Opposition to the concentrated wealth of the aristocracy has been to a large extent dissipated by the spread of owner-occupation and the growth of the ideology of home ownership. Radical support for land reform now tends to focus on the property speculator (or finance capitalism more generally) rather than the landed aristocrat. For historians, the major difference over the course of the twentieth century has been the way other forms of rent extraction has replaced the rent income from land. By the end of the century a wider range of other owners of property extract rent from any commodity, including land that can be tradeable in local, national or global markets. Ownership of residential property is no longer confined to a small group of powerful landlords but spread throughout the population reaching a high point of 71% of total households by the beginning of the twenty-first century. While the 'bundle of rights' that make up a legal claim to ownership of non-residential land has been constrained by the state over time, especially during the first half of the twentieth century, the rights of residential owner-occupiers have been to a large extent protected in the name of a property-owning democracy and its accompanying ideology of home ownership during the second half of the century.

Since 1945, the state has intervened in a number of different ways to reduce the rights of private property owners to use or transfer land by such measures as confiscation, compulsory purchase for town and country planning purposes, taxation of land as a capital asset including its inheritance, attempts to recover the 'unearned increment' from development land, and the strengthening of the rights of leaseholders and sitting tenants over the rights of freeholders. Governments have also, for example, nationalised

1 Piketty, *Capital in the Twenty-First Century*, pp. 113–39.
2 Ryan-Collins et al., *Rethinking the Economics of Land and Housing*, p. 9 and p. 190.

different types of natural resources above and below the land surface, such as coal and oil or gas, sometimes with compensation to the owners, for example underground coal deposits in the 1930s, and sometimes without compensation, for example open-cast mining and on-shore deposits of oil and gas after the Second World War. But in other respects, the rights of property owners have been strengthened, especially during the last quarter of the twentieth century as owner-occupation and the ideology of home ownership has spread.[3] These rights have been reinforced and financial investment in owner-occupied housing now underpins the performance of the economy as a whole through the integration of property and financial markets in a global economy. Such investment guarantees the financial security of a very large proportion of the population through equities and pension funds, a process which accelerated after 1980, described by economists as the financialisation of housing and land.[4]

As a result, the interventionist powers of the state with regard to land-ownership have been progressively reduced. Town and Country planning has been diluted in favour of landowners, the rights of agricultural tenant farmers have been taken away, inheritance tax and other taxes on capital and land have been relaxed, and a strong property-owning ideology 'supported by the practice of deregulation', has developed.[5] Right of centre think tanks in favour of the free market now argue that compulsory acquisition of private land by the state is a threat to individual liberties, a strand of thinking now strongly represented in the United States and the United Kingdom, where neo-liberalism as a system of economic thought has been most dominant.[6] By the end of the twentieth century the right to private property has been reinforced by neoliberal ideology. In the powerful tradition of laissez-faire economics, land is now commonly regarded as no different to capital or labour and can be traded in a free market like any other commodity. According to this perspective, land should not be treated as a special case in the way advocated before 1914, when many reformers from across the political spectrum saw land as belonging to all members of society in common, which differentiated it from capital or labour.[7]

The situation at the beginning of the twenty-first century is very different. Land reformers who seek to challenge the primacy of private property are very much in the minority. In America there is a body of academic literature, which sees the protection of private property as a constitutional right, arguing that private ownership of land is a guarantor of liberty and the rule of law.[8]

3 Ronald, *The Ideology of Home Ownership.*
4 Ryan-Collins et al., *Rethinking the Economics of Land and Housing,* pp. 109–58.
5 Marsden, 'Property-State Relations in the 1980s', pp. 126–45; Harvey, *A Brief History of Neoliberalism.*
6 Denman, *Land in a Free Society.*
7 Offer, *Property and Politics,* pp. 1–7; Vogel, 'The Land Question: A Liberal Theory of Communal Property'.
8 Pipes, *Property and Freedom;* Ely, *The Guardian of Every Other Right.*

In terms of legal protection, the Universal Declaration of Human Rights, adopted by the United Nations in 1948, states that everyone has the right to own property alone as well as in association with others, and that individuals should not be arbitrarily deprived of it. Such rights are more understated in an English context given the absence of a written constitution. The European Convention on Human Rights defines the protection of property rights as 'the right to peaceful enjoyment of possessions', but places greater emphasis on 'the right of the state to enforce such laws ... to control the use of property in accordance with the general interest or to secure the payment of taxes or other contributions or penalties'.

In historical terms, therefore, property is a changing and dynamic concept subject to shifts in political power and changes in technology and the economy.[9] To take one crucial example, the abolition of slavery in the nineteenth century saw the almost total elimination of the concept of private property in human beings, although such practices continue to survive on a wide scale but without the ideological or political justification they once enjoyed. The 'bundle of rights' and legal obligations of owners, whether they be an aristocratic landlord, an owner-occupier or a property developer, have been subject to different levels of government intervention during the twentieth century. This book will explore such trends in relation to the ownership and control of land, with particular reference to the controversial question of compensation and betterment.

Historical interpretations of land reform in twentieth-century England

There is a considerable body of historical studies on the land question in Britain before 1914 covering England and taking into account the different nationalist experiences of Scotland, Ireland and Wales.[10] Radical opposition to the concentration of aristocratic landownership was a major feature of Victorian politics as can be seen in the campaigns to abolish the Corn Laws in the 1840s; or to achieve free trade in land and the end of primogeniture in the 1860s; or to introduce the taxation of land values and to create smallholdings and allotments in the period after 1870. Land reform reached a climax at the beginning of the twentieth century, especially in Ireland where the issue was closely associated with the demand for home rule. This controversy was serious enough in the 1880s to split the Liberal Party of its unionist supporters who joined the Conservative Party over the issue of Irish home rule. By the Edwardian period, the parameters of the

9 Ryan-Collins et al., *Rethinking the Economics of Land and Housing*, p. 223.
10 Cragoe and Readman, *The Land Question in Britain*; Readman, *Land and Nation in England*; Packer, *Lloyd George, Liberalism and the Land*; Bowie, *The Radical and Socialist Tradition in British Town Planning*; Bronstein, *Land Reform and Working-Class Experience in Britain and the United States, 1800–1862*.

land question had also expanded to include not only traditional agrarian demands, such as the creation of smallholdings and the taxation of land values, but new reforms designed to appeal to newly enfranchised voters in urban as well as rural areas. Keeping rural labour on the land was seen as a solution to urban unemployment and housing shortages in overcrowded cities as well as a means of encouraging agricultural self-sufficiency in an era of increasing international tension and anxieties. Early advocacy of garden cities on publicly owned land was also a feature of the Edwardian urban land question and helped give birth to the modern town and country planning movement.

Much attention has been given by historians to the confrontational and rhetorical manner in which Lloyd George sought to revitalise his political appeal by attacking the entrenched power and privilege of the ennobled aristocracy, most notably in his 1909 budget, which sought to introduce new types of land taxation, and in his ambitious rural land campaign launched in 1912. Such a radical programme posed a real political threat to the power of landed wealth at the time and created a constitutional crisis leading to the Parliament Act of 1911, which reduced the powers of the House of Lords to block financial legislation. At the same time, Lloyd George sought to lay the foundations for a potential progressive alliance built on a strong case for radical land reform in both rural and urban areas for the forthcoming general election scheduled for 1915.[11] The outbreak of war destroyed such plans, and severely weakened the Liberal Party which had championed land reform up to that time. It never recovered thereafter to enact such a programme.

There is a noticeable absence of published work on the history of land reform after the First World War, when as an issue of acute political controversy, it quite suddenly declined in importance for reasons that have not been adequately explored by historians. Land reform experienced a dramatic decline after 1918, and as one historian noted it 'dropped out of the history books too'.[12] This 'strange death' has been initially explained by historians as the result of a combination of both short- and long-term factors. By far the most significant long-term trend has been the declining political, if not social, influence of the landed aristocracy during the first half of the twentieth century, and the almost total disappearance of the gentry as a rural class, replaced in the main by owner-occupiers, especially farmers. Of crucial long-term importance is that land declined as a source of wealth and political power. In his survey of English landed society in the twentieth century, the historian F. M. L. Thompson, argued that the disappearance of the landed aristocracy from the parliamentary scene

---

11 Packer, *Lloyd George, Liberalism and the Land*; Gilbert, 'David Lloyd George: The Reform of British Landholding and the Budget of 1914', pp. 117–41; Bruce K. Murray, *The People's Budget, 1909/10*.
12 Thompson, 'The Strange Death of the English Land Question', p. 259.

was a straightforward result of a loss of power, influence, and social relevance, and simply records their ejection from the political machinery by the business, professional, and working-class groups with control of voting power, and thus their descent into political obscurity.[13]

But he went on to suggest that the landed aristocracy had not so much disappeared as a class but had become either practically invisible, apart from the hunting field and hunt balls, or had voluntarily withdrawn from politics. Those estates that had managed to survive the difficult economic circumstances of the interwar period were sustained thereafter by self-help, economic diversification, government subsidies and not least the rediscovery of the 'stately homes of England'.[14]

Historians have suggested a number of other reasons that also need to be taken into account. The extension of the franchise in 1918 and the mass sales of aristocratic land to owner-occupiers in the early 1920s arising from the impact of death duties, which according to contemporaries saw up to a quarter of the country change hands, was the beginning of a slow reduction in the perceived political influence of aristocratic landed wealth. The spread of owner-occupation after the war also created a significant block of middle and working-class property holders in urban areas, owning both the house and the land on which it was built. This constituted a powerful electoral interest group which would have in practice opposed any attacks on the principle of private ownership, a situation acknowledged if not encouraged by both mainstream political parties after 1918. The growth of owner-occupation, although only occupying fewer than 10% of the total acreage of the country, and the dream of widespread home ownership, made possible by the availability of mortgages, defused the issue of land reform and made it appear largely irrelevant to an electorate increasingly concentrated in urban areas. However, the question of local rates, and other taxes on property, including inheritance tax and death duties, has ensured that land taxation remains an important if somewhat hidden aspect of land reform during the twentieth century.

Other reasons also need to be taken into account. The growth of institutional landlords, such as the Forestry Commission, set up in 1919, and other government departments, especially the Ministry of Defence, and the later land acquisitions by, for example, the National Trust, distracted attention away from the concentrated land-holdings of the aristocracy and its association with political power. As a result of these trends, historians have argued that the land question no longer played such an important role in British politics after 1918. Moreover, Irish independence in the early 1920s removed the

---

13 Thompson, 'English Landed Society in the Twentieth Century, 1, Property: Collapse and Survival', p. 4.
14 Thompson, '2, New Poor and New Rich', pp. 1–20; '3, Self-Help and Outdoor Relief', pp. 1–23; 4, Prestige without Power?', pp. 1–22.

question of home rule as a highly contentious party issue in British politics and reduced the relevance and urgency of the land question after the war.

Changes to party politics were also influential. Historians have generally accepted that the rise of the Labour Party after 1918, and the way in which it replaced the Liberal Party as the main opposition, was partly responsible for the demise of land reform, although it is not always appreciated that the Labour Party continued to support different schemes of reform for most of the twentieth century. As one historian of rural policy (Burchardt) has commented, 'the politics of capital against labour replaced those of people against aristocracy. Land permanently lost the political centrality it had had between 1880–1914'.[15] Another historian (Perkin) has also drawn attention to the way in which all three major parties were divided on the question of land reform. He argued that by the end of the nineteenth century the Liberal Party had lost the support of landlords and many business men, who transferred their allegiance to the Conservatives after 1880, without gaining working-class voters and thereby losing their hope of office. Similarly, he noted that the Conservatives were not just the party of landowners: Its constituency widened during the twentieth century to include not only landowners but also developers, the construction industry and the beneficiaries of a property-owning democracy. He further pointed out that the Labour Party 'was divided between the protagonists of land nationalisation and the pragmatists who saw the best hope of solving the housing shortage and winning a fair share of capital gains created by the community, in a judicious combination of planning regulation, compulsory purchase and taxation of betterment'. For Perkin, all three parties pursued 'their vacillating policies with little regard to the constraints of the market and the powerful interest groups which could defeat government pressure by withholding land or development funds or construction skills in what amounted to a strike of capital'.[16]

Although the economic, political and social influence of the landed aristocracy declined after 1918,[17] the case for land reform did not completely disappear as an issue of political controversy. There have been key moments when the rights of private property in both town and country have been brought into question, particularly in times of war when the state played an interventionist role in land-use control. Although such challenges did not succeed in undermining the general principle of private ownership, they deserve to receive more attention from historians. The history of land reform after 1918 is not one of total failure or obscurity in the face of the domination of private property. As Perkin has pointed out, despite the divisions between the political parties and the consequent twists and turns of policy, landowners have experienced during the course of the twentieth century a significant reduction in absolute property rights as a result of town planning legislation and the

15 Burchardt, *Paradise Lost*, p. 86.
16 Perkin, *The Rise of Professional Society*, p. 383.
17 Cannadine, *The Decline and Fall of the British Aristocracy*.

nationalisation of mineral rights. 'Although they have not been constrained or penalised nearly as much as some of their critics desired or opponents threatened, there can be no doubt that the rights which landowners enjoyed for upwards of three centuries have been severely curtailed in the twentieth.'[18]

Historians have also noted that the definition of land reform is wider than just a question of tenure or taxation. After the First World War it encompassed a number of important issues relating to urban development, rural preservation and our relationship with the countryside. Two main general policy areas can be identified – the preservation of the countryside as rural heritage and the control of land use for urban development. While the former has received more attention from historians, the latter has been relatively neglected. Historians have identified the romantic idealisation of the countryside by a predominantly urban population as one of the factors driving interest in land reform before the First World War. It has been suggested that this accounts to some extent for its declining political importance after the war, when it became increasingly irrelevant to a predominantly urban electorate divorced from the land.[19] But this romantic tradition continues to exercise a significant influence to this day. During the course of the twentieth century, public interest in land changed from one of ownership to preservation of the countryside and the rescue of the 'stately homes of England'. As Burchardt has pointed out, 'the decline in practical interest in the politics of land was paralleled by an equally striking interest in aesthetic interest in the appearance of the countryside'.[20]

These environmental concerns were nascent elements of the land reform movement before 1914 but assumed greater importance during the twentieth century, as demonstrated by town and country planning legislation safeguarding the distinction between town and country, such as the green belt and the creation of garden cities and new towns. Public pressure also guaranteed access to the countryside and the setting up of national parks, long-distance pathways and areas of outstanding natural beauty. The very high levels of popular support for the role of the National Trust and other organisations in owning and preserving the landscape and rural heritage is a measure of the influence of the rural idyll in English history in particular, and the way it defined a particular view of 'Englishness'.[21]

But the urban land question, especially political attempts to recover betterment through town and country planning to counter uncontrolled property speculation, has not received the same detailed consideration by historians. It has been an important feature of the professional and specialist literature on town and country planning, but it has not been given any

18 Perkin, *The Rise of Professional Society*, p. 384.
19 Packer, *Lloyd George, Liberalism and the Land*, pp. 2–4; Offer, *Property and Politics*, pp. 328–49; Howkins, 'The Discovery of Rural England', pp. 62–88; Weiner, *English Culture and the Decline of the Industrial Spirit*.
20 Burchardt, *Paradise Lost*, p. 88; Mandler, *The Fall and Rise of the Stately Home*.
21 Matless, *Landscape and Englishness*; Williams, *The Country and the City*.

detailed consideration in either general histories of the twentieth century or in more specialist studies of housing, where to a large extent the question of landownership has been absent or ignored. But the twentieth century saw various political attempts to address the issue of ownership and control of land. The Labour Chancellor of the Exchequer, Philip Snowden, tried unsuccessfully to reintroduce land taxes in his budget of 1931, although this is seen by some historians as the last gasp of interest in an irrelevant and outdated attempt at reform no longer relevant to the circumstances of the interwar industrial crisis.[22]

But the control of land for development purposes, including the complex question of taxation of land values, became an issue of acute political controversy during the Second World War and the debate over post-war reconstruction, especially the behaviour of property developers speculating in the redevelopment of bombed sites. It resurfaced again in the town and country planning legislation of the post-war Labour government through the creation of a Central Land Board responsible for collecting a betterment levy seeking to capture increases in development land values for the community. Land reform also attracted very high levels of political and public attention in the 1960s and 1970s, with attempts to control the development of urban land in the public interest, especially in relation to housing, and to counter the effects of uncontrolled land and property speculation.[23]

The question of land reform has also been noticeably absent from histories of the Labour Party. Up to 1945, the Labour Party had supported a policy of land nationalisation, although not always consistently, continuing a strong tradition of nineteenth century agrarian radicalism.[24] On their election in 1945, the Labour government enacted town and country planning legislation, including the attempt to recover increases in land values arising from development through a betterment levy. While the Town and Country Planning Act of 1947 has remained on the statute book to this day, the betterment clauses were repealed by the incoming Conservative government in the early 1950s on the grounds that they were not only too difficult to collect but were in any case an attack on private property. Interest revived again in the 1960s and 1970s when the unprecedented property boom, and the negative repercussions of speculation in land, raised the matter of the control of land for community and public purposes, such as municipal housing. But attempts by Labour governments to reform the way land was controlled in the public interest were consistently repealed by returning Conservative administrations. The 'Right to Buy' policies of the 1980s, combined with the deregulation of financial

---

22 Skidelsky, *Politicians and the Slump*.

23 Weiler, 'Labour and the Land: From Municipalisation to the Land Commission, 1951–1971'; 'Labour and the Land: The Making of the Community Land Act, 1976'; 'The Rise and Fall of the Conservatives' Grand Design for Housing', 1951–64'.

24 Tichelar, 'The Labour Party, Agricultural Policy and the Retreat from Rural Land Nationalisation' and 'The Conflict over Property Rights during the Second World War'.

markets, buried land reform as a political demand for a generation thereafter. The Labour Party after their election in 1997 did not try and revive their previous policy of seeking to recover increases in the value of land for the community on anything like the same scale or with the same ambition. These questions have been absent from general histories of the Labour Party. But it has taken the financial crash of 2008 to put the question of land reform back on the political agenda of the party.

New interpretations of land reform in the twenty-first century

New questions are now being asked at the beginning of the twenty-first century about the control and development of land in the context of the financial crash of 2008 and the related housing crisis. Marxist commentators have started to draw attention to the role of the market in land and property in creating the crisis conditions of 2007–2009, arguing that an understanding of urbanisation and the built environment needs to be integrated into general economic theory.[25] Thus interest in land reform has revived as a response to the crisis in neoliberal economic thinking. At a local level, a range of new popular movements have emerged questioning our relationship to land, such as the 'Right to the City' movement inspired by the visionary writings of Henri Lefebvre and related occupy movements opposed to the privatisation of public space. This has widened out into a critique of the way financial institutions are trading in land as a commodity and redeveloping urban communities to the detriment of the majority of citizens.[26] Anarchist and squatting groups still challenge authority by occupying buildings, land or public spaces in opposition to threats to the environment posed by road building and other ecologically damaging schemes, such as fracking.

A number of historians have recently highlighted the way land in rural areas at the end of the twentieth century remains concentrated in large estates, the ownership of which is mostly hidden from public awareness. Such concerns continue to drive demands for land reform. A survey of 'who owns Britain' at the end of the twentieth century calculated that for England 'fewer than 5,000 families own over 13 million acres, about 40% of the surface area of the country'.[27] It has been estimated that 'landed wealth is still concentrated in relatively few hands … with an estimated 200,000 individuals (mostly comprising the monarchy, aristocracy and gentry) owning about two-thirds of the land'.[28] The same survey also drew attention to a 'rigged and overpriced land market, a farming sector maintained in existence almost wholly by

---

25 Harvey, *The Ways of the World*, p. 278.
26 Harvey, *Rebel Cities*; Vasudevan, *The Autonomous City*.
27 Cahill, *Who Owns Britain?*
28 Home, 'Land Ownership in the United Kingdom', pp. 103–8; Blinkhorn and Gibson (eds.), *Landownership and Power in Modern Europe*; Norton-Taylor, *Whose Land Is It Anyway?* Rubenstein, *Men of Property*.

public subsidy, diverted ultimately into the pockets of large landowners, and a defective Land Registry to conceal the ownership of the UK'.[29]

Other commentators have also highlighted the use and abuse of the system of landownership and its very damaging effect on housing and the environment.[30] Radical economists are beginning to take a similar interest in this question, and the role of land is being restored to a more central place in the study of economics.[31] In a similar way some radical town planners are now revisiting the land issue and advocating a programme embracing planning reform, public land acquisition, disposal and taxation.[32] The taxation of land values is attracting more public attention along with other possible ways of realising the wealth in land for the public good. Some housing reformers are advocating that council tax should be gradually transformed into a 'national property tax'.[33] Mainstream think tanks like the Institute of Fiscal Studies have come out in favour of better land value taxation.[34] Land reform in Scotland is undergoing a renewal of interest following the electoral success of the Scottish National Party and the strength of the tradition of political opposition to the concentration of landownership in the Highlands and islands.[35] Different schemes of community landownership are now becoming a realistic political possibility. Furthermore, despite the long-term failure of the smallholdings and allotments movement to achieve its original objectives of reviving small farming in England, allotments have continued to thrive as urban phenomena addressing ecological and community building concerns in the early twenty-first century, and they represent an active type of land reform, but one which does not challenge the rights of private property.[36]

Historians are now also taking a renewed interest in land reform in the context of the financial crisis of 2008. Weiler has revisited the Labour Party's support for land nationalisation in the 1960s and 1970s, seeing it largely as a response to the rampant property speculation of those decades. He has identified new levels of support for a campaign to tax land values as the best way of addressing the housing crisis in the south of England.[37] Linklater was inspired to write his recent history of global landownership in order to understand the circumstances of the economic crash and the political failure of financial regulation. His book started with him questioning the Austrian school of economics and led him in turn to examine the link between the ownership of land and the concept of liberty, which is so firmly established in England and

29 Cahill, *Who Owns Britain?* p. 215.
30 Hetherington, *Whose Land Is Our Land?*
31 Ryan-Collins et al., *Rethinking the Economics of Land and Housing.*
32 Bowie, 'Revisiting the Land Issue'; Bowie, *Radical Solutions to the Housing Supply Crisis.*
33 Dorling, *All That Is Solid*, p. 308.
34 Mirrlees et al., *Tax by Design*, p. 481.
35 Wightman, *Scotland: Land and Power.*
36 Nilsen, *The Working Man's Green Space*, p. 176.
37 Weiler, 'Labour and the Land: The Making of the Community Land Act, 1976'.

the United States. He was critical of historians who have neglected the history of landownership:

> To Nineteenth Century Whig historians who took property to be the foundation-stone of democracy and their Marxist successors who identified possession of the means of production as the central agent in shaping society and class consciousness, the impact of ownership across history was obvious. But that context is largely ignored by today's historians.[38]

In a similar way, there is now renewed interest by American historians in Henry George, and his influential book *Progress and Poverty* (1879) which played a crucial role in increasing support for the taxation of land values (the single tax) on both sides of the Atlantic during the last quarter of the nineteenth century. George's reform programme resonates in contemporary ways as a response to growing inequality and wealth disparity. One historian has set the context for a new biography of Henry George in the so-called *New Gilded Age* of poverty and inequality created in the wake 'of the great financial meltdown of 2008 and the subsequent deep economic recession'.[39]

Summary

This chapter has reviewed the way historians have interpreted land reform movements in England during the twentieth century, taking into account the way the meaning of landed property has changed in response to economic and social change. The demands of land reformers have been either partly forgotten or altogether lost during the twentieth century as a result of the decline in the political influence of the aristocracy, the ideological triumph of private property and the spread of individual owner-occupation. To a large extent interest in changing or restoring lost land rights or introducing new systems of land tenure (through, for example, squatting movements, creating allotments, small farms or land colonies, or by controlling, redistributing, publicly owning or taxing land for the common good), have tended to be regarded by contemporary mainstream thinking, including some historians, as a type of historical aberration from the forward march of a property-owning democracy and its links with ideas of freedom. Marxist theory or liberal concepts of communal property, such as natural rights, are seen as economically unviable (large farms are more economic than smallholdings), politically unrealistic or even backward-looking, pastoral or nostalgic. This book will seek to restore a discussion of land reform to a more central place in political debate at the beginning of the twenty-first century by exploring the reasons why attempts to tax 'the unearned increment' failed.

---

38 Linklater, *Owning the Earth.*
39 O'Donnell, *Henry George and the Crisis of Inequality*, p. xxiv.

2 Land reform movements before 1914

Land reform movements up to the First World War represented a wide variety of intellectual and class-based traditions responding in different ways to the long-term growth of capitalist property relationships. Land reform underpinned wider demands for radical political change, especially the campaign for the vote. It was influenced by communitarian, socialist and utopian thought, natural rights theories and classical political economy. This chapter will describe the early growth in England of a private land market creating the circumstances for the eventual triumph of private property as the primary form of land tenure. It will then outline the way that land reform movements developed from the seventeenth century in response to the loss of rights to common land and in opposition to the concentrated political power of the landed classes. The demand for land reform became a major feature of nineteenth-century politics, reaching a climax in the late Victorian and Edwardian period with the 'People's Budget' of Lloyd George in 1909, which included for the first time an attempt by central government to tax the unimproved value of land. The demand for taxation of land values survived into the twentieth century as a powerful idea. It remains a viable but untested policy to this day. But it failed to be successfully implemented for reasons that will be explored in this book.

Before 1914 the 'land question' occupied a central place in the political programmes of all parties and formed an important part of debates on political economy. The nineteenth century had witnessed a series of radical campaigns by reformers, representing both middle and working-class interests, to reduce the disproportionate political power and influence of aristocratic landowners, whose wealth was derived mainly from rent, in favour of a more equitable distribution of land in the name of economic development, greater democracy and political justice. The matter of landownership rights was a vitally important strand of this controversy. It informed much wider issues concerning urban and rural development and influenced debates about the state of agriculture, housing reform and early pressure for town and country planning. Land reform inspired movements seeking to build new communities, such as garden cities and other planned developments involving wider control of land use in the public interest.[1] While the defenders of private property argued that the state had no right to intervene in questions of ownership, and encouraged the spread of owner-occupation as a bulwark against radical social reform and potential political unrest, land reformers from a wide range of different perspectives pressed for greater state control and intervention. This political controversy manifested itself in the twentieth century as a fundamental conflict between a Conservative Party wedded to the idea of a property-owning democracy and a Labour Party committed to state control of land for public benefit, although the aim of private home ownership was adopted by both parties after 1979, representing the triumph of private property.

In the earlier part of the nineteenth century the writings of Thomas Spence and Thomas Paine continued a tradition of working-class agrarianism which was carried forward into the Chartist movement and later working-class organisations like the Labour Party. In the second half of the century, the campaigns of the Victorian philosopher John Stuart Mill and the American 'single taxer' Henry George sought to recover for the community a tax on the increased value of land but to preserve private property as a natural right. Both Mill and George argued that increases in land values were created largely by the actions of the community rather than by any effort of the landowners themselves. The profits (or the 'unearned increment') that they obtained from rent were therefore unproductive ('they spin nor neither do they weave') and they could be taxed without affecting the productive capacity of the rest of the economy. It was this body of thought which exercised a powerful influence on land reform movements before 1914 and inspired a series of political attempts to introduce taxation of land values in the late Victorian and Edwardian periods. The aim of recovering 'the unearned increment' went on to become the ideological justification for the Labour Party's attempt to tax land values in the interwar period and to nationalise development rights in land after 1945.

Political responses to the development of a private market in land

The demand for land reform was primarily a response to the growth of capitalist property relationships. Private ownership was a system of land tenure that started as early as the thirteenth century. There is strong evidence to suggest that land was increasingly treated as a commodity and that full private ownership became established much earlier in England than in some other parts of Europe, including Scotland and Ireland, where feudal relationships of communal property took much longer to disappear.[2] In England the various

---

1 Bowie, *The Radical and Socialist Tradition in British Planning.*
2 Macfarlane, *The Origins of English Individualism.*

systems of copyhold tenure, which had ensured certain customary obligations and rights to land use, were slowly replaced by the development of a private market in land. This preceded the onset of enclosure.[3] However, it is clear that after the seventeenth century, and with the beginnings of large-scale parliamentary enclosure in the eighteenth century, the majority of the rural poor lost their rights to the use of common land. What is understood as the peasantry only survived in certain areas but slowly disappeared, subject to regional variations, to be replaced eventually by a tripartite system of aristo-cratic landlord, tenant farmer and agricultural labourer.

Some land reform movements were very radical, calling for the common ownership of land and its redistribution or its taxation. Other more socially conservative movements sought to create owner-occupied smallholdings or peasant proprietorships ('Three Acres and a Cow') which were seen as a potential bulwark against more revolutionary solutions attacking private property.[4] Before 1914, working-class demands were partly driven by the vio-lent experience of agricultural enclosure or clearances, and the memories of the dispossessed rural population of their lost rights to common land. As the historian Edward Thompson has commented, 'enclosure, in taking the commons away from the poor, made them strangers in their own land'.[5] It was the loss of such customary rights that turned populist politics towards a variety of land schemes that attempted to restore pre-enclosure communities.[6]

Land reform was also an important aspect of mainstream liberal thinking before 1914, inspired by the classical political economy of Adam Smith and David Ricardo. Middle-class interests were opposed to the monopoly exercised by the landed aristocracy and their support for protectionist Corn Laws, keeping the price of bread artificially high and preventing the operation of a free market. During the nineteenth century, middle and working-class opinion converged into a widespread criticism of the system of land tenure and the political power of landowners.[7] Nationalist sentiment in Ireland and to a lesser extent in Scotland and Wales also played a role in creating intense bitterness towards aristocratic English landlords, many of them absentee. The eviction of the rural population from the land where they had common rights, in order to bring about agricultural improvements and extract higher rents, generated a long-lasting tradition of opposition to aristocratic landownership.

In a country undergoing rapid and unprecedented urban growth during the nineteenth century, the memory of a lost rural past in England became part of an urban tradition of agrarian land reform as rural workers migrated to towns and cities to benefit from better economic conditions. Thus, land

3 E. P. Thompson, 'The Grid of Inheritance', pp. 263–300.
4 Collings, *Land Reform*, p. 180 (fn); Burchardt, *Paradise Lost*, pp. 35–45 and 77–88.
5 E. P. Thompson, *Customs in Common*, p. 184.
6 Rosenman, 'On the Enclosure Acts and the Commons', *BRANCH: Britain, Representation, and Nineteenth-Century History*, Web, 20 (2014).
7 Perkin, 'Land Reform and Class Conflict in Victorian Britain', pp. 177–217.

reform became a feature of radical urban politics during the nineteenth century. There was only a limited demand from agricultural workers and tenant farmers for reform unlike in other more rural societies, such as Ireland and large parts of Europe where the population retained stronger connections with rural life, where the cities offered fewer opportunities for higher paid employment and where smaller-scale ownership was more prevalent. In England higher agricultural productivity provided at above subsistence level income to the smaller farmers, as well as wages to rural workers, tended to defuse radical demands for reform in rural areas.

The only major exception to this trend in the United Kingdom has been Ireland, where the creation of a class of small peasant farmers, enacted by a series of land acts at the end of the nineteenth century in response to insurrectionary land wars against absentee English landlords, significantly changed the pattern of land-holdings in the twentieth century. 'In 1845 the native Irish peasantry owned less than half of one per cent of the land of their country.... By 1997, 87% of the citizens of the Irish Republic ... owned 97% of the land, either as home owners or family farmers'.[8] In Scotland the tradition of land reform was also different to that in England, given the degree of concentrated ownership by landlords in the Highlands and islands and the historical legacy of the clearances, leading to high levels of emigration. But unlike in Ireland, the system of land tenure has remained broadly unchanged with aristocratic landlords still owning large estates. This continues to fuel a more vibrant demand for land reform in Scotland today in comparison to England, where the issue has not attracted the same level of public support.[9]

Most attempts to resist enclosure or demand land reform since the mid-seventeenth century failed in the face of the long-term triumph of private property rights. This was despite occasional and short-lived outbursts of resistance to the enclosure of common land.[10] It was the loss of customary rights that tended to trigger violent opposition rather than the issue of enclosure itself.[11] After 1918, landownership became more widely dispersed amongst a variety of different individual owner-occupiers and institutions. There are now very high levels of owner-occupation in comparison with some of our European neighbours, despite a recent reversal of trends, although very large tracts of rural land continue to be owned by a small group of mainly institutional landlords, including the surviving aristocracy.[12] Land is now taken for granted as an important economic commodity to be traded in a free market. In Britain, as in the majority of Western countries, the rights

8 Cahill, *Who Owns Britain?* p. 186.
9 Wightman, *Scotland: Land and Power*; Wightman, *The Poor Had No Lawyers*.
10 E. P. Thompson, *The Making of the English Working Class*, pp. 233–58; Neeson, The Opponents of Enclosure in Eighteenth-Century Northamptonshire', pp. 114–39; Neeson, *Commoners: Common Right Enclosure and Social Change in England, 1700–1820*.
11 Stevenson, *Popular Disturbance in England, 1700–1832*, pp. 51–5.
12 Rubenstein, *Men of Property*, pp. 278–302.

of private property are seen as an unquestioned part of what is understood to live in a free and democratic society, or a 'property-owning democracy', a term coined by the Scottish Tory MP Noel Skelton in the interwar period as a challenge to socialism, but building on a long-term tradition of Conservative support for small-scale ownership which emerged during the 1880s.[13] Such a belief is supported by a body of philosophical and economic thought that has developed over time to guarantee such freedoms.[14]

Thus before 1914 the concentrated nature of land tenure in England generated a tradition of ideological engagement with the question of land-ownership, and what it means in terms of democracy, natural rights and political participation. The belief that 'the earth originally belonged to all mankind in common' dominated the thinking of many British philosophers and political economists, as well as reformers representing many shades of different political opinion. It served as the starting point from which the philosopher John Locke derived the legitimacy of private property but conversely, it also 'inspired numerous radical schemes of collective ownership and redistribution of land, from the Diggers to Thomas Spence, Thomas Paine and the Owenite communities'.[15]

The controversy over land reform in England began in the seventeenth century during the Civil War. This witnessed a revolutionary if short-lived debate about natural rights, democracy and landownership, and in particular whether male non-property owners (the poor, servants, peasants, indentured workers) had the right to vote as demanded by some of the more radical Levellers in Cromwell's army. However, the triumph of the men of property was one of the primary outcomes of the Civil War. The principle of private property was in part validated by the philosophers John Locke and James Harrington, who were also active in politics and whose ideas were strongly influenced by the revolutionary circumstances of the Civil War. They tended to see private property as a defence against the anarchy and radicalism generated by the Civil War and the uncertainty of republican government. They sanctified landownership as a vital aspect of freedom and democracy won at the expense of the divine right of kings. However, this triumphalist view was less explicit about the loss of rights of non-property owners to common land, such as servants and wage earners with no legitimate stake in land or property. The dispossessed did not form part of any political settlement until the beginning of the extension of the franchise in the nineteenth century, and even then, full suffrage rights were not achieved until the twentieth century when the link between the right to vote and ownership or renting of property was finally, if not totally, broken.

---

13 Torrance, *Noel Skelton and the Property-Owning Democracy*; Offer, *Property and Politics*, pp. 148–59.
14 Macpherson, *The Political Theory of Possessive Individualism*.
15 Vogel, 'The Land Question: A Liberal Theory of Communal Property', p. 107.

As is now well documented, the Civil War gave rise to a radical strand of land reform in the form of the Levellers, known as the Diggers (or the True Levellers). Their leader was Gerard Winstanley, and his influence continues to inform land reform movements today.[16] He advocated the ending of private property in opposition to enclosure. 'Looking both backwards and forwards, the Levellers believed that true equality could be established only by means of an attack on the institution of property as such.'[17] The Levellers emerged during the Midlands rising of 1607 (referred to by Shakespeare in *Coriolanus*) against the growing pace of private enclosure and they represented the culmination of a century of unauthorised encroachments on forests and waste grounds by squatters and local commoners.[18]

In 1649 Winstanley occupied a tract of unpromising land on Saint George's Hill in Surrey and planted subsistence foods as part of the more general aim of establishing an egalitarian society based on natural rights and Christian principles.[19] A number of further Digger colonies followed in central and southern England. But after having lost the protection of the army, this experiment in radical reform did not last longer than a few months before the Diggers were physically dispersed by local landlords and parsons threatened by the attack on the principle of private property, and the challenge to their authority that this represented.[20] After the execution of the King in 1649, Cromwell defeated the Levellers and other radical opponents and confirmed the primacy of landownership as the qualification for political participation in the new republic.

The violent experience of the Civil War influenced a range of different intellectual views justifying private property. This has been well covered by historians tracing the development of ideological support for private property.[21] For Locke, who had been closely involved in seeking legal resolution to a series of controversial land disputes as a government servant in South Carolina, 'Government has no other end than the preservation of property'.[22] The legal defence of private property was consolidated during the eighteenth century as evidenced by William Blackstone's *Commentaries on the Laws of England*, published in the 1760s. He observed that 'so great is the regard of the law for private property, that it will not authorise the least violation of it'. Moreover, the growth in the number of capital offences (known as The Bloody Code) from fifty to over two hundred between 1688 and 1820 was also

16 Howkins, 'From Diggers to Dongas: The Land in English Radicalism, 1649–2000'.
17 Hill, 'The Norman Yoke', p. 93.
18 Hill (ed.), *Winstanley: The Law of Freedom and Other Writings*.
19 Hill, *The World Turned Upside Down*, pp. 113–50.
20 Hill, *The Experience of Defeat*, pp. 35–40.
21 Linklater, *Owning the Earth*, pp. 39–74.
22 Locke, *The Second Treatise of Government* (1690), sections 85 and 94; Macpherson, *The Political Theory of Possessive Individualism*.

a reflection of a genuine concern by the landed classes about the real danger posed to their property by protest and riot.

The threat to property rights from an absolute monarch had to a significant degree diminished after the constitutional settlement of 1688. Thus, the development of common law and the 'bloody code' were concerned in the main with offences against property committed by the poor, including forgery which was seen as a direct challenge to legal claims of ownership. Transportation for enclosure rioters was also introduced to protect the interests of landlords seeking agricultural improvements and higher rents.[23] A radical tradition of land reform which challenged private property in land, as represented by the Diggers, did not revive again until the end of the eighteenth century as a result of a combination of a century of enlightenment thinking on political economy, the memory of lost rights to common land and the specific economic and political circumstances which helped forge English working-class consciousness after 1800.

The origins of the concept of the 'unearned increment'

The enlightenment gave birth to a set of radical ideas about land and its economic utility. These ideas went on to inform both a liberal and socialist tradition of English land reform. This manifested itself in two ways. First it provided further intellectual and legal validation of the principle of private property (the growth of possessive individualism). Second the writings of Adam Smith and David Ricardo also argued for the first time that the concentration of landed wealth was a potential obstacle to economic growth, laissez faire and free trade. They regarded land as qualitatively different in certain important respects to capital and labour. Out of this line of thought emerged the growth of anti-landlord sentiments that were taken up by future land reformers, especially those arguing for taxing land as a means of generating government revenue, reducing inequality and removing obstacles to free trade. Opposition to protectionism in general, and the Corn Laws in particular, were strongly influenced by such anti-landlord sentiments. Thus, the new political economy sought not only to preserve the principle of private property but it also laid the foundation for ideas about land reform, and in particular the taxation of the value of land, especially those increases arising naturally in society through no effort or input from the landowners themselves.

For Adam Smith the foundation of civil society was the ownership and protection of property. The *Wealth of Nations* (1776) defines one of the main purposes of government as the defence of the natural and inalienable right to possess property. This built on the natural right philosophy of John Locke. Smith saw society as divided into three great constituent orders – landlords,

---

23 Hay, 'Property, Authority and the Criminal Law' in Hay et al. (eds.), *Albion's Fatal Tree*, pp. 17–63.

capitalists and wage labourers. This division mirrored the growing reality of economic relations in eighteenth-century England, with each order deriving rent, profits and wages from a growing capitalist economy, where it was argued unfettered competition resulted in significant economic benefits. But Smith regarded rent as a different type of return to profits or wages. This became a vitally important distinction taken up by other economists and later land reformers.

Smith defined rent as the price paid for the use of land. But he argued that it should reflect its productive use and not become a monopoly and a barrier to economic improvement. His key idea was that rent was a pure surplus in that it was a benefit to the owner of land independent of any effort or investment made by the owner. Landlords were 'the only one of the three orders whose revenue costs them neither labour nor care, but comes to them, as it were, of its own accord'.[24] Smith went out of his way to criticise those restrictive practices that inhibited competition and free trade, including the way landlords monopolised land through primogeniture, leading to an over-concentration of political power and an under-representation of industrial and middle-class interests. He considered that a tax on rent 'was no discouragement to any sort of industry'. He speculated that 'ground rents and the ordinary rent of land are, therefore, perhaps, the species of revenue which can best bear to have a peculiar tax imposed upon them'.[25]

The initial idea of taxing what became known as 'the unearned increment' went on to directly inspire future generations of economists and radicals. It remains current today in a number of think tanks and pressure groups, such as the Henry George Foundation, which campaigns for a land value tax (LVT) and publishes *Land and Liberty*.[26] One of the most influential thinkers in this respect was the economist David Ricardo, who developed a marginal theory of rent in his ground-breaking *Principles of Political Economy and Taxation* (1817). Of equal influence was his contemporary, the historian and political theorist James Mill, who took Ricardo's theory and turned it into a practical proposal to tax any future increase in rents arising from government legislation or future increases in population (*The Elements of Political Economics*, 1821). Ricardo's definition of 'pure ground rent', which proved later to be very controversial amongst economists, gave rise to the concept that rent is a 'free gift of nature', creating the possibility that it could be taxed or even confiscated by the state. Although he never publicly called for such a radical course of action, he did campaign along with James Mill for the repeal of the Corn Laws and for democratic reform in order to reduce the influence of the landed aristocracy and their support for protectionist measures.

Mill's son, the liberal philosopher John Stuart Mill further developed the idea of a land tax in his *Principles of Political Economy* (1948). He called

---

24 Smith, *Wealth of Nations*, p. 64 and p. 249; Linklater, *Owning the Earth*, pp. 55–74.
25 Smith, *Wealth of Nations*, Book V, Chapter 2, Article 1.
26 www.henrygeorgefoundation.org.

for a valuation of all land in the country so that its present value could be exempted from taxation, prior to the introduction of a comprehensive system of the taxation on future increases in value. He argued that 'landlords grow rich in their sleep without working, risking or economising. The increase in the value of the land, arising as it does from the efforts of an entire community, should belong to the community and not to the individual who might hold title'.[27] As the pre-eminent philosopher of Victorian England, he turned this potentially revolutionary idea into a practical political proposal through the formation of the Land Tenure Reform Association (LTRA) in 1869. It campaigned for free trade in land, the abolition of primogeniture and the taxation of the unearned increment.[28] The movement represented by the Anti-Corn Law League was thus continued by Mill in his quest for the taxation of land values, reflecting very similar and strong anti-landlord sentiments. But while the League succeeded in abolishing the Corn Laws in 1846, the LTRA failed to achieve free trade in land or to dent the entrenched power of the landed aristocracy after 1850. In fact, the height of their political influence was not reached until the last quarter of the nineteenth century and only started to decline during the twentieth century as other sources of wealth replaced land as the foundation of political power.

Apart from a tradition of working-class agrarianism (see below), the interests of aristocratic landed power were not ideologically or politically challenged in a serious way until the parliamentary land survey of the early 1880s exposed the extraordinary concentration of their holdings and the Irish land wars posed a serious political challenge to their legitimacy. This led to a major realignment of British politics as the Liberal Unionists joined the Conservative Party over the issue of home rule for Ireland and the related question of land reform. After this split, the Liberal Party embraced the radical policy of taxation of land values during the 1890s, influenced to a large extent by the campaigns of the American land reformer Henry George and the need to appeal to growing urban and rural electorate newly enfranchised by the 1884 Reform Act. Henry George's attack on private property as a cause of poverty, promoted during a series of highly publicised and almost evangelical popular lecture tours in the early 1880s, had a major impact on the radical wing of the Liberal Party and the emerging Labour movement, building on a long-term tradition of agrarian and communitarian thought.

Support for the idea of the taxation of land values reached its culmination with Henry George and his book, *Progress and Poverty* (1873). He transformed the idea into the practical proposal of the single tax, inspiring both socialists and liberal reformers on both sides of the Atlantic in the last quarter of the nineteenth century. He achieved this more by his rhetoric about poverty than his laissez-faire economic theories.[29] *Progress and Poverty* was an attack on

27 Mill, *The Principles of Political Economy*, Book V, Chapter 2, Section 5.
28 Burchardt, *Paradise Lost*, pp. 78–9; Offer, *Property and Politics*, pp. 182–3.
29 Blaug, 'Henry George: Rebel with a Cause', pp. 270–88.

the idea of private property in land, building on the natural right philosophy of John Locke and the laissez-faire principles of Adam Smith. Although he maintained that the remedy for the unequal distribution of wealth (defined as poverty) was 'to make land common property', he concluded that it was not necessary to confiscate land, but that it was only necessary to confiscate rent and to abolish all taxation save upon land values (defined as progress). He later went on to refer to this as the single tax in order to differentiate his idea from those calling for full land nationalisation (as advocated at the time by the naturalist Alfred Russel Wallace) and from the campaign for peasant pro-prietorship in Ireland. In essence his single tax was a confiscatory levy on the unimproved value of ground rent, but which avoided questioning the rights of private property. *Progress and Poverty* became the most widely read book on economics in the nineteenth century. At the time of its publication, it also proved highly attractive to a generation of working and middle-class radicals during the 1880s as it reflected an earlier tradition of rural agrarianism that flourished from the beginning of the nineteenth century. This was equally influenced by natural right theories and reluctance to attack the principle of private property.

The influence of working-class agrarianism

A tradition of radical working-class agrarianism developed in Britain and America at the end of the eighteenth century, inspired by the rebellion of the American colonies and the French Revolution as well as the intellectual legacy of Thomas Harrington, whose ideas about property and political freedom was reflected in the American Declaration of Independence. Recent research has demonstrated how working-class radicals ranging from Thomas Paine and Thomas Spence in the 1790s, to William Cobbett in the 1820s, and the Chartist Feargus O'Connor in the 1840s 'claimed that every man had a nat-ural right or a birth right in the soil, and linked the distribution of land to the balance of political power or the existence of corruption in society'.[30] Land reform was inextricably linked to wider demands for political reform. The ideas of these working-class reformers persisted throughout the nineteenth century and played a long-term role in popular politics, influencing the pol-icies of the Labour Party at the end of the century. The historian of Thomas Spence (Chase) has shown how:

> industrialisation did not replace the landlord with the capitalist as the object of radical scorn. Rather it led to an enhanced awareness of how inequality in the ownership of land, 'the womb of wealth', reinforced inequalities in all other spheres of economic activity.... Recourse to the land was a means of resisting the imposition of increasingly

30 Bronstein, *Land Reform and Working-Class Experience*, p. 23.

capitalist work-forms; to campaign for such access was one means by which labour sought to negotiate what shape industrialising society should assume.[31]

The intellectual influence of James Harrington was present in the ideas of Thomas Spence (1750–1814), and other radicals such as William Ogilvie (1736–1813) and Thomas Paine (1737–1809).[32] For Harrington, agrarian equality guaranteed political liberty. The distribution of land and the exercise of power were linked. The demand for universal adult male suffrage was thus the primary objective of working-class radicals at this time who were opposed to the concentration of political power based on aristocratic landed wealth. This was a view shared by middle-class reformers equally opposed to economic protectionism and mercantilist theories. In these circumstances land reform underpinned wider political reform in a way that it failed to do in the twentieth century after universal suffrage had been finally achieved. This may perhaps help to account for the way in which the 'land question' declined in political importance after 1918.

The most influential proponent of working-class land reform was the millenarian Thomas Spence, whose ideas went on to inspire a tradition of agrarian reform in the middle decades of the nineteenth century. He was the most radical and least respectable of such reformers and was active in revolutionary politics in London during the 1810s as a member of the London Corresponding Society, before his arrest for treason. He was in a minority in advocating the common ownership of all land, while many other reformers tended to accept the principle of private property as a natural right.[33] For Spence private property in land was theft, and should be repossessed and administered by parish government in the democratic tradition of local city states, for which there should be no compensation to landowners, maintaining that 'each parish is a little polished Athens'.[34]

An agrarian outlook influenced other working-class reformers involved in the radical politics of the time, but they did not all share the confiscatory approach of Spence, supporting instead more pragmatic attempts to tax or redistribute the ownership of land for the common good. In fact the majority of such reformers rejected any ideas that threatened the sanctity of private property, tending to regard the labour of working people, especially the produce of artisans as a form of natural private property that should be equally defended as ownership of land, as long as it was equitably distributed and led to political reform.[35] Such thinkers were above all opposed to the concentration of landed wealth and the economic and political power this gave

31 Chase, *The People's Farm*, pp. 4–5.
32 Beer, *The Pioneers of Land Reform*.
33 Chase, *The People's Farm*, p. 29.
34 Bonnett and Armstrong (eds.), *Thomas Spence*, p. 8.
35 Bronstein, *Land Reform and Working-Class Experience*, p. 33.

to the aristocracy, as clearly illustrated in the writings of Thomas Paine, a contemporary of Spence, and better known for his *Rights of Man* (1791). He was the author of a relatively unknown pamphlet, entitled *Agrarian Justice*, written after his release from prison in France in 1797.[36] Paine was more of a radical liberal who popularised the laissez-faire writings of Adam Smith. He made a distinction between 'natural property', such as the earth, air and water, which exists in primitive societies, and 'artificial property', created by mankind in more advanced economies. But since it was not possible to revert to a form of landownership based on a natural birth right as in primitive societies, 'Paine proposed that those who owned land should pay a lump sum and an annuity to all those deprived on their birth right'.[37]

The ideas of Spence and Paine, along with other radical commentators such as the journalist and free-thinker Richard Carlile, who like Paine supported a single tax on land, formed part of a body of political writing about land distribution as a solution to social and political inequality. The methods which they suggested for implementing land redistribution diverged widely, but they provided various propositions from which practical solutions were generated – 'not only by ... land-hungry Chartists, and American homesteaders, but also by a host of other thinkers who grappled with the issue between the turn of the nineteenth century and the 1840s'.[38] They promoted a range of ideas from the radical to the conservative, the paternalistic to the fiercely independent, centring on land as a solution to poverty and overpopulation. They shared a number of concerns, many of which continue to be features of contemporary life in modern English culture, such as anti-urbanism, the virtuous benefits of landed independence (yeoman farmers and smallholders), and 'back-to-the-land' movements as a remedy for unemployment, bad health and alienation caused by factory production.[39]

Evidence of working-class agrarianism can also be seen in the community experiments of the utopian socialist and philanthropist Robert Owen (New Lanark and New Harmony) in the 1820s. The experience of such practical experiments in community formation was absorbed by the Chartist movement and can be seen in their Land Plan adopted in 1845. The radical language employed by the Chartists demonstrated the strength of the idea that their 'politically enforced expropriation from the land remained the ultimate source of the condition of the working classes and the growing tyranny of the money and factory lords'.[40] The Chartist Land Company is by far the clearest and most ambitious example of working-class land reform in the nineteenth century. As Chase has pointed out, it was originally intended as a relatively small-scale enterprise demonstrating the economic and social benefits of a

---

36 Paine, *Agrarian Justice*.
37 Claeys, 'Paine's Agrarian Justice', p. 21.
38 Bronstein, *Land Reform and Working-Class Experience*, p. 33.
39 Ibid., pp. 37–51.
40 Jones, *Languages of Class*, p. 153.

movement back to the land by industrial workers, but its objectives were much more fundamental, namely:

> To purchase land on which to locate such of its members as may be selected ... to demonstrate to the working classes of the kingdom, firstly the value of land, as a means of making them independent of the grinding capitalist; and secondly, to show them the necessity of securing the speedy enactment of the 'People's Charter'; [and] the accomplishment of the political and social emancipation of the enslaved and degraded working classes.[41]

The Society attracted enormous enthusiasm, with 20,000 shareholders, 70,000 weekly subscribers, 600 local branches and five estates. But it spiralled out of control and was wound up by the government in 1851 for breaking friendly society rules, resulting in the early death of its founder, Feargus O'Connor. It generated much recrimination within the movement itself, including many later historians who have dismissed the experiment as an aberration from the correct socialist course of working-class political reform. It set back the cause of such reform for a generation, although the tradition of agrarianism was kept alive through a series of smaller and more successful but ultimately short-lived experiments in rural living.[42]

Of more success were the freehold land societies, established during the late 1840s to provide plots of land for building houses, including the creation of smallholdings, which were increasingly seen as guaranteeing a degree of economic independence to those dispossessed of their rights by enclosure and industrialisation. In their early phase they provided an opportunity for purchasers to obtain the vote as forty shilling freeholders under the 1832 Reform Act. But these societies soon lost their radical edge as they became vehicles for the aspirations of important sections of the middle and upper working classes seeking respectability and security in the more prosperous decades after 1850. They developed into early versions of building societies, ensuring the spread of later owner-occupation and the political decline of land reform as a popular political issue.[43]

But support for radical land reform did not disappear with the decline of Chartism after 1850 and before the socialist revival in the 1880s. It remained a distinctive feature of working-class politics, especially in the London clubs, inspired by Thomas Spence and the Chartists. Working-class radicals tended to support land nationalisation in opposition to the moderate demands for the taxation of land values advocated by John Stuart Mill's LTRA. It was these radicals rather than the influence of intellectuals that helped introduce

41 Rules of the Chartist Co-Operative Land Society (1845) quoted in Chase, '"Wholesome Object Lessons": The Chartist Land Plan in Retrospect', p. 59.
42 Chase, 'Out of Radicalism'.
43 Ibid., pp. 319–45.

ideas of the common ownership of land into the programmes the socialist groups formed during the 1880s, and eventually the Labour Party.[44]

Anarchist and socialist influences on land reform

In contrast, other strands of intellectual opinion supporting the full nationalisation of land, such as the ideology of the early European socialist movement, proved to have less resonance in English radical political movements during the nineteenth century. The slogan of the anarchist and utopian socialist Pierre-Joseph Proudhon that 'Property is theft', published in his book *What is Property* (1840) during a period of revolutionary turmoil in France, argued that property is *murder* and *robbery*. But like many English agrarians, in his view this did not extend to the exclusive possession of property generated by labour-made wealth. For this reason, he was very sympathetic to the peasantry and supported small-scale private ownership. 'His agrarian socialism was indeed a socialism for the peasants.'[45] Marx initially welcomed Proudhon's attack on property as a critique of existing capitalist society, but he later condemned Proudhon as part of his intellectual attack on political economy in general and the formulation of his labour theory of value in particular. His views on the origins of private property remained part of a philosophical body of work confined in the main to a narrow circle of fellow thinkers, although they became more widely known in British socialist circles during the early 1880s.[46]

In terms of mainstream socialist thinking, theories of natural rights in relation to property were more influential in the development of socialist thought in England than Marxist theory. For example, in his discussion of private property, the socialist Edward Carpenter argued that true ownership cannot exist without some living and human relationship to the object owned. Private ownership of land may be legal, but it was dead and harmful because it lacked this human quality. In his book *England's Ideal*, he gave a clear example of a natural rights understanding of private property, which applied to land and any other material object which was created by human hands. He maintained that this would seem to be

> ...the original type of private property. If I cut a stick in the wild woods, whittle it, peel it, polish it, and transform it into a walking stick, the universal consent of mankind allows me a right to that stick. And Why? Because as far as it is a product of anything besides Nature, it is a product of my *work*. I have entered into the closest relationship to it; I have put myself into it; it has become part of me – one of my properties.[47]

44 Bowie, *The Radical and Socialist Tradition in British Planning*, pp. 74–91.
45 Mitrany, *Marx against the Peasant*, p. 21.
46 Jones, *Karl Marx*, pp. 173–5.
47 Carpenter, *England's Ideal*, p. 147.

In practical political terms, Marx criticised the Chartist Land Company and its advocacy of small-scale proprietorship as a distraction from real working-class land reform, namely the nationalisation of land.[48] Marx argued in the *Communist Manifesto* that the theory of communism could be summed up in a single sentence – the abolition of private property, by which he meant bourgeois private property. He went on to support the working-class Land and Labour League, founded in 1869 and which called for full land nationalisation. But the League did not succeed in gaining any widespread political support in the period before the socialist revival of the 1880s.[49] Marx was against small-scale peasant proprietorships as for him socialism would be achieved by the urban working class taking over the commanding heights of the industrial economy which was essentially characterised by concentrated and efficient large-scale production. The first Marxist organisation in Britain, the Social Democratic Federation, founded in 1881, supported large-scale farming organised on a state collective basis in opposition to the growing demand for independent smallholdings administered and owned at a local level, differentiating themselves from the more reformist Fabian Society and the non-Marxist Independent Labour Party, which went on to establish the Labour Party.[50]

Edwardian climax

After 1880 the campaign for land reform became an increasingly important part of the political programmes of mainstream parties as well as the emerging Labour movement. Following the defeat of Chartism after 1850, working-class demands for land reform (including other radical if not revolutionary policies such as republicanism) were channelled into the more reformist politics represented on the left wing of the Gladstonian Liberal Party. However, land reform did not diminish as a result. A number of developments contributed to the continuing strength of these political demands – the socialist revival of the 1880s, the lecture tours of Henry George, the revelatory results of the parliamentary land surveys showing the concentration of aristocratic ownership published in the early 1880s, and not least the insurrectionary land wars in Ireland. Other factors also played a part, including the growth of local government and its need for financial resources to pay for local services. The extension of the franchise in both rural and urban areas after 1884 made political parties more aware of the need to adopt policies that would appeal to a wider and more working-class electorate.

48 Marx and Engels, Collected Works, Vol. 6, pp. 358–60, p. 686 quoted in Bronstein, *Land Reform and Working-Class Experience*, p. 216.
49 Harrison, *Before the Socialists*; Bowie, *The Radical and Socialist Tradition in British Planning*, pp. 82–4.
50 Tichelar, 'Socialists, Labour and the Land'.

In these circumstances, two major policy areas dominated land reform debates in the period leading up to 1914. The first was the demand for taxation of land values as a source of new government revenue, and the related campaign for land nationalisation as advocated by the Land Nationalisation Society, set up by Alfred Russel Wallace in 1882. The second was the demand for smallholdings and allotments ('Three Acres and a Cow'). These two policy areas combined to form part of a radical programme of reform, reaching a climax in the immediate pre-First World War period in the Land Campaign of Lloyd George and the People's Budget of 1909.[51]

The latest historical research has emphasised how land reform reflected a range of different nationalist, patriotic and ideological traditions which tended to overlap and sometimes contradict each other. The radical wing of the Liberal Party, free from its unionist MPs after their defection to the Conservative Party in 1886 over Irish home rule, looked to the taxation of land values and the revival of agriculture as the remedy for a number of political challenges facing a governing party, especially the need for new sources of government revenue and the consolidation of its electoral base in both urban and rural areas. The Conservative Party began to look more favourably on the promotion of small-scale peasant proprietorships as a response to social unrest, as long as this did not threaten the fundamental interests of private landlords. In fact, many Conservatives began to see the wider encouragement of small-scale ownership as a potential bulwark against socialist attacks on private property and as a possible solution to rural unemployment during a period of agricultural depression. Keeping labour on the land was also seen as an answer to the growing crisis of unemployment and poverty in urban areas. These were policies which appealed equally to the emerging Labour movement, especially some trade union interests. Such views underpinned the demand of Jesse Collings, the Liberal MP and close friend of Joseph Chamberlain, for peasant proprietorships.[52]

Many reformers believed that the detrimental effects of city life were leading to a deterioration in the health and efficiency of the race. The preservation of a rural way of life would bring about a reversal of these dangerous trends. The garden city movement, for example, which emerged at this time was driven by a similar tendency to idolise rural life.[53] It also looked to the taxation of land values as an essential foundation for their growth and development. Ebenezer Howard was explicit in *Garden Cities of Tomorrow* in arguing that capturing the 'rent' on which garden cities were built would pay for the infrastructure and services of new communities combining the best features of both rural and urban living.[54]

51 Packer, *Lloyd George, Liberalism and the Land*; Gilbert, 'David Lloyd George: The Reform of British Landholding and the Budget of 1914', pp. 117–41; Bruce K. Murray, *The People's Budget, 1909/10*.
52 Bone, 'Legislation to Revive Small Farming in England, 1887–1914', pp. 653–61.
53 Bowie, *The Radical and Socialist Tradition in British Planning*, pp. 141–69.
54 Howard, *Garden Cities of Tomorrow*, chapter 11.

The political views of the new socialist organisations set up during the socialist revival of the 1880s were equally inspired by a number of different intellectual and working-class traditions. The Fabian Society founded in London in 1883 was initially enthusiastic about Ricardian economic thought. They developed their own theory of rent to differentiate themselves from the Marxist labour theory of value during debates with the Marxist Social Democratic Federation (SDF). While rejecting the economic basis of the single tax, some leading members of the Fabian Society were much taken by the power of George's rhetorical attacks on the causes of poverty. The leading Fabian George Bernard Shaw proclaimed that 'public property in land is the basic economic condition of socialism'.[55] In practical political terms, the Fabians developed a series of pragmatic and gradualist policies seeking to tax 'unearned incomes', including taxation of land values and death duties. They supported local government schemes to set up allotments and smallholdings, and in particular attempts by the London County Council, where they exercised some progressive influence, to recover an early form of betterment. This was a special rent-charge imposed in cases where improvements carried out by state action increased the value of land in adjacent areas.[56]

Other socialist organisations, like the Independent Labour Party (ILP) and the SDF, devoted a great deal of energy to considering how to revitalise British agriculture and prevent, and even reverse, rural depopulation at a time of agricultural depression and falling rent rolls. Controversy centred on the virtues of smallholdings as opposed to the merits of a collectivised, state-run agricultural system. The ILP supported the former while the SDF advocated the latter, though both aimed to raise the condition of the agricultural labourer. Much of this socialist literature was imbued with criticism of industrialisation, and reflected the influence of Ruskin, Arnold, Morris, Carpenter, Blatchford and Kropotkin. The dream of running a small farm, or being the owner of a small rural estate, free from the influence of squire and parson, represented a strong emotive response which drew inspiration from a long-term tradition of agrarianism. The ILP in particular campaigned to get the Labour Party to adopt a socialist programme for the countryside. To the ILP the legitimate labour vote in the rural districts, and the border lands between town and country which, for example, characterised many mining communities, included both the farm labourer and the small tenant farmer. British socialists were not necessarily constrained by the same strategic considerations in relation to political campaigning in the countryside as were their European counterparts, where a socially conservative peasantry protected by tariffs frequently comprised a large and politically powerful bloc opposed to radical reform.[57]

55 Shaw (ed.), *Fabian Essays in Socialism*, p. 24.
56 McBriar, *Fabian Socialism and English Politics, 1884–1918*, chapters 2 and 4.
57 Tichelar, 'Socialists, Labour and the Land', pp. 131–2.

The last twenty years of the nineteenth century witnessed an acceleration of political interest in the taxation of land values and the creation of rural smallholdings. During the early 1880s the situation in Ireland, and the impact of the lecture tours of Henry George, gave rise to the formation of two new organisations. The Land Nationalisation Society was set up in 1881 by the naturalist Alfred Russel Wallace and initially called for the public ownership of all land with full compensation to the owners. The English Land Restoration League was set up in 1883 as a rival organisation to support the views of Henry George. Both organisations toured the country in their respective yellow and red vans generating a great deal of local enthusiasm and support. But it took the controversy over Irish home rule and the influence of Joseph Chamberlain's 'unauthorised programme', supported by his ally Jesse Collings's demand for peasant proprietorships, to convert the Liberal Party, now free from its unionist associations after the split of 1886, to a policy of unhindered advocacy of taxation of land values and the municipal letting of smallholdings. This was confirmed when the National Liberal Federation adopted the 'Newcastle Programme' in 1891. While Conservative legislation on allotments and smallholdings was enacted in 1887 and 1892, it would take the landslide victory of the Liberal Party in 1906 before a radical programme of land reform became a realistic political possibility for the first time and a major threat to the interests of private property.[58]

By the beginning of the twentieth century, land reform encompassed a wide range of progressive issues, from a desire to protect the special role of agriculture in society and reverse the deterioration of rural life (such as the minimum wage for agricultural workers), to finding solutions to the problems created by rapid urbanisation and the unregulated growth of metropolitan areas. This was superimposed on the highly controversial issue of how to pay for welfare reform at a time of significant increases in local rates and national taxation. Lloyd George saw the taxation of land values as a potentially new source of revenue for central and local government. The discretionary power to collect betterment was included in the 1909 Housing and Town Planning Act. The 1909 budget contained proposals for a tax on the capital value of land as well as a 20% tax on the unearned increment to be introduced after a full evaluation, alongside increases in death duties, first introduced in 1894, and a new super tax. Very controversially, Lloyd George set in train the valuation of all land in England opening up the possibility for a further and radical extension of taxation of land in the future. The landed aristocracy found it in their interest to vigorously oppose this attack on their economic and political power. The House of Lords rejected Lloyd George's budget precipitating a major constitutional crisis, two general elections in 1910 and

58 Burchardt, *Paradise Lost*, pp. 77–85.

the Parliament Act of 1911 which reduced the power of the Lords to amend finance bills. Building on this success, Lloyd George launched an ambitious land campaign in 1913 in order to keep the political momentum of his attack on landed interests going. But the outbreak of the First World War put paid to his aim of forming a progressive alliance with the Labour Party, to fight the general election scheduled for 1915. Land reform as a potential unifying issue did not recover after the war.

At this time, the Labour Party was not in a strong enough position either in the country or in the House of Commons to influence the outcome of Lloyd George's land campaign. It published its own policy on the land question in 1913 at the height of the Liberal Party's rural campaign in order to differentiate itself from the potentially more radical policies of Lloyd George. It resisted socialist demands to adopt a clear and unequivocal policy on land nationalisation declaring instead that public ownership of land was a long-term goal to be achieved when Labour enjoyed a majority in Parliament and could raise sufficient revenue through the taxation of land to be able to subsidise smallholders on a large enough scale to break the monopoly of the big landowners. The taxation of land values was regarded as the main source of revenue for this purpose. It was suspicious of an overtly centralised role for the state and was more comfortable with the idea of power and ownership of land being devolved and exercised at a local level through district and parish councils, thereby guaranteeing the status of the free and independent rural artisan, both labourer and tenant farmer. Its rejection of immediate land nationalisation and its stress on independence and local democracy placed it firmly with a tradition of radical agrarianism.[59]

Summary

By 1914, the land reform policies of the Liberal Party, and the emerging Labour Party, reflected the strength of a powerful tradition of rural agrarianism, the intellectual origins of which can be traced back to the seventeenth century. One important strand of this tradition was the idea of taxing the unearned increment, a concept first elaborated by Adam Smith, taken forward by David Ricardo and John Stuart Mill and popularised by Henry George. Taxing the unimproved value of sites, known later as land value tax (LVT) had become the official policy of the Liberal Party, and Lloyd George introduced such a tax in his 'People's Budget' of 1909.

However, the land taxes proved difficult to either administer or collect during the domestic emergency of the First World War and were eventually repealed by the post-war coalition government in 1920 without generating much political controversy. But the question of the value of land and the amount the state

59 Tichelar, 'Socialists, Labour and the Land'.

had to pay to purchase it for development, either compulsorily or on the open market, went on to become an ongoing and highly controversial aspect of land reform in the twentieth century, especially given the remarkable increase in the price of land after the Second World War. The quest to recover the 'unearned increment' was the ideological justification for the various attempts by Labour governments since 1924 to introduce radical land reform.

Part II

The land question and taxation of land values, 1914 to 1939

3 The impact of the First World War and the spread of owner-occupation

This chapter will discuss the changes that took place in agriculture and land tenure during the war and interwar period, looking at patterns of landownership and the spread of owner-occupation. These changes help account for the decline in political importance of the land question after 1918. Most notably they go some way to explain the withdrawal of the landed aristocracy from politics following the sale of their estates during the period from 1909 to 1927. Of equal importance was the domestic impact of the First World War, which influenced public opinion on the use of land in the national interest. The continuing economic decline of agriculture during the interwar period also contributed to less adverse public attention being directed towards landowners as a class, especially after the withdrawal of wartime agricultural protection in 1921, regarded by many farmers as 'The Great Betrayal'. As a result, land reform attracted less public controversy as a political issue after 1918, particularly as more farmers became owner-occupiers on an increasing scale. The following chapter will assess the political implications of these developments and argue that town and country planning eclipsed the policy of land taxation.

The impact of the First World War

The countryside underwent some remarkable changes after 1914 as a result of the domestic impact of the war and the scale of government intervention in the control and use of land. The outbreak of war had put an end to the ambition of Lloyd George to fight the general election scheduled for 1915 on a platform of radical land reform, possibly in alliance with the Labour Party, but appealing to the wider urban electorate, especially those members of the enfranchised working class transferring their allegiance to the Labour Party. Plans for the valuation of all land-holdings by a combined government department (a new Domesday office, for England and Wales, long campaigned for by land reformers), were initiated by Lloyd George before the war for the purposes of laying the groundwork for introducing the taxation of land values, including a compulsory system of land registration.[1] But these plans were put on hold as civil servants were redirected to the war effort and the relevant legislation was subsequently repealed after the war with little opposition.

For the first two years of the Great War the management of land as a resource was carried on very much as business as usual, with the country relying on traditional free trade to import cheap food to feed the nation. But by the end of 1915, the policy of laissez faire was no longer a viable way to fight a prolonged war on the economic and industrial scale required, especially when the belligerent nations employed economic blockades through submarine warfare.[2] The formation of a more effective wartime coalition led by Lloyd George in 1916 ushered in unprecedented levels of state intervention in the economy and the organisation of society, including the management of agriculture through the county council War Agricultural Executive Committees and the requisitioning of large tracts of land for use by the War Office. As a result, public attitudes to the countryside and land underwent some significant changes. Political antagonism towards the landed aristocracy was mitigated by wartime collectivism and the social mixing of the classes in the trenches. The literary journal, the *Athenaeum* (forerunner to the *New Statesman*) commented in April 1918 that

> Land shares with Ireland, Beer and Religion the somewhat doubtful distinction of having been one of the subjects of perpetual political controversy in this country. But, as in so many matters, the effect of the War has been to produce much greater unanimity than would have been thought possible four years ago. For instance, the comparatively smooth passage of the minimum wage clauses of the Corn Production Act (1917) and the general approval of large schemes for smallholdings for discharged soldiers have illustrated the advance in public opinion.[3]

The war required the urgent requisitioning of land for military purposes. This was achieved largely by compulsory means through the Defence of the Realm Act. Such intervention posed a potentially dangerous precedent for post-war reconstruction along radical lines, although the scale of such hopes never materialised in practice in the climate of post-war austerity. The new Ministry of Reconstruction set up a Land Acquisition Committee in 1917, chaired by Sir Leslie Scott, the barrister and Conservative MP for Liverpool. He became a key figure in the interwar preservation movement and one of the founders of the Council for the Preservation of Rural England.[4] His committee

1 Offer, *Property and Politics.*
2 Dewey, *War and Progress: Britain 1914–1945*; Marwick, *The Deluge*; Dewey, *British Agriculture in the First World War.*
3 *The Athenaeum*, April 1918, p. 18.
4 Leslie Scott Papers MSS 119/3/5/TP/1–9.

recommended a streamlined and simplified mechanism for the compulsory purchase of land for public works after the war, overcoming the archaic and time-consuming system of seeking permission through private members bills in Parliament, a process no longer regarded as fit for purpose in the expanding post-war market for land.[5] His final report, published in March 1918 at a very dangerous moment in the war, and only a few months after the Russian Revolution, was however at pains to point out that its recommendations did not involve any new principles attacking private property or any element of confiscation.[6]

By the end of the war three million acres of grassland had been ploughed up as part of 'A Dig for Victory Campaign' and the expansion of smallholdings in urban areas had made a significant contribution to supplies of home-produced food, ensuring a degree of self-sufficiency not matched by other European belligerent nations. The historian of the 'Countryside at War' (Dakers) has summarised the key wartime developments:

> Thousands of acres were requisitioned for army and prison camps, munitions factories and airfields; extensive areas of woodlands were devastated to provide extra timber for use at home and abroad; some country towns and villages were filled to over flowing with officers, soldiers and the machinery of war; country houses were turned into hospitals and their parks were churned up by gun-carriages and tanks; in the fields labourers were replaced by truant schoolchildren, land girls in breeches, able-bodied pacifists, Belgium refugees and German prisoners.[7]

The war demonstrated the need for state intervention in agriculture to ensure food supplies during a period of rapidly increasing prices and potential food shortages caused by the wartime restriction on imports. By 1915 the government had set up the War Agricultural Committees, managed by county councils, to control the labour supply through military exemptions, and to monitor levels of production. Rents were frozen, food prices soared and the income of farmers went up as a result, shifting property rights back from the landowner to tenant farmers.[8] Although the impact of the committees was initially limited they laid the foundations for a greater level of intervention during the last two years of the war, setting a precedent for the continuation of guaranteed prices and a minimum wage for agricultural workers after the war.[9]

5 *First Report of the Committee of the Ministry of Reconstruction Dealing with Law and Practice Relating to the Acquisition and Valuation of Land for Public Purposes*, Cd. 8998 (1918).
6 *The Times*, 12 March 1918, p. 3.
7 Dakers, *Forever England: The Countryside at War*, p. 17.
8 Offer, 'Farm Tenure and Land Values in England, 1750–1950', p. 17.
9 Howkins, *Reshaping Rural England*, p. 255.

In December 1918, the Ministry of Reconstruction, influenced by the spirit of wartime collectivism, summarised the remarkable changes that had taken place in terms of rural development and outlined an agenda of future government intervention.[10] It noted accurately that by far the most significant wartime intervention was the passing of the Corn Production Act in 1917, as an emergency measure to combat food shortages arising as a result of the impact of submarine warfare. The Act guaranteed the minimum price of corn and set up wages boards to pay minimum wages, reversing a long period of agricultural depression. The ministry had drawn up plans to continue the not always effective county council War Agricultural Executive Committees after the war on the assumption that the state might want to exercise some supervision over increased food production in the national interest. These plans employed arguments in favour of more government intervention in agriculture production, smallholdings, village reconstruction and transport. They represented a new type of land reform but also echoed the agrarianism and pastoralism of pre-war concerns by calling for 'the establishment of a permanent reservoir of healthy and contented men and women from which the physical strength of the nation can be perpetually renewed, ... the security of their food supply for the whole people even in times of peril, and the reestablishment of a proper social and political balance between the urban and rural community'.[11]

While such essentially agrarian notions were not fulfilled after the war, other developments did become part of a programme of permanent change. The most significant was the creation of the Forestry Commission, in 1919, which became the largest landowner in terms of acreage during the course of the twentieth century (2.8 million acres by 1990). It was set up in 1919 as a state-run organisation under the chairmanship of Lord Lovat, a catholic aristocratic landowner and war hero. It is an early example of the nationalisation of a natural resource, unlike the coal industry which had to wait until 1946. The Acland Committee, set up by Asquith in 1916 to look at the best ways of growing home-grown timber to meet severe wartime shortages, especially necessary for the building of trenches and supporting coal mining, had identified by 1918 between three and five million acres of existing waste land that could be used to grow coniferous trees. The war had exposed the nations over-reliance on imported timber, mainly from Russia and Canada, made into a crisis by the interruption of imports after the Russian Revolution in 1917. In the end a target of 1,770,000 acres of conifers to be planted over a period of 80 years was agreed, a figure which was far exceeded by the outbreak of World War Two.[12]

State ownership of land also increased after the war as the government retained large tracts of the countryside for military use. In the 1870s the War

---

10 *Report of the Work of the Ministry of Reconstruction* (December 1918) Cd. 9231.
11 *Second Part of the Report of the Agricultural Policy Committee* (December 1918), Cd. 9079, p. 35.
12 Cahill, *Who Owns Britain?* pp. 140–5.

Department owned just 165,000 acres and this had increased to over 250,000 acres by 1939. This expanded dramatically to over 11 million acres during the Second World War, or 20% of the country. The retention of such sites, although much reduced, continues to be an issue of controversy to this day, as the Ministry of Defence owns or leases large tracts of land on Dartmoor, Salisbury Plain, and the Northumberland Peak District and Pembrokeshire national parks.[13] The War Office after both world wars managed to retain land in Wiltshire and Dorset, including Lulworth Cove, for military training purposes, an ongoing and unresolved controversy which has generated acute public controversy over access to the countryside and protection of the land-scape.[14] Such concerns reflect the way land reform took new directions during the course of the twentieth century. In terms of public perception, aristocratic landownership no longer attracted the same level of radical opposition as it had done before the war. The growth of other forms of landownership, such as state requisitioning and owner-occupation in both urban and rural areas, mitigated concerns about the political power of a landed aristocracy which was experiencing severe economic difficulties. Moreover, the gentry as a rural ruling class either sold their holdings or emigrated to the outposts of Empire on an unprecedented scale.

The war also saw a remarkable increase in the number of urban allotments for producing home-grown food. For the first two years of the war no rationing was imposed or serious concerns expressed about food shortages, but inflationary pressures and the threat of submarine warfare finally led to government action in December, 1916. An order for the cultivation of land in urban areas was issued under the Defence of the Realm Act, empowering local authorities to acquire land for allotments. Unoccupied land could be acquired compulsorily, while occupied sites could be taken by agreement with the permission of the owner. Common land could also be commandeered as long as their natural beauty was not damaged.[15] The land reformer Gerald Butcher described this measure in 1918 as 'the most drastic statute of land reform', declaring that such state appropriation of land for the common good had not been possible politically before the war.[16] By 1918 the number of allotments had increased from 450,000 in 1914 to over 1,500,000 (occupying over 200,000 acres).[17] 'Every bit of spare land was commandeered: undeveloped building sites, front and back gardens of empty houses, corners of parks and commons, golf courses and tennis courts. Lloyd George made it known that he had turned his Surrey garden over to growing potatoes.'[18]

13 Cahill, *Who Owns Britain?* p. 145.
14 Wright, *The Village that Died for England.*
15 *The Times*, 13 December 1916, p. 12.
16 Butcher, *Allotments for All: The Story of a Great Movement.*
17 Nilsen, *The Working Man's Green Space*, p. 41.
18 Willes, *The Gardens of the British Working Class*, p. 273.

The government also turned its urgent attention to the settling of discharged sailors and soldiers on rural smallholdings after the war. The Board of Agriculture appointed a specialist committee in the summer of 1915, chaired by Sir Harry Verney MP, a baronet, large landowner and Liberal MP for Basingstoke. He was given the task of recommending the best way of employing discharged sailors and soldiers on the land. The motives for this policy were influenced by pre-war agrarianism and concerns about the deleterious effects of city life on the health of the population, and especially the physical condition of the troops. The committee took evidence from a range of well-known land reformers and published its findings in 1916, concluding that

> The stability and physical strength of a nation depend largely on those classes who have either been born or brought up in the country or have had the advantages of country life. It is certain that the physique of those portions of our nation who live in crowded streets rapidly deteriorates and would deteriorate even further if they were not to some extent reinforced by men from the country districts. If therefore we desire a strong and healthy race, we must encourage as large a proportion of our people as possible to live on the land. The demobilisation of the navy and army at the close of the war will afford a unique opportunity of developing agriculture in this country.[19]

By the end of the war the government had established colonies of smallholdings, including the Farm Settlements Estates in Lincolnshire owned by the Ministry of Agriculture. It had also enacted the Land Settlement (Facilities) Act in 1919 which further encouraged local authorities to acquire land for the settlement of ex-servicemen, but these were for rent rather than purchase, unlike earlier pre-war legislation that sought to create a property-owning peasantry. By 1924, county councils had bought and leased a quarter of a million acres and nearly 50,000 men and women had applied for smallholdings. But many tenants were found to be unsuitable and only half-hearted in their commitment to a life on the land, although by 1920 over 14,000 had been settled.[20]

In reality, rural smallholdings did not provide an answer to the problems of agriculture during the interwar period, which experienced a period of further depression after the removal of guaranteed prices for corn in 1921. In fact, country districts continued to experience significant rural depopulation. The UK agricultural labour force declined from 27% in 1851 to 11% in 1911. By 1931 it had fallen to only 8.7%.[21] For one historian, 'the socially stabilising provision of carefully controlled access to land for the working

19 Verney Committee, *The Settlement or Employment on the Land in England and Wales of Discharged Sailors and Soldiers* (1916), Cd. 8182.
20 Dakers, *Forever England: The Countryside at War*, p. 196.
21 Dewey, *British Agriculture in the First World War*, pp. 240–1.

class was a means for the landed class to defuse social unrest and retain both their estates and their political power'. She argued that access to a plot of land emulated, on a small scale, the benefits of landownership and fostered adhesion to the existing social order.[22] Such an interpretation supports the idea of a 'ramparts' strategy, a proposition first proposed by the Conservative Prime Minister Lord Salisbury in the 1880s, designed to protect the unequal distribution of property by erecting a rampart of small property owners.[23]

However, after the war, small farms did not provide an answer to agricultural productivity.[24] In their review of the value of smallholdings, carried out in the early 1930s, the social reformers and researchers, Viscount Astor and Seebohm Rowntree reluctantly came out against their extension on economic grounds, concluding that:

> The old rigid separation between town and country is being rapidly broken down. The agricultural labourer is coming to increasingly enjoy many of the facilities and conveniences of the townsman. The industrial worker is being brought increasingly into contact with the amenities of the countryside. Do not these tendencies ... represent more hopeful possibilities than those which some Continental countries are attempting to realise by the extension of a peasant economy? ... By the increasing contact which is springing up between town and countryside, are we not likely to secure a sounder basis for social stability than is offered by the clash of antagonistic standpoints associated in so many countries with the sharply divergent structures of industry and agriculture.[25]

The growth in the size of farms became one of the primary features of the transformation of agriculture in the West during the twentieth century.[26] In contrast, the demand for town-based allotments ('lungs in the city'), rather than rural smallholdings, grew into an urban phenomenon during the twentieth century as the population became ever more divorced from country life. They became an important means of providing recreation and a way of reconnecting to nature for a population confined to urban areas.[27]

Post-war changes in rural development and landownership

Some wartime changes were a continuation of pre-war trends, such as the sale of landed estates, the promotion of smallholdings and the idealisation of

22 Nilsen, *The Working Man's Green Space.*
23 Offer, *Property and Politics*, chapter 9 and pp. 405–6; Daunton, *House and Home in the Victorian City*, pp. 223–4.
24 Bone, 'Legislation to Revive Small Farming in England, 1887–1914', pp. 653–61.
25 Astor and Rowntree, *The Agricultural Dilemma*, p. 91.
26 Grigg, *The Transformation of Agriculture in the West.*
27 Nilsen, *The Working Man's Green Space*, p. 3; Crouch and Ward, *The Allotment.*

the countryside for literary, nationalistic and nostalgic purposes. Others were new developments, such as the state requisitioning of land for war purposes, changes in the way the traditional landowning class were perceived in class and political terms, and government intervention to increase agricultural production through guaranteed prices and wages. Some of these trends continued after the war, such as the sale of landed estates to owner-occupying famers and the influence of a pastoral tradition in popular culture and literature accentuated by the experience of the trenches. But other changes were soon reversed in the climate of post-war austerity and restoration of free trade. The withdrawal of agricultural protection led to the return of pre-war depression and deteriorating economic and social conditions in the countryside, increasingly blighted by ribbon development, unregulated advertising and suburban sprawl. As a result, public concern shifted away from a preoccupation about the political power of the landed aristocracy, whose sons had paid a high price in the trenches, towards the need to conserve and protect the countryside from despoliation and to introduce more centralised planning to control urban development (see chapter 4).

After the war the sale of landed estates accelerated reaching a peak in the early 1920s. A large number of them were broken up and individual farms sold to tenant farmers, leading to a significant increase in owner-occupation. Historians have disputed the claim by F. M. L. Thompson that the sale of landed estates immediately after the war, which the *Estates Gazette* claimed in 1921 allegedly saw up to one-quarter of England change hands in a very short period of time, was nothing short of a revolution in landownership. Thompson had argued that

> such an enormous and rapid transfer of land had not been seen since the confiscations and sequestrations of the Civil War, such a permanent transfer not since the dissolution of the monasteries in the sixteenth century. Indeed, a transfer on this scale and in such a short space of time had probably not been equalled since the Norman Conquest.[28]

Some historians have suggested that landlords were so demoralised 'by the prospect of diminished post-tax incomes and lost power over their land that they were selling out in droves'.[29] Others have criticised Thompson's apocalyptic language as an exaggeration. They insisted that this did not reflect the real revolution in landownership on the eve of the First World War caused by agricultural depression, the introduction in 1894 of death duties and the fears posed by Lloyd George's land tax proposals after 1909.[30] Leaving aside the technical aspects of this debate, Thompson responded by maintaining that

---

28 Thompson, *English Landed Society in the Nineteenth Century*, p. 352; *Estates Gazette*, 31 December 1921.
29 Perkin, *The Rise of Professional Society*, p. 154.
30 Beckett and Turner, 'End of the Old Order?', pp. 269–88.

however the level of sales was measured, 'it seems possible that something not far short of "a quarter of England" may actually have changed hands in 1918–21'.[31] The important issue for Thompson was that there was little evidence after 1918 to indicate a resumption of the pre-war assault on land-owners. Although the threat of Bolshevism did seriously alarm the propertied classes following the Russian Revolution, the radical political attack on land-lordism was not repeated after the war, with reformers confining their imme-diate demands to the provision of smallholdings for ex-servicemen. Other historians have also commented on the abdication of radicalism at this time in relation to land reform measures. For example, Offer has suggested that the 'the apathy of Liberals and Labour made it easier ... to push through the policy which culminated in the Law of Property Act 1925', a reform of land tenure and registration arrangements which fell far short of Victorian and Edwardian demands for reform.[32]

However the transfer of land-holdings, which between 1909 and 1927 may have amounted to between six and eight million acres, 'was certainly a water-shed in the history of landownership and rural life'.[33] Most agree that the beginnings of these sales started before 1914 on a smaller scale arising from agricultural depression, falling rent rolls and the burden of taxation, and not helped by the taxation of land values and the new surtax introduced in Lloyd George's budget of 1909. But it is clear that the war created a real financial crisis for many landowners and was the primary reason for their decision to sell their estates, either entirely or in part. Incomes from rent had been roughly halved as a result of the rent freeze introduced by the government. Many owners decided to sell their land, especially divesting themselves of holdings on the edge of large estates, taking advantage of high land prices and the ability of tenant farmers to purchase their farms. There had been significant increases in the income of farmers due to government intervention to fix prices during the war, a situation which many thought would continue after the end of hostilities. The budget of 1919 introduced death duties of 40% on estates valued over £2 million and although few were directly affected, 'for most land-owners selling was simple good sense'.[34] The example of the journalist farmer A. G. Street has been cited, who taking over his late father's farm in 1918, 'was faced with an increased rent demand from the estate agents of nearly 100%, on a take it or leave it basis. He took it, borrowing the working capital at 5%, a move he regretted shortly afterwards, in the depression of 1921–3'.[35]

The onset of agricultural depression after the repeal of the Corn Production Act in 1921 saw the collapse of agricultural prices. By 1925 the large-scale disposal of rural estates had significantly slowed down. Many farmers got

31 Thompson, 'The Land Market, 1880–1925', pp. 289–300.
32 Offer, 'The Origins of the Law of Property Acts, 1910–25', pp. 505–22.
33 Dewey, *British Agriculture in the First World War*, p. 242.
34 Dakers, *Forever England: The Countryside at War*, p. 201.
35 Street, *Farmer's Glory*, p. 219, quoted in Dewey, *British Agriculture*, p. 242.

into financial difficulties during the years that followed and struggled to repay their mortgages, some selling their farms to builders and developers. But the process of the spread of owner-occupation precipitated by the war continued, resulting in a remarkable transformation in land tenure arrangements with important consequences for the fortunes of land reform. By 1961 the percentage of farmers who were owner-occupiers in England and Wales had increased to 56%. These levels were on a par with the Low Countries, but significantly less than Ireland, France, Denmark and Germany, where occupancy was much higher.[36] In these circumstances it became increasingly difficult for politicians from the left to attack the principle of private property. The proportion of agricultural holdings occupied by their owners had expanded from 13% in 1909 to 37% by 1927, with the majority of the sales taking place between 1919 and 1921.[37] This was the largest single shift out of tenancy into owner-occupation – from one-tenth to one-third.[38]

The spread of owner-occupation in urban areas

While farming and the countryside remained depressed during the interwar period, urban land markets boomed and provided rich investment opportunities for both the new institutional landlords and the larger landowners capable of diversifying, particularly those owning estates on the fringes of the main towns and cities. By 1939 about four million new houses had been built, two and a half million for private sale, mainly in suburban locations on prime agricultural land. The rest was built by local authorities to rehouse the families of the armed services following demobilisation after the war, and as part of a concerted political attempt for the first time to clear the slums. The Addison Act of 1919 and Labour's Wheatley Housing Act of 1924 saw the birth of local authority provided housing, financed by central government funding. The interwar period thus witnessed a significant shift from private to social renting. 'Although 77% of households were renting in 1919, only 1% of households were doing so from social landlords (either councils or the charities established by reforming philanthropists). As a result of direct state action to build council homes, by 1939 the percentage of households socially renting had risen to 10%.'[39]

A policy of cheap money and readily available mortgages, combined with growing middle-class incomes, and aided by electrification and development of road transport, created a remarkable expansion in suburban housing for those capable of escaping from the crowded city centres. Cheap land prices and the low wages of building workers, together with minimal state regulation of private housebuilding, including weak town and country planning, made

---

36 Grigg, *The Transformation of Agriculture in the West*, p. 81.
37 Sturmey, 'Owner-Farming in England and Wales, 1900–1950', pp. 283–306.
38 Offer, 'Farm Tenure and Land Values in England, 1750–1950', p. 19.
39 Office of National Statistics, *A Century of Home Ownership*.

building for owner-occupation a particularly profitable activity during the interwar years. Owner-occupied housing became an ideal investment for new entrants in the financial sector, such as insurance companies and new building societies. Such investment provided a higher return than government bonds and the manufacturing industry.[40] Similar developments were taking place in the market for commercial property, giving rise to a new group of financial companies supporting the building boom.[41] By 1938 about 35% of all houses in Britain were owner-occupied and concentrated in the suburbs and boom-towns such as Slough, Dagenham, Coventry, Oxford and Bristol.[42]

Although almost two-thirds of all householders continued to rent their house from a private landlord, owner-occupation also became common amongst the working classes in certain areas. By 1939 such owner-occupation stood at almost 20%, particularly 'in the Lancashire cotton towns, the mining regions of South Wales, shipbuilding towns such as Jarrow, and to a lesser extent the Yorkshire Wool districts and some isolated working-class suburbs of south-east London'.[43] The early building societies had been working-class institutions set up specifically to help house purchases, although the need for regular repayments meant in practice that by 1939 it was still only the elite of the working class that could afford home ownership. For those in the rented sector, poor rent controls fuelled anti-landlord sentiments and the demand of Labour councils for municipal housing.[44] But by the outbreak of the Second World War, even the Labour Party could not afford to ignore the needs of an important minority of its traditional political constituency that owned their own houses. On the eve of the 1945 general election, Clement Attlee privately observed that the working and middle classes had small but significant investments in insurance schemes, savings and property, as well as 'co-op' shares and post office and bank deposits, which they were eager to protect. He cautioned against the Labour Party mouthing 'Marxian shibboleths about the proletariat having nothing to lose but their chains'.[45]

For those people unable to obtain a mortgage after 1918, other options were available to become property owners in areas characterised as marginal, semirural or coastal. Without strict planning control many were able to acquire or squat plots of land in areas where it was low in value, such as on river estuaries and coastal strips. They put up shacks or disused railway carriages, and built weekend cottages, holiday homes or more substantial buildings, usually without permission and connection to services. These sites acquired the label of 'makeshift landscapes', and although they did

40 Ball, *Housing Policy and Economic Power*, pp. 29–42.
41 Scott, *The Property Masters*, pp. 68–98.
42 Swenarton and Taylor, 'The Scale and Nature of the Growth of Owner-Occupation in Britain between the Wars', p. 377.
43 Ibid., p. 378; Benson, *The Working Class in Britain, 1850–1939*, pp. 72–91.
44 Stevenson, *British Society, 1914–45*, pp. 221–30.
45 Bew, *Citizen Clem*, pp. 334–5.

not occupy extensive areas of land, they became a feature of the changing pattern of land tenure in the interwar period, particularly in the South East. The introduction of effective town planning legislation in 1947 brought such developments to an abrupt end. They have been described as being part of a 'Quest for Arcadia', informed by long-term traditions of pastoralism and agrarianism, and fulfilling the strong twentieth-century desire for owning a property of one's own.[46]

However, such makeshift landscapes were viewed with some horror by the growing preservationist movement, represented by the National Trust and the Council for the Preservation of Rural England, set up in 1926 to safeguard a very particular view of landscape, including the type of responsible citizenship required to benefit from access to the countryside.[47] These organisations coalesced to form a powerful lobby group that created a climate for more effective town and country planning. The conflict between the desire for property ownership and the aesthetic control of the landscape was an important development in the formation of new land reform policies after 1918, especially the control of urban development. Unregulated ribbon development by speculative builders and unsightly advertising hoardings were heavily objected to by the preservationists whose influence increased during this period. This conflict fed into demands for the preservation of the countryside against urban intrusion, controlled access to mountain and moorland, and the establishment of national parks, creating class and cultural divisions that cut across traditional political allegiances.[48]

The growing influence of town and country planning

As a result of the boom in housebuilding, the interwar period saw an 'unprecedented increase in the scale and rapidity of land-use change. By the mid-1930s, an estimated 60,000 acres of rural land in England and Wales were covered each year by buildings'.[49] Undesirable ribbon development in the countryside created pressure for conservation and control of urban sprawl, and a growing political awareness of the need to preserve the beauty of the countryside against urban intrusion.[50] Support for town planning and garden cities increased, particularly in the 1930s amongst middle-class intellectuals wishing to preserve a specific and on the whole nostalgic image of the English countryside. Certain of the larger metropolitan local authorities were also keen to rehouse urban slum dwellers in council estates built to garden city principles on cheaper suburban land.[51] However, such municipal intrusions

---

46 Hardy and Ward, *Arcadia for All*.
47 Matless, *Landscape and Englishness*.
48 Moore-Colyer, 'From Great Wren to Toad Hall' and 'A Voice Clamouring in the Wilderness'; Walker, 'The Popularisation of the Outdoor Movement, 1900–1940'.
49 Sheail, 'The Restriction of Ribbon Development Act', pp. 501–12.
50 Jeans, 'Planning and the Myth of the English Countryside in the Interwar Period', pp. 249–64.
51 Heathorn, 'An English Paradise to Regain?'

into the countryside met significant opposition from adjacent county councils resistant to the expansionist tendencies of, for example, the London County Council (LCC) and other metropolitan conurbations. As a result, the focus of local authority housing policy shifted in the 1930s from suburban to inner-city redevelopment, particularly the building of four storey tenement blocks to rehouse working-class families relocated from slum clearance areas.[52]

The erection of inner-city blocks of flats increased the anxiety of certain town planners about urban congestion and added weight to the demands of the garden cities lobby for decentralisation and the building of houses with gardens at a density of twelve houses per acre. The flats versus houses debate came to the fore in the 1930s, with the emergence of a modern school of British architecture calling for flats to be built on modern lines in urban areas. Influential town planners like Thomas Sharp emphasised the need to pre-serve 'towns as towns and countryside as countryside'.[53] The controversy over flats or houses, and the degree of decongestion that was thought neces-sary to achieve the desired balance between town and country, split the town planning movement in the 1930s. Such conflicts became an important feature of debates on popular housing provision into the 1940s and thereafter.[54]

Although the scope of town planning legislation was widened in 1919 and 1925 and extended to cover all areas of the country in 1932, it remained, like the Restriction of Ribbon Development Act in 1935, very limited in its application.[55] The interests of private property fought successful rear-guard actions in both Houses of Parliament to reduce the effectiveness of the legis-lation, particularly its financial provisions relating to betterment and com-pensation. All the acts reaffirmed the principle of betterment created by the preparation of planning schemes (50% in 1919 increased to 75% in 1932), but in practice no betterment was ever collected and the geographical pattern of industrial and urban development continued to be shaped largely by market forces.[56] The legislation was entirely permissive, and although local author-ities had the power to stop undesirable development, the high cost of com-pensating landlords prevented real control of land use, particularly at a time when economic depression reduced local authority rate income. By 1942 only 3% of the area of Britain was covered by a planning scheme.

The leading planners of the day, John Dower, Patrick Abercrombie, Thomas Adams, Frederick Osborn and Raymond Unwin, criticised the existing planning system for its permissive character; its lack of regional and

---

52 Yelling, *Slums and Redevelopment*, pp. 164–83.
53 Sharp, *Towns and Countryside* (London, 1932) and *English Panorama* (London, 1936).
54 Tsubaki, 'Post-War Reconstruction and the Questions of Popular Housing Provision, 1939–1951' (University of Warwick, PhD, 1993).
55 Cherry, 'The Town Planning Act, 1919'; Ward, 'The Town and Country Planning Act, 1932', pp. 681–9; Sheail, 'The Restriction of Ribbon Development Act', pp. 501–12.
56 Reade, *British Town and Country Planning*, p. 42; Sheail, 'Interwar Planning in Britain: The Wider Context', pp. 335–51.

national coordination and involvement with other agencies; and above all its financial weakness. They were especially critical of 'the provision that compensation for reduction in property values through planning shall be paid by the authority in full and immediately, while betterment for increase in property values shall be paid to the authority only as to 75 per cent and on realisation, through change of use or ownership during a limited period'.[57]

While planning legislation remained largely ineffective as a result of the power of property interests in Parliament, the intellectual influence of the garden city movement gained ground in the 1930s. This was part of the growth of political interest in centralised planning. Town planning was quickly recognised by 'middle opinion' as an essential ingredient of the broader demand for political and economic planning.[58] By the late 1930s, the continuing and chronic problems of the distressed areas gave added weight to the demand for national planning as did the examples of central government intervention embodied in the American New Deal and the building programmes of the fascist regimes of Germany and Italy. The need for national coordination became a rallying cry of numerous middle-class pressure groups, such as the Council for the Preservation of Rural England set up by Patrick Abercrombie in 1926.[59] The popular writings of H. J. Massingham lent an anti-urban and reactionary flavour to these debates in his lament for a lost English peasantry. Similar myth-making was encouraged by H. V. Morton in his widely read *In Search of England*.[60] These 'back-to-the-land' views were not shared by more progressive elements within the town planning lobby and political parties (see chapter 4).

Many town planners were highly critical of the inadequacies of local government in dealing with preservationist issues. They campaigned for stronger central direction and more powers for the larger local authorities. Support for regional planning also grew with the creation of regional planning committees under the 1932 Act. Although limited in their powers, some progress was made by the LCC, Liverpool and Manchester in building municipal housing estates on the suburban fringes (e.g. Becontree, Wythenshawe), where land was cheaper. But these were not garden cities as advocated by the town planners who wished to see significant decentralisation of industry and population through the building of satellite towns within a clearly defined green belt. After Labour gained control of the LCC in 1934, policy shifted

---

57 Dower et al., 'Positive Planning in Great Britain'. Paper submitted to the Royal Institute of British Architects, *Journal of the Royal Institute of British Architects*, 13 July 1935.

58 *Planning*, the broadsheet issued by *Political and Economic Planning*, devoted to a critique of Town and Country Planning, No. 2, 9 May 1933.

59 Abercrombie, 'The Preservation of Rural England'; Williams-Ellis, *England and the Octopus* (Portmeirion, 1928) and *Britain and the Beast* (London, 1938).

60 Massingham, *The English Countryman*; Morton, *In Search of England*; Moore-Colyer, 'A Voice Clamouring in the Wilderness'.

away from building municipal housing in the outer areas to building tenement blocks within LCC borders, thereby avoiding the problem of land speculation.[61] At the same time, the LCC under Herbert Morrison was successful in buying up a green belt (or 'green girdle') around London to prevent suburban sprawl. After 1934, the LCC spent about '£1,820,000 and local councils three times that much, in buying around 72,000 acres of green land and preserving it for recreational or agricultural use'.[62]

By 1939, the agenda of the Garden Cities and Town Planning Association had become widely accepted by 'middle opinion' as offering a comprehensive solution to the physical and economic problems of both town and countryside. It included demands for:

(1) a national policy to guide future land use and the creation of a national planning body;

(2) the maintenance of a distinction between town and country through the discouragement of development in agricultural areas, and the protection of recognised beauty spots and wild areas through the creation of national parks;

(3) country (or green) belts preserved around all cities and towns, and the density of urban areas limited to permit the building of houses with gardens;

(4) new industrial or urban development to be restricted to existing centres in the green belt and to new towns, taking into account the needs of industry and agriculture, with ribbon development prevented, and any new development in congested areas strictly controlled;

(5) reasonable compensation to be paid to owners deprived of prospective building value and the creation of a national compensation fund financed by the values of land zoned for building.[63]

Thus, by the late 1930s, land-use planning had encompassed calls for the protection of the countryside for access and recreation. During the interwar period, as fewer people worked on the land for agricultural purposes and migrated to the towns and cities, more of the urban population began to seek access to the land for recreation and spiritual fulfilment. The expansion of paid holidays was one of the main factors in the growth of working-class interest in the countryside. The Workers' Travel Association, the Ramblers' Association and the Youth Hostels Association were the main channels through which the idyll of the countryside spread from an elite upper-class

---

61 Young and Garside, *Metropolitan London: Politics and Urban Change, 1837–1981*.

62 Inwood, *A History of London*, pp. 723–4.

63 Printed in *Town and Country Planning*, 7, 28 (July–September 1939), p. 95; Evidence of the TCPA in the *Minutes of Evidence Taken before the Royal Commission on the Geographical Distribution of the Industrial Population*, 15 June 1938.

interest at the end of the nineteenth century to a mass outdoor movement by the late 1930s.[64] Rambling peaked in enthusiasm between 1926 and 1932 and the Ramblers' Association was formed in 1935. More militant hiking by working-class groups gave rise to mass trespass movements seeking greater access to mountains and moor land.[65] Anti-landlord sentiments were particularly strong in the north of England, Wales and Scotland and fuelled pressure for national parks and rights of way. An Access to Mountains Bill was finally enacted in 1939, albeit in a limited form, weakened by property interests in both Houses of Parliament. For many, the countryside came to be perceived as a closed place of aristocratic sport and privilege (the weekend country house party attended by the 'smart set') rather than as being economically useful or accessible to a mass urban populace.

The movement for the creation of national parks also gained momentum in the 1930s following Ramsay MacDonald's appointment of a committee of enquiry in 1929, chaired by Christopher Addison, to look at ways of preserving areas of outstanding natural beauty.[66] The Council for the Preservation of Rural England became an important umbrella group campaigning for national parks, although other rural pressure groups, such as the Ramblers' Association perceived such bodies as backward-looking and cranky, drawn from the rural and academic elite, and 'hell-bent on preserving the countryside for those who lived in it'.[67] Struggles over access channelled traditional anti-landlordism into new political movements differentiated by class and culture. 'The withdrawal of the aristocracy from the land paved the way for the re-appropriation of the countryside by urban society.... After the First World War, as political conflict between aristocracy and people died down, the countryside became more available for reconnection with a national identity.'[68] Stanley Baldwin capitalised on the public interest in rural nostalgia to consolidate his appeal to the middle classes that no longer looked to the landed aristocracy as leaders of society.[69]

Summary

After 1918, concern about land began to focus on other issues of more relevance to a population concentrated in urban and suburban areas and perceiving the countryside in different ways. Pre-war pressure for land reform did not disappear entirely but was channelled into new political directions. While

---

64 Walker, 'The Outdoor Movement in England and Wales, 1900–1939'.
65 Lowerson, 'Battles for the Countryside'; Walker, 'The Popularisation of the Outdoor Movement, 1900–1940', pp. 140–53.
66 Morgan, *Portrait of a Progressive*, p. 186.
67 Moore-Colyer, 'From Great Wren to Toad Hall', pp. 105–25.
68 Mandler, *The Fall and Rise of the Stately Home*, p. 226.
69 Schwarz, 'The Language of Constitutionalism'.

important sections of the working classes wanted access to the countryside for recreation following the extension of paid holidays, other influential middle-class interests wanted to protect rural areas from the despoliation arising from unregulated advertising, makeshift settlements and ribbon development by speculative builders. There was pressure for better access to the countryside and more centralised town and country planning to control development.

The relationship between town and country underwent significant changes in the interwar period and anti-landlord sentiments expressed themselves in new political ways. While the countryside experienced a profound economic and social crisis, urban society began to develop an agenda towards the land that sought to preserve and rescue it as a place of beauty, health and recreation. This was matched by a growing if slow political awareness of the need to protect agriculture as an industry amongst others from further economic decline, while seeking to safeguard the policy of cheap imported food for the urban population. Land reformers no longer regarded agriculture as special in contrast to other industries. Farming was perceived less as a way of life, possessing virtues which were different to urban living, and more like any other industry requiring support and state protection.

By the eve of the Second World War many of these new developments influenced the way in which the land question was interpreted as a political issue. Other factors also contributed to this process. In terms of domestic politics, Irish independence in 1921 may also have played a role by removing the contentious issue of home rule and its vital relationship to land reform. The political threat of Bolshevism and the extension of the franchise, almost certainly added to the cocktail of ruling-class concerns about the future of royalty and aristocratic landed wealth. In many other areas of Europe, the large landowners experienced confiscation or much worse. However, the potential for social unrest was largely unrealised in the United Kingdom. Revolution was avoided and the landed aristocracy survived, but with reduced political power and a much lower public profile. Thus after 1918, the landed interest no longer provided a focus of opposition to those who were radicalised about the concentration of their political power. Rent income and agricultural productivity had been the economic foundation of their power. But after the war, agriculture as an industry declined in economic importance and was left to face cheap imports leading to falling rent income and a general deterioration of conditions in the countryside.

Those who argued that agriculture should be treated as a special industry for wider social reasons, such as the injurious effects of unhealthy city life, the need for a peasantry or the security of domestic food production, lost out to the views of a political establishment increasingly wedded to austerity, free trade and the economic benefits of large-scale farming. In the face of agricultural depression, there was a move towards limited protectionism, imperial preference and better marketing of basic food stuffs during the 1930s, but not on a scale sufficient enough to restore economic prosperity to the large landowner. But above all, it was the spread of owner-occupation, especially amongst farmers, and the lower middle classes in urban and suburban areas during the interwar housebuilding boom in the South East and the Midlands, which helped defuse the question of land reform. It made the idea of a property-owning democracy into a reality for an increasing proportion of the population able to obtain mortgages. This was a trend which politicians from governing parties found difficult to ignore in a new age of mass democracy after the extension of the vote in 1918.

4   The rise of town planning and the demise of site value rating

The politics of land reform changed in the interwar period in response to the demographic and social changes outlined in chapter 3. This chapter will trace the way that town and country planning, including the collection of betterment through land-use control, eclipsed the more traditional policy of site value taxation. While the Conservative Party consolidated its position as the defender of private property and came to be seen as more clearly representing the interests of both the countryside and the new property-owning democracy, Labour inherited the progressive mantle of the ideology of social reform represented by the 'New Liberalism' of Lloyd George, which emphasised the connections between land, housing, poverty and unemployment, and advocated the rating of site values as the primary solution to the housing question.[1] But after 1918, Labour took land reform in new directions, losing some aspects of the pre-war tradition of agrarianism and embracing with more enthusiasm town and country planning, and slum clearance and the building of public housing for rent. In contrast, the Conservative Party became more closely identified with the idea of a property-owning democracy while also appointing itself 'as the rightful representative of the countryside – an appropriation which reached its apogee under Stanley Baldwin, with his styling of England as the country, and the Conservative Party as its friend'.[2] At the same time the Labour Party came to be seen as representing the interests of the working class in urban and metropolitan areas, but not necessarily in the new suburbs. It struggled to obtain much of a foothold in the countryside, apart from certain areas where agricultural trade unionism was relatively strong.

There was little scope for returning to the politics of the New Liberalism after 1918, with its emphasis on combining personal freedom and property ownership with state obligations to address social needs. The Liberal Party

---

1 Freeden, *The New Liberalism*, p. 140; Harris, 'Labour's Political and Social Thought', pp. 18–21.
2 Griffiths, *Labour and the Countryside*, p. 43; Burchardt, *Paradise Lost*, p. 105.

failed to regain power after the war. It was replaced by the Labour Party as the left-wing opposition representing the newly enfranchised and predominantly urban working class, and it was elected on a pragmatic programme of state intervention to build public housing and enact welfare reform. After the extension of the franchise in 1918, the link between property and voting rights became less important and Labour looked more towards the conscription of wealth, including large concentrations of landed property, as the solution to the land question while not directly attacking the principle of private property. Liberal land policy after 1918 sought to target the agricultural worker for fear of the potential influence of the Labour Party in rural areas while it wrote-off the farmers as already three-quarters Conservative. But Lloyd George's electoral strategy failed to withstand the ongoing decline of the rural population and the onset of agricultural depression after 1921.[3]

The spread of owner-occupation in both town and country and the return of agricultural depression, pushed land reform policy towards more state intervention, such as stronger town and country planning and the protection of the countryside from urban development. The interwar period also saw the introduction of some limited protectionist measures for agriculture. However, there were two elements of Edwardian land reform that did survive after the First World War. First, there was a continuing demand for smallholdings for rural workers. Returning soldiers and sailors were added to the list after the war as they were considered to be suitable for resettlement on the land following demobilisation, a policy promoted by politicians from all parties. Similarly, the unemployed were also considered to be ideal recipients of a 'back-to-the-land' policy. Second, there were two unsuccessful attempts to reintroduce taxation of land values (the rating of site values on unimproved land) by the Labour Chancellor of the Exchequer, Philip Snowden, in his budgets of 1924 and 1931.

However, by the outbreak of the Second World War, both these policies had failed. Smallholdings and allotments did not really provide a viable answer to the problems of a depressed agriculture. Taxation of land values was no longer considered a practical means of generating central government revenue and had been dropped for lack of support. Instead, Labour-controlled local authorities, especially the London County Council captured by the party in 1934, tried to enact local schemes of betterment under the permissive powers granted to them by town and country planning legislation (while having to pay compensation at market rates for any land compulsorily purchased).

This chapter will review the record of both of the main political parties, concentrating in particular on the Labour Party as the inheritor of the tradition of radical agrarianism. It will discuss four key areas of reform. First, it will note the lack of radical engagement in the way in which property law

---

3 Dawson, 'The Liberal Land Policy, 1924–1929', p. 273.

was reformed in 1925, and the missed opportunity this represented to achieve the registration of title, a long-standing demand of Victorian and Edwardian reformers campaigning for free trade in land. Second, it will trace the way in which support for a more economic approach to agriculture was adopted in the face of foreign competition, and the way in which smallholdings were slowly replaced by a more state-interventionist approach to protect agriculture. Third, it will describe the way in which taxation of land values was eclipsed by growing support for land nationalisation, as part of an ideological move towards more centralised state planning. Finally, it will explore how stronger town and country planning started to gain support, particularly in the Labour Party, as a means of protecting the countryside from urban despoliation and addressing the problems of the distressed areas. These developments represented a partial rejection of the 'back-to-the-land' policies of pre-war land reform. This did not however reduce the cultural idealisation of the countryside as an escape from the worst features of industrial and urban life, a view which could be found represented across the political spectrum.[4]

Land law reform

Pre-war demands for the registration of title, a measure seen by reformers as necessary to break the political monopoly of the landed aristocracy, failed to generate any significant level of political controversy after 1918, when moves were made by the House of Lords to simplify the highly complex system of property law. Its complexity may have been one reason for the lack of political engagement. Popular novelists like Dorothy L Sayers referred to this so-called 'simplifying Act' as continuing 'to cause a shocking lot of muddle' (in a Lord Peter Wimsey murder mystery concerning inheritance rights).[5] The failure of political radicalism may also have played a part, as did the reduced circumstances of the landed aristocracy. The extension of vote in 1918 to all adult men and married women over thirty had altered the balance in the political battle between landed wealth and 'the people' in favour of those without property. The link between property ownership and the vote had been closely linked in the minds of working-class radicals before 1914. But the extension of the vote as a universal entitlement to all adult men and women in 1928 finally broke this connection.

In many respects the land law legislation did not achieve a radical reform of tenure arrangements as hoped for by earlier reformers. In reality, the Law of Property Act of 1925 and its accompanying consolidating legislation assisted in the badly needed simplification of conveyancing. The legislation abolished the last vestiges of feudal tenure arrangements, such as copyhold,

4 Jeans, 'Planning and the Myth of the English Countryside in the Interwar Period', pp. 249–64; Burchardt, *Paradise Lost*; Williams, *The Country and the City*.
5 Sayers, *Unnatural Death*, p. 165.

and corrected some of the complexities of Victorian land law. But it was a far cry from the demand for free trade in land. There has, as one historian confirmed, never been a fundamental reform of the land system. Expectations were high after the war, but 'in the event nothing came of it, apart from the legislative spring-cleaning of 1925, designed to adapt the forms of land law to the realities of landownership'.[6] There had been continuous pressure to abolish archaic practices, such as primogeniture and overly complex convey-ancing arrangements (ridiculed by Charles Dickens in his description of the case of Jarndyce versus Jarndyce in *Bleak House*). But the legislation of 1925 was limited. Its primary objective was to ease the transfer of land to meet the realities of the changing property market after the war, when the number of sales increased with the beginnings of the spread of owner-occupation. For radical land reformers the legislation was a missed opportunity.

The failure to introduce the compulsory registration of title, for example, was one indication of the limited scope of this legislation, which attracted little public attention and was not debated in the House of Commons. The history of land registration in England has been one of procrastination and delay, and this continues to this day with a Land Registry that as Kevin Cahill has noted 'is defi-cient of 2 million titles, covering up to half of England and Wales, and with no ... prospect of that deficit ever being remedied'.[7] The legal profession as a vested interest has been held largely responsible for thwarting the pressure for reform. Solicitors had resisted attempts to end their monopoly over conveyancing for decades before 1914, but the profession had come to recognise after the war that their restrictive practices were not in their long-term financial or professional interests.[8] The official history of the Land Registry stated that such opposition could be traced back to the seventeenth century, when reformers looked, for example, to Holland, which had introduced land registration in 1529, resulting in higher land values and the achievement of more efficient mortgages. 'In the Commonwealth era' it continued 'hopes were high that something could be done to remedy what Oliver Cromwell called "an ungodly mess". ... Registration of deeds bills were introduced but talked out of parliament by the opposition of the judiciary in 1653 and 1656'.[9]

While conveyancing was simplified, the pressure for land registration was resisted. The compulsory registration of title was seen as an important part of the campaign for free trade in land during the nineteenth century. It was promoted by middle-class radicals such as Richard Cobden, who wished to extend the principle of free trade to the market for land. This was taken up by John Stuart Mill and the Land Tenure Reform Association in the 1860s and found considerable support in both main political parties after 1885.[10]

---

6 Perkin, 'Land Reform and Class Conflict in Victorian Britain', p. 178.
7 Cahill, *Who Owns Britain?* p. 53.
8 Ball, *Housing Policy and Economic Power*, pp. 29–30.
9 Land Registry, *A Short History of Land Registration in England and Wales*, p. 4.
10 Offer, 'The Origins of the Law of Property Acts, 1910–25', p. 505.

The free trade in land movement sought to abolish primogeniture and the costly and uncertain conveyancing practices that characterised the Victorian land market and which were held responsible for entrenched aristocratic power and economic inefficiency. 'For men who believed in the superiority of market forces to solve social problems it was imperative to remove "artificial" impediments to a system of private property based upon individual initiative and responsibility.'[11] Their aim was to simplify the transfer of land and make land like any other commodity for sale in a free market. Its attraction for middle-class reformers was that it could lead to the break-up of the big landed estates, reduce the power of the landed aristocracy and then bring about the wider distribution of landownership without extending the vote to the working classes.[12] For class-conscious radicals, the registration of land

> was a means of dismantling in the instruments of aristocratic identity and separateness. ...Registration was a perquisite of an interventionist policy of tenure reform, peasant proprietorships, allotment provision, home ownership for the working classes; it was an accessory of land taxation, sanitary reform and compulsory purchase. These connections are manifest in subsequent Liberal Proposals and measures in the 1880s and thereafter.[13]

While support for registration of title had enjoyed some success during the latter part of the nineteenth century, it was only made compulsory in the London area and remained a voluntary scheme in the rest of the country following lobbying by provincial solicitors. Offer has described in detail how pressure for the registration of title failed to be achieved in the legislation of 1925 despite the head of steam for land reform generated by Lloyd George in the immediate pre-war period. Lloyd George had sought to enact the principle of compulsory registration in 1911, endorsed by a Royal Commission, which under pressure from solicitors refused to support compulsion. His aim was to form a Domesday office for England and Wales, amalgamating the existing Land Registry with the Land Values Department, with the ultimate objective of undertaking a comprehensive cadastral type survey of land-holdings as a prerequisite for the introduction of taxation of land values.[14]

However, the outbreak of war interrupted these ambitions in the same way that it thwarted Lloyd George's plans for a radical land reform programme unifying the progressive left. Although wartime collectivism created new opportunities for registration of title, the machinery set up by the Ministry of Reconstruction in 1917 rejected compulsory registration, despite the political awareness of its chairman, Lord Scott, that such a system would cut

11 Anderson, *Lawyers and the Making of English Land Law, 1832–1940*, p. 161.
12 Thompson, *English Landed Society in the Nineteenth Century*, p. 283.
13 Offer, *Property and Politics*, pp. 33–4.
14 Offer, 'The Origins of the Law of Property Acts, 1910–25', pp. 508.

the ground from under the feet of the 'bolshevists (sic)'.[15] There was some hope immediately after the war that progress could be made. But while '1919–20 was a period of hope ... , 1921–25 was a period of humiliation'.[16] Certain important members of the legal profession acted as a powerful lobby group to prevent compulsory registration, motivated in part by pecuniary interests, although other wider professional interests may also have played a part.[17]

Certainly after 1921 concerns about public expenditure put paid to an enhanced Land Registry with compulsory powers. *The Times* complained that such extravagant plans for the creation of a Land Registry Department were detrimental to the taxpayer.[18] Offer concluded that 'ruling class retrenchment after the First World War defeated the prospects of registration' and that this can be accounted for by the abdication of radicalism, with single taxers like Josiah C. Wedgwood and other members of the Labour Party not putting up any significant opposition.[19] In fact, he has suggested that the Labour Party may have been bought off by an amendment to the Law of Property Bill in 1921, allowing trade unions to lease or buy more than one acre of land (which had been forbidden by the Trades Union Act of 1871). In the opinion of the Solicitor General at the time, this would give the trade unions a 'proprietary interest which would disincline them to revolution'.[20]

From smallholdings to agricultural protection

The repeal of the Corn Production Act in 1921 in the name of free trade led to agricultural depression, falling prices and rents and further rural depopulation. The sales of landed estates, the destruction of many country houses and the disappearance of large numbers of the gentry, with many emigrating to the outposts of Empire, combined to create a neglected and run down countryside blighted by well-publicised examples of urban despoliation.[21] Historians have described in detail the way the economic crises of the interwar period gave rise to pressure for tariff protection, imperial preference and better marketing of basic food stuffs, made more urgent after the economic crash of 1929.[22] The Conservative Party and the national coalition government after 1931 were as equally divided on how to respond to this crisis as was the Labour Party, which had traditionally supported free trade. The Conservative Party moved away during this period from thinking about agriculture in terms of guaranteeing social stability. It looked to the

15 Offer, 'The Origins of the Law of Property Acts, 1910–25', p. 514.
16 Ibid., p. 520.
17 Anderson, *Lawyers and the Making of English Land Law, 1832–1940*.
18 *The Times*, 8 January 1921, p. 4.
19 Offer, 'The Origins of the Law of Property Acts, 1910–25', p. 522.
20 Offer, 'The Origins of the Law of Property Acts, 1910–25', p. 519.
21 Jeans, 'Planning and the Myth of the English Countryside in the Interwar Period', pp. 249–64.
22 Perren, *Agriculture in Depression, 1870–1940*.

introduction of partial economic protection of agriculture, allied with a preference for trading with the Empire, and the adoption of better marketing to protect home-grown produce, such as milk. This marked the end of the way in which an agrarian vision had influenced policymakers, despite the rhetoric employed by politicians like Stanley Baldwin who continued to extoll the virtues of an idealised country life.[23] The Labour Party responded in a not dissimilar way to these economic pressures. Their land reform policies changed after 1918 in favour of a more state-interventionist approach, away from free trade towards producer marketing, and as a result rejecting previous 'back-to-the-land' remedies.[24]

The social role of agriculture had been one of the primary features of the Edwardian 'land question'. Mainstream thinking sought to reverse rural depopulation through smallholdings which it was hoped would revive the economic fortunes of agriculture and the countryside, as well as achieving certain social objectives relating to the general health and well-being of the nation. However, after 1918 this position became increasingly problematic. Calls for the creation of a Continental-style peasant economy were slowly and tentatively displaced during the interwar period by a more economic approach to the problems of agriculture, with a growing recognition of the need for larger-scale production and investment. For example, smallholdings had been a primary feature of Labour's agricultural policy before 1914, although the agricultural trade unions looked to other more pragmatic reforms to improve working conditions.[25]

The period before 1914 witnessed significant legislative activity, with over 20,000 smallholdings created by local authorities. This was continued during and after the war. Interest in the development of smallholdings remained intense during the 1920s, especially as a means of settling discharged soldiers and unemployed men on the land. Further minor legislation was enacted in 1925 and 1926 to ensure the provision of allotments in town planning schemes, although by the end of the 1920s the number of allotments had fallen to below one million.[26] Lloyd George looked in particular to the revival of agriculture in the post-war period as the cure for unemployment and rural depopulation. He believed, 'until proved wrong in 1925, that the land would be a popular vote winning issue'.[27]

Although the Labour Party was committed to smallholdings in the 1920s, its attitude was more ambivalent.[28] 'Whether the future lies with small holdings, with the present medium sized farms or huge capitalist production

23 Cooper, *British Agricultural Policy, 1912–1936*.
24 Tichelar, 'The Labour Party and Land Reform in the Inter-War Period'.
25 LP/AG/30/24, LPA: Part 6.
26 Departmental Committee of Inquiry into Allotments (Thorpe Report, 1969), Cmnd. 4166.
27 Campbell, *Lloyd George: The Goat in the Wilderness, 1922–1931*; Dawson, 'The Liberal Land Policy, 1924–1929', pp. 272–90.
28 Griffiths, *Labour and the Countryside*, pp. 270–4.

on much larger farms, no one can at present foresee' commented Arthur Henderson, the party's General Secretary in 1922.[29] Throughout the interwar period, party policy supported the setting up of 'one fair-sized experimental farm in each district, to be cultivated on business lines in such a way as to demonstrate what could be done by the most improved methods'.[30] However, this did not prevent others in the party, such as the ardent single taxer Josiah C. Wedgwood, who had joined the Labour Party in 1921, from continuing to refer to 'land hunger' and 'Three Acres and a Cow': 'Does anyone doubt' he argued 'that hunger for land is the one permanent craving of the farm workers? ... tillers of the soil will even attempt to take the land by force'.[31] Such views did not find favour with the General Secretary of the Agricultural Workers Union.[32]

In the 1930s, emphasis shifted in Labour Party thinking to land settlements as a means of addressing mass unemployment. The Labour government in 1931 sought, through the Land Utilisation Act to set up a corporation to purchase tracts of land for large-scale experiments in farming and reclamation. The Act also gave the Minister of Agriculture new powers to create up to 100,000 new small farms. The Conservatives attacked this measure as creeping nationalisation, but failure to provide any significant funding led to these schemes becoming an irrelevancy.[33] One final attempt to put unemployed men on the land was made in 1934 with the creation of the Land Settlement Association, which became part of the special areas policy in 1935.

The Labour Party continued to support smallholdings and allotments after 1931 as a means of giving the agricultural worker independence, but opinion both inside and outside the party was beginning to recognise the limitations. In 1935 the Oxford Agricultural Economics Research Institute concluded that there was 'no more justification for raising the cry of "back-to-the-land" in the mining villages of Durham or the shipyards of Barrow and the Tyne, than for raising the cry of "back-to-the-village-blacksmith's-shop", in Sheffield, or of "back-to-the-handloom", in Lancashire'.[34] Other opinion formers were also reluctantly driven to the conclusion that 'the possibilities of large-scale land settlement were far smaller than some of us had believed ... the results of settling large numbers of workers on the land ... [was] likely to prejudice our whole national economy, our relations with the Dominions and our international relations in Europe'.[35]

---

29 'The Labour Party and Agriculture', a speech made by Arthur Henderson at Cromer on 17 March 1922, LPA: Part 1, 21/19; The Labour Party and Land Reform.
30 'The Labour Party and the Countryside' (1921), p. 4, LPA: Part 1, 21/24.
31 Wedgwood, 'Labour and the Farm Worker' (1925), p. 6, LPA: Part 1, 25/46.
32 Ibid., p. 3, foreword by R. B. Walker, General Secretary of the Agricultural Workers Union.
33 Skidelsky, *Politicians and the Slump*, pp. 256–9.
34 Orwin and Drake, *Back to the Land*, pp. 92–3.
35 Astor and Rowntree, *The Agricultural Dilemma*, pp. x–xi.

In his review of British agriculture published in 1939, Labour's Christopher Addison took an international perspective. He admitted that only about 30,000 smallholdings had actually been created by legislation since 1908 out of a total of 280,000 small farms of less than fifty acres. The total number of such holdings only represented about 7% of cultivable land in comparison with France where it was 42% and Germany where it was 30%. 'I have become convinced that [smallholdings] are not in fact the easiest and most promising method' of production, 'although sound National policy should provide for its development on the grouped ... colony system under unified direction where the land was appropriate'. For Addison, the future lay with market-garden production 'on a scale big enough to make proper provision for skilled direction and management'.[36] By 1939 therefore, smallholdings, which had dominated Labour Party agricultural policy since the turn of the century, had almost been abandoned. They no longer offered the possibility of social engineering and political stability that had so captured the imagination of land reformers before 1914.

The most contentious aspect of Labour Party policy concerned pressure to compromise over free trade. Such a change represented a fundamental shift of policy. The Labour Party from its inception had been committed to free trade almost as an act of faith. It was the party of cheap food for a rapidly expanding urban population. However, the experience of the First World War in subsidising the income of farmers greatly influenced post-war developments and had a considerable impact on politicians like Christopher Addison, a Liberal convert to Labour in the early 1920s, who played a leading role in the development of Labour's agricultural policy after the war.[37] Despite the pressure for protection, majority opinion in the party remained staunchly pro-free trade. In 1918 Philip Snowden, the party's future Chancellor, repudiated 'all proposals for a Protective Tariff ... and strenuously opposed any taxation, of any kind, which would increase the price of food'.[38] The repeal of the Corn Production Act in 1921 was condemned more for its abolition of agricultural wages boards and fair rents than for its abandonment of subsidised incomes to farmers. Labour pledged to reintroduce the minimum wage for rural workers, reduce agricultural rates, give state help to farmers who bought their land at the height of the great land sales, and introduce fair rent courts.[39] In its first major policy statement after the war it proposed, apart from a long-term ambition to abolish 'landlordism', a reform of wages and housing, rating reductions and above all else 'no protective tariffs'.[40]

---

36 Christopher Addison, *A Policy for British Agriculture*, pp. 241–60.
37 Morgan, *Portrait of a Progressive*; Cline, *Recruits to Labour.*
38 Labour and the New Social Order (1918) p. 14; 'Why the Labour Party is Opposed to All Protective Tariffs (1918), LPA Part 1, 18/57.
39 'Agricultural Wages – Who Killed Cock Robin?' (1922); 'What Labour Will Do on the Land' (1922); 'Labour's Policy for the Farmer' (1923), LPA: Part 1, 22/1, 22/67 and 23/41.
40 'The Labour Party and the Countryside' (1921), LPA: Part 1, 21/24.

But the onset of agricultural depression after 1921 gave added weight to demands for protection. It was Christopher Addison who brought to Labour an enthusiasm for the marketing of food and the use of import boards, the provision of which were seen by many as the socialist answer to improved home agriculture, replacing a previous reliance on smallholdings.[41] Support for marketing appeared for the first time in Labour's second major policy statement on agriculture published jointly with the Trades Union Council (TUC) in 1926.[42] A proposal for import boards was also included in the party's new national programme in 1928, *Labour and the Nation*. It was argued that such boards represented the best means to safeguard domestic agriculture without admitting the need for tariffs.[43] When Labour formed its second minority government in 1929, agricultural policy, and in particular the controversy over import quota and marketing schemes, was to lock the Treasury and the Ministry of Agriculture in conflict over the next eighteen months. Tensions within the government centred on the debate that quota, while better than tariffs, were still an infringement of the principle of free trade. Philip Snowden regarded quota as political suicide.[44]

The Labour government was too divided on the question to take any action but introduced instead the highly successful Agricultural Marketing Act of 1931. Labour's commitment to producer marketing and price stability for farmers was confirmed in its third major policy statement on agriculture published in 1932. This advocated the establishment of a commodity board as part of a system of national planning.[45] Hugh Dalton, the architect of Labour's policy transformation in the 1930s, saw Addison's Marketing Act as an essential element of the economic planning of external trade.[46] Tom Williams, a future Labour Minister of Agriculture, advocated a National Marketing Commission, price-fixing and import boards.[47] Dalton played a key role in encouraging the party to adopt practical policies to take control of finance, land, transport, coal and power. These proposals were included in *Labour's Immediate Programme* in 1937.[48] This trend was particularly noticeable in Labour's agricultural policy. *Labour's Policy for Our Countryside*, written by Christopher Addison in 1937, advocated guaranteed prices for domestic produce, the control of imperial produce and marketing boards.[49]

---

41 Morgan, *Portrait of a Progressive*, p. 170.
42 'A Labour Policy on Agriculture' (1926), p. 15, LPA: Part 1, Pamphlet and Leaflets, 26/19.
43 Griffiths, *Labour and the Countryside*, pp. 217–57.
44 Marquand, *Ramsay MacDonald*, pp. 557–61.
45 'The Land and the National Planning of Agriculture' (1932), LPA: Part 2, 32/9; Stafford Cripps, 'The Economic Planning of Agriculture' (1934), LPA: Part 2, 34/13.
46 Dalton, *Practical Socialism for Britain*, p. 307.
47 Williams, *Labour's Way to Use the Land*, pp. 91–9.
48 *Labour's Immediate Programme* (1937); Morgan, 'The Planners' pp. 105–18.
49 'Labour's Policy for Our Countryside' (1937); 'Labour's Policy of Food for All' (1937), LPA: Part 2, 36/39 and 37/17.

Support for marketing and control of agricultural produce developed in parallel with a growing interest in nutrition. The marketing of domestic milk and fresh vegetables at a price affordable for urban working-class consumers became an important new feature of both Conservative and Labour Party agricultural policy in the late 1930s.[50] This emphasis on cheap fresh food was a new urban demand on the British countryside which undermined a sentimental approach to agricultural reform, as evidence increasingly indicated that milk production and market gardening were best carried out on a larger-scale economic basis.[51] Together, the policies of producer marketing and nutrition combined to represent a partial rejection of the 'back-to-the-land' option, and a historic abandonment of free trade. These were developments that Labour shared with the direction of Conservative policy in the same period. An economic view of agriculture increasingly replaced the belief in the superior virtue of country life.

From taxation of land values to land nationalisation

Although demands for the taxation of land values survived into the 1920s, and in particular the rating of site values which had been an important part of Lloyd George's People's Budget of 1909, by 1939 this policy no longer attracted the same level of political support. Attempts to introduce site value rating had been made by the London County Council by way of a private bill in 1901, and it had presented evidence in support of such a policy to the Royal Commission on the Housing of the Working Classes in 1885 (which recommended land taxation) and the Royal Commission on Local Taxation in 1899. Also, a number of private bills on the rating of site values were introduced without success during the Edwardian period, which would have taxed the value of the land rather than the property built on it.[52] After 1918, this policy was to a large extent superseded by a growing emphasis on land nationalisation and town and country planning, including more specific policies in relation to the recoupment of betterment in the urban land market through land-use control. The rating of site values never obtained sufficient political support during the twentieth century to ensure any legislative success. Land reformers increasingly looked to town and country planning to recoup betterment and determine levels of compensation for the compulsory purchase of development land.[53]

After 1918 the Liberal Party and Lloyd George, in particular, continued to press for the rating of site values. He set up the *Land and Nation League* in 1925 and relaunched another ambitious land campaign based on the publication

50 'Nutrition and Food Supplies' (1936); 'Labour's Policy of Food for All' (1937), LPA: Part 2, 37/1 and 37/13; Cooper, *British Agricultural Policy, 1912–1936*.

51 Christopher Addison, *A Policy for British Agriculture*, pp. 241–60.

52 Prest, *The Taxation of Urban Land*, pp. 64–73.

53 Prest, *The Taxation of Urban Land*, pp. 73–6.

of two reports – *Land and the Nation* (Green Book), targeted at the agricultural labourer, and *Towns and the Land* (Brown Book). Both advocated the rating of site values. But many land taxers were suspicious of Lloyd George for a range of personal and political reasons. Some like J C Wedgwood MP had migrated to the Labour Party in the hope of finding a better platform for the promotion of the single tax. However, the Liberal Party was split between those who looked to the land question as a means of consolidating their electoral support in rural areas, through smallholdings and peasant proprietorships, and those who gave a higher priority to the mainly urban issues of town planning and leasehold reform. These two approaches were not easy to reconcile and the party failed to regain their support in either rural or urban areas.[54]

Similar tensions existed in the Labour Party. Its policy on the land question before the First World War was characterised by various tensions. 'How to deal with the economic and political implications of vast concentrations of property (particularly land) constituted one of the most obdurate of theoretical questions for a party committed to large-scale structural change by peaceful and constitutional processes.'[55] Labour had shared with radical liberalism vehement opposition to the concentration of landed wealth while supporting small-scale personal ownership of property as a means of conferring political freedoms. It supported both the nationalisation of land as a long-term measure and the taxation of land values as a pragmatic short-term route to full nationalisation. In relation to urban land, policy concentrated on seeking greater powers for local authorities to clear slums and build working-class housing for rent, following the introduction of exchequer subsidies in 1919. The early town planning movement was viewed with some class suspicion, as was the role of the central state. The taxation of land values was regarded as a potential source of revenue, once in government, to acquire land for smallholdings and urban housing, although a minority in the party also regarded land taxation as a long-term alternative to nationalisation.[56]

Before 1914 the party resisted demands for the adoption of a radical policy of land nationalisation. It did so not only for fear of antagonising agricultural trade union support, but because such a centralist approach ran counter to the idealised view it held about the independent rural artisan renting or buying a plot of land from the local parish council. Pre-war ambivalence towards land nationalisation persisted throughout the war, and it was not included as an immediate demand in *Labour and the New Social Order* in 1918. The taxation of land values proved to be more appealing than land nationalisation, mirroring wider party debates about the need for raising additional government revenue to pay for the enormous level of wartime debt though a

54 Douglas, *Land, People and Politics*, pp. 184–97.
55 Harris, 'Labour's Political and Social Thought', pp. 18–19.
56 Tichelar, 'Socialists, Labour and the Land'.

capital levy and the conscription of wealth.[57] The legislative model offered by the Lloyd George land taxes, with its system of Inland Revenue valuation, was still in place (if not operating) during the war. The party looked to the 'appropriate direct taxation of land values' in order to bring into the Public Exchequer 'the steadily rising unearned increment of urban and mineral land'.[58] The Trades Union Congress was also a strong advocate of the taxation of land values in 1917 and 1918 in order to finance the war, although it reverted to a policy of long-term land nationalisation after the war.[59]

However, the war had proved to be profoundly damaging to the cause of the single tax, due mainly to the break-up of the Liberal Party. Many 'single taxers' joined Labour in the 1920s as the Liberal Party no longer provided a politically viable base for their cause.[60] As a result land taxation held a prominent place in Labour policy statements after the war: 'The steadily rising unearned increment of urban and mineral land ought, by an appropriate direct Taxation of Land Values, to be wholly brought into the Public Exchequer'.[61] In 1923 a party committee recommended the re-establishment of the land valuation department. It also sought the introduction of a national flat rate land tax of one penny in the pound on the full unimproved capital value of all land, with local authorities having the power to levy rates on land values within their areas.[62]

The most ardent campaigner in Labour's ranks for land taxation was Josiah C. Wedgwood, a Liberal convert to Labour in the early 1920s, who pressed for taxation as a short-term measure pending, or even as a substitute for, long-term nationalisation.[63] In 1924 Philip Snowden came under intense pressure from single taxers in the party to implement these policies in his budget.[64] Accordingly, he announced a tax of 1d in the £ on land values to deal with the scandal of the private appropriation of land values created by the enterprise and industry of the people and by the expenditure of public money. 'This', he argued 'marked one further stage towards the emancipation of the people from the tyranny and injustice of private land monopoly', a classic statement of pre-war land reform ideology. The Country Landowners' Association (CLA), set up in 1907 to combat Liberal land reform, expressed concern about the attacks on land by the Labour Party during the election of 1923.[65] Its remedy to combat what it saw as communism was improved

57 Dalton, *The Capital Levy Explained*.
58 Douglas, *Land, People and Politics*, p. 15 and p. 169.
59 TUC Registry Files MSS292/830.3/7 (Warwick University).
60 Douglas, *Land, People and Politics*, pp. 169–83.
61 'Labour and the New Social Order' (1918), p. 15.
62 TUC Registry Files MSS 292/830.3/5.
63 Wedgwood, *The Land Question: Taxation and Rating of Land Values* (1925) and (1929), LPA: Part 2, 25/47 and 29/103, 62; Wedgwood, *Memoirs of a Fighting Life*.
64 Luckhurst Scott, 'The Labour Party and Land Value Taxation' and *Land and Liberty*, February 1929, LPA: Part 2, 29/83.
65 The Country Landowners' Association was formed following the publication of a pamphlet by Algernon Turnor, *The Land and the Social Problem* (1907). It was quickly followed by the

working conditions for rural workers and resistance to any measures such as taxation which interfered with competitive market conditions.[66] In practice Snowden's new tax was, for one historian, 'a feeble and relatively harmless sop to demands for action against parasitical capital'. It made little sense, he argued to seek to unite industry and labour against such landowners when they and industrialists were already allies in the Conservative Party, 'and many in the Labour Party saw the tax as merely part of a wider campaign against socially created wealth' (such as the capital levy).[67]

Labour's 1929 Manifesto continued to support a policy of land taxation, playing down the issue of land nationalisation. It pledged that while land remains in private hands, 'the Party will deal drastically with the scandal of the appropriation of land values by private owners'.[68] Snowden repeated the attempt again in his budget of 1931. In pursuit of Treasury orthodoxy, he was reluctant to increase income tax or surtax proposing instead a tax on land values. The proposals met fierce opposition from the Conservative Party and its allies. Conservatives argued that Lloyd George's land taxes, which they pointed out he had voted to abolish in 1920, had only yielded £1.3 million, while the cost of collection was estimated at £5 million. 'Experience seems to indicate', an internal report noted, 'that the valuation of land is an expensive process, and that the net yield of any duty based upon such valuation would be out of all proportion to the cost of collecting'.[69]

The CLA deplored the tax as a move towards state ownership of all land. It lobbied to have agricultural land exempted. It also objected at the time to clauses in the Town and Country Planning Bill giving local authorities powers to collect betterment, arguing that full compensation should be paid to owners whose property was affected.[70] The Conservatives also supported the view of the Land Union, another organisation set up just before the war in 1909 to defend the rights of private property.[71] It maintained that land, which had been lawful property for centuries, was already taxed heavily by death duties and local rates, and that advocates of land taxation 'aim at nothing short of the absolute confiscation of all private property in land'.[72] But Snowden's budget did not survive the formation of the national government. He was isolated over his uncompromising support for land taxation and was in serious conflict with the rest of his cabinet who did not share his enthusiasm for such traditional Liberal laissez-faire policies at a time of acute economic

National Farmers Union in 1908, representing the interests of mainly tenant farmers, and the Land Union in 1909 set up to defend private property.
66 CLA: Minutes of the Council, 14 December 1923 (SR: CLA AD1/3).
67 Daunton, *Just Taxes*, p. 157.
68 *Labour and the Nation* (1929), p. 42.
69 CPA: CRD 1/42/4 – Land Taxation.
70 CLA: Report of the Executive Committee, 23 July 1931 (SR: CLA AD1/8).
71 *The Spectator*, 14 May 1910, p. 3.
72 CPA: CRD 1/42/1&2 – Land Taxation.

crisis. But his party was terrified he might resign over the issue precipitating a general election during a time of economic crisis.[73]

But this aspect of land reform, which had been such a vital component in the armoury of Liberal-Radical attacks on the landed interest, was a casualty of the worldwide economic crisis. It disappeared from view during the 1930s with the partial demise of free trade.[74] Labour's 1932 policy statement on agriculture devoted only one short dismissive paragraph to the issue: 'It is a matter for consideration, how far it is practicable to apply a scheme of land value taxation to land, rural or urban, not transferred to national ownership'.[75] During the 1930s there was growing emphasis on the public ownership of agricultural land as part of a system of national planning. This pushed the issue of land taxation into the background as almost an irrelevance. For Hugh Dalton, it was beyond the scope of government 'to restore to the public the unearned private increments of the past. That restoration can only be made by taxation, and in particular by death duties. But ... we can control in the public interest the use of land, and so plan future development'.[76] Supporters of taxation of land values continued to press their case within the party, although a distinction was increasingly made between the merits of taxing urban rather than rural land. A land value taxation group was formed by the Parliamentary Labour Party in 1937. The London County Council (LCC), captured by the Labour Party in 1934, introduced a private bill to rate site values as a means of generating extra income for local services.[77]

But such attempts failed and the cause of taxation of land suffered a series of setbacks with Hugh Dalton describing the policy as out of date and a waste of effort.[78] By 1939 this aspect of land reform, which had dominated radical thinking on the land question since the late nineteenth century, had diminished in political importance. The demand for land nationalisation, particularly of agricultural land, or at least the control of land use in the national interest, had replaced it as the answer to a range of economic and social questions. The limited introduction of protectionist economic measures for agriculture had undermined the intellectual argument for taxing land values, which had always been closely associated with the demand for free trade and cheap food. Interest had shifted from the rural land question to the control of development in urban areas and the related question of the inadequate resource base of urban local government. By 1938, Attlee, who had no objection in principle to the taxation of land values, placed a higher priority on the

73 Snowden, *An Autobiography, Vol. 2*, 1919–1934, pp. 905–16.
74 Skidelsky, *Politicians and the Slump*, pp. 307–8.
75 'The Land and the National Planning of Agriculture' (1932), p. 9, LPA: Part 2, 32/9.
76 Dalton, *Practical Socialism for Britain*, pp. 152–3.
77 *The Times*, 28 July 1938; LPA: Policy Committee, 18 October 1938; *Labour Research*, 28:2, February 1939, 35; Daunton, *Just Taxes*, p. 349.
78 Tichelar, 'The Labour Party and Land Reform in the Inter-War Period', pp. 85–101; Griffiths, *Labour and the Countryside*, pp. 301–4.

ability of the government at a local or national level to purchase land at an affordable price for public housing.[79]

Growing support for town and country planning

During the 1930s the Labour Party came out in support of stronger town and country planning. This was in contrast to the Conservative Party, which sought to protect the rights of private property posed by the threat of state control of land use in both town and country. The Labour Party modified their policies towards the land question after 1918 in three important areas reflecting the economic and social realities of the interwar years. First it came out more strongly in favour of garden cities, overcoming some initial concerns about their middle class and suburban nature. Second, it adopted a more centralised approach to preservation and town and country planning, dropping an earlier emphasis on local democratic control based on a suspicion of the role of a centralised state. Third, it campaigned consistently throughout the period for increased access to the countryside and the creation of national parks.

The ideal of the garden city, partly based on a virtuous urban view of combining the best of town and country advocated by Ebenezer Howard's inspirational writings, was the founding idea of the emerging town and country planning movement during the interwar period, although the historical origins of the movement had longer antecedents.[80] The Labour Party embraced centralised land-use planning with more enthusiasm during the 1930s as a means of achieving such ideals. The initial idea for garden cities was based on the state purchase of the land required for building together with the taxation of land values to finance infrastructure and services. Such an approach coincided to some extent with the aims of the preservationist lobby, represented by the Council for the Preservation of Rural England, which pressed for more centralist solutions to the problems of uncontrolled industrial and urban growth. Before 1914, the party did not strongly identify with the principles of garden cities because they offered no immediate hope of alleviating urban slums or providing working-class housing at affordable rents in the short term. But the party began to share with the early town planners a common interest in broader political solutions to the land question. This not only encompassed the long-term aim of land nationalisation but included the taxation of land values and other systems to tax speculative landlords (or betterment).

---

79 Richard Stokes Papers, Box 1: General Correspondence – Letter from Stokes to Attlee, 2 March 1938.
80 Howard, *Tomorrow: A Peaceful Path to Real Reform*; Bowie, *The Radical and Socialist Tradition in British Planning*; Burchardt, *Paradise Lost*, pp. 58–66, pp. 89–111; Griffiths, *Labour and the Countryside*, pp. 305–9.

During the interwar period the Labour Party's policy towards town and country planning was also influenced by the perceived inadequacies of local government, particularly its small-scale nature and limited financial base at a time of economic depression. In the debate on the Town and Country Planning Bill in 1931, Arthur Greenwood, Labour's Minister of Health, argued for a policy of national planning and intervention to build new houses, and for limiting compensation to landlords and increasing betterment to 100% to local authorities. He maintained that garden cities and satellite towns should be part of properly planned regional schemes but recognised that there would be insurmountable conflicts with property interests in dealing rationally with land-use control.[81] The question of compensation and betterment began to climb up the political agenda of Labour local government, especially after Labour captured control of the London County Council in 1934. The meaning of compensation and betterment became more clearly defined during this period. It was concerned with what level 'the state should compensate land owners whose land is acquired (either by agreement or compulsion) for public or community purposes; and whether or not, and at what level, the state should seek to collect increases (betterment) in land values created by private capital or government action'.[82]

Although garden cities and the dispersal of industry and population away from congested urban areas were official party policy, there were various interests in the party that looked upon such developments with concern. Labour local authorities saw dispersal as a threat to their already limited rate base and were anxious that declining urban populations and the removal of industry from their areas would reduce rate income further. In practice, the Labour Party was opposed to the building of 'huge dormitory cottage estates in outlying districts', such as Becontree in Essex, with their inadequate social and transport infrastructure, and pressed for the construction of smaller estates which fitted in with existing buildings.[83] Even the LCC, which under Herbert Morrison championed the green belt and satellite towns, argued in its evidence to the Royal Commission on the Geographical Distribution of the Industrial Population that any relocation of industry should take careful account of the total volume of employment in Greater London, in order to maintain it at an adequate level. He also pointed out that a reasonably large concentration of population enables such services as education and public health to be economically developed to a high degree.[84]

Opposition to garden cities was also expressed in class terms. When George Hicks, the Secretary of the Amalgamated Union of Building Trade Workers,

---

81 *Parliamentary Debates* (Official Report), 251, 15 April 1931, cols. 193–205.
82 McKay and Cox, *The Politics of Urban Change*, pp. 69–106.
83 Labour Party, 'Up with the Houses, Down with the Slums' (1934).
84 Minutes of Evidence of Royal Commission on the Geographical Distribution of the Industrial Population, 16 February 1938, p. 421.

addressed the Garden Cities and Town and Country Planning Association in 1928 he stated that:

> Garden cities are becoming, as it were, a practical ideal of bourgeois villadom; a rest haven or happy valley of the higher paid strata of workers, professional workers, civil servants and so on. ... I am not in favour of establishing little town paradises, while the most hideous aspects of life in our big industrial cities remain untouched, and thousands are compelled to dwell in black and squalid regions of misery and desolation ... We do not want a lot of little garden cities tucked away in the country districts, and the big ugly messes which we call towns and cities to continue as they are.[85]

It was the problems of the distressed areas, and the continuation of economic depression, which led the Labour Party to embrace centralised state planning by the late 1930s. This put paid to any hope of decentralised solutions or the granting of enabling legislation to local authorities.[86] By this date, local politicians such as Herbert Morrison, who had campaigned for home rule for London in the 1920s, argued that town planning should be in the hands of the larger county councils and the Ministry of Health. 'Is it not amazing' he stated 'that in 1939 very small local authorities should be preserved as supreme statutory town-planning authorities?'[87] By 1934 George Lansbury, the party's new leader after MacDonald's defection, and a long-time supporter of land colonies for the unemployed, advocated a national planning authority with the powers to create new industrial areas with residential districts beyond. 'I visualise England, Scotland and Wales as a carefully planned pattern of garden land, farm land, well-defined and sharply limited industrial areas.... The homes of the workers of all kinds should be away from pits and factories in prettily laid-out garden cities.' This was to be achieved by nationalising the land and taxing land values.[88] In 1937 the party's new leader, Attlee, stated that 'the country must, through a national organisation, say where particular industries are to be located, where land is to be kept for residential development, and where there are to be parks and open spaces'.[89] By 1939, others had dismissed even regional planning maintaining that it was only the government acting as a central authority that could plan and re-equip the country in the light of impending war.[90]

---

85 'Garden Cities and the Workers', *Garden Cities and Town Planning* (April 1928) pp. 61–3.
86 Rowett, 'Labour Party and Local Government: Theory and Practice in the Inter-War Years', unpublished DPhil thesis, University of Oxford, 1979, p. 331.
87 *The Times*, 2 March 1939, p. 11.
88 Lansbury, *My England*, (London, 1934), pp. 58–72; see also Lansbury, *My Life* (London, 1928), pp. 99–109, for his support for land colonies for the unemployed.
89 Attlee, 'A National Plan for Town and Countryside', *Town and Country Planning*, 6 (1937).
90 'A Plan for Greater London', *Town and Country Planning*, 7, 26 January–March 1939, pp. 7–19.

A further aspect of Labour's approach to land reform, which had become linked to support for town and country planning, was the demand for access to the countryside and the creation of national parks. *How Labour Will Save Agriculture*, issued in 1934, painted a depressed picture of 'our countryside', but acknowledged the need for preservation to combat the danger of uncontrolled urban despoliation and intrusion:

> From the window of a railway carriage, slow decay is everywhere apparent: empty, untilled fields; miserable cottages; farm houses in bad repair. These are common features throughout the English countryside, with here and there the 'big house' – the sign of a land owning class which has long outlived its function. And if you go by road, what do you find? Long lines of 'ribbon development' leading out of every town. Innumerable and intolerable villas, the slums of the 1940s, stretching far out into the fields – spoiling the countryside, but contributing little to it – bringing ugliness without prosperity. The countryside of Britain – neglected, wasted and destroyed – is becoming a mere convenience for the townsman to drive out into on Sunday evenings and listen to his radio in the open air.[91]

Labour Party demands for increased access centred on moorland and mountains rather than the southern downlands and the 'national heritage' of the country houses in park land. Again, this was mainly a matter of social class. Despoliation of the countryside was seen as the result of middle-class suburban developments and recreation use, arising as a result of the intrusion of the motor car and the building of golf courses, uncontrolled development and neglect by a traditional landowning elite that was deserting the land and its responsibilities. The demands of working-class hikers and walkers for access to the mountains and moorlands, especially in the countryside of the north of England and Scotland, met with concerted opposition from landlords wishing to preserve such places for sport and privacy.[92]

Labour supported the various attempts to introduce an Access to Mountains Bill in 1908, 1926, 1927 and 1931. A bill was finally enacted in 1939, albeit in a very limited form following powerful opposition from landowners.[93] MacDonald was particularly sympathetic to the demand for national parks and appointed a committee of enquiry chaired by Christopher Addison in 1929. But such pressure met similar opposition in the 1930s from landowners and the Conservative Party to what was seen as potential backdoor nationalisation.[94] Despite the myth of an idealised 'southern counties' countryside,

---

91 'How Labour Will Save Agriculture' (1934), LPA: Part 2, 34/23; see also Griffiths, *Labour and the Countryside*, pp. 209–15.

92 Lowerson, 'Battles for the Countryside'; Stephenson, *Forbidden Land*.

93 Papers of Philip Noel-Baker 3/203, 'Access to Mountains Bill, 1939'.

94 Sheail, *Nature in Trust*, pp. 68–88.

Labour in this period was more interested in 'the call of the wild' than in more middle-class preservation movements represented by the Council for the Preservation of Rural England, although support for the latter was not entirely absent. The party's leading advocate of planning, Hugh Dalton, regarded the National Trust as an example of practical socialism in action, but his interest was always more in areas of outstanding natural beauty rather than the country house, unless of course such buildings could be bequeathed to the nation in lieu of death duties.[95]

Summary

The 'land question' had undergone some significant changes during the interwar period. The Conservative Party defended property interests against growing pressure for land-use control and encouraged the spread of a property-owning democracy as a bulwark against socialism. The Liberal Party had attempted to revive their land campaign in the 1920s but failed to attract electoral support. By the 1930s, the Labour Party had to a large extent rejected the 'back-to-the-land' option as an economic remedy for the ills of British agriculture and as a means of attacking the landed aristocracy as a social class.

The policy of smallholdings was largely but not entirely replaced by support for producer marketing, import boards and better nutrition to be achieved by larger-scale production and market gardening. Agriculture therefore began to be treated as an important industry amongst others requiring state support, and not as a special case based on an agenda of other strategic social and political concerns such as unemployment and national hygiene. By 1939 the Labour Party had developed a set of rural policies that enabled it to appeal more successfully to countryside interests, and with the support and influence of Christopher Addison, in particular, 'was at last making real headway as the party of the countryside as well as industrial regions of Britain'.[96]

Politicians continued to hold an idealised if not pastoral view of rural life. Those on the right looked to the land as a source of political stability and social conservatism. Those on the left shared this idyllic view, but this idealism expressed itself not so much in terms of a general desire to 'return to the land' but in demands for access and preservation, and in the growing movement for garden cities and town and country planning. Labour policy, in particular, had shifted from anti-landlordism to a greater emphasis on the control of land use through centralised physical planning. In terms of urban land policy, the party had largely adopted the agenda of the Garden Cities and Town Planning Association, which combined the demand for centralised planning

95 Dalton, *Practical Socialism for Britain*, p. 292; Mandler, *The Fall and Rise of the Stately Home*, pp. 334–40.
96 Morgan, *Portrait of a Progressive*, pp. 225–6; Griffiths, *Labour and the Countryside*.

with the dispersal of population and industry, together with a reform of compensation and betterment to counter speculative urban landlords.

Thus, by the outbreak of the Second World War, the Labour Party had lost its earlier support for decentralisation in favour of centralised economic and physical planning. After 1931 the party embraced the politics of planning, influenced by the New Deal in America and Soviet 'five-year plans', although it was divided on the means to implement such policies in practice.[97] As a result, land nationalisation became a prominent feature of Labour Party policy during the 1930s. Taxation of land values, which characterised the pre-1914 land question, had almost disappeared from political view. Interest had shifted from the taxation of all land, including the traditional agricultural landlord, as a radical panacea for the land question, to the taxation of rising land values in urban areas as a means of generating additional income for local authorities. The focus of policy had moved in the direction of compensation to landowners and the collection of betterment and away from taxing the landed aristocracy to extinction.

97 Harris, 'Labour's Political and Social Thought', pp. 23–6.

Part III

The political conflict over landed property rights, 1942 to 1979

5   The impact of the war on town and country

The war revived the question of land reform and changed public attitudes towards the countryside, property speculators and town and country planning. In particular, the Blitz had the effect of linking the question of the cost of land to the specific issue of rebuilding city centres destroyed by enemy bombing after the war. For reconstruction to take place, the Labour Party argued that land needed to be purchased at less than market prices, a problem that had severely restricted town planning and council house-building in the interwar period. The recovery of the 'unearned increment' therefore became associated with post-war reconstruction and the need to control property speculation. As a result, the traditional land reform demand for the rating of site values, as championed by Lloyd George, and Henry George before him, was supplanted by other ways of control-ling land use and recovering betterment. The rating of site values on unim-proved land never recovered its radical credentials thereafter (although it is experiencing some renewed interest currently as one possible answer to the housing crisis).

The chapter will describe the changes that took place during that war in the market for rural and urban land. It will also look at how public attitudes changed with regard to the countryside and town and country planning. As in the First World War, the government intervened in agriculture to guarantee prices and wages in order to increase production to meet a wartime emer-gency. But unlike the first war, urban land reform became a source of bitter political conflict which nearly undermined the wartime coalition. Debates over the rights of property and compensation to landlords were highly con-troversial and divisive. The controversy centred on the level of compensation to be paid to landowners after the war, when sites purchased by speculators during the Blitz were bought out compulsorily by local authorities wishing to rebuild. There was less controversy over the future of rural land and the role of agriculture. Indeed, a political consensus emerged about the need to protect agriculture and the countryside from urban development, including the creation of the green belt and national parks. Moreover, the popularity of farmers had been greatly enhanced during the war by the way that farming was run like 'a national social service'. By 1945 the position of the farmers as guardians of the countryside was assured, including the safeguarding of their property rights as owner-occupiers.

The Blitz and the demand for land-use control in urban areas

The Blitz channelled political interest in land reform into new directions. This was quite different from the impact of the First World War. As we have seen, government intervention in agriculture, for example, did not survive the first few years of peace. The repeal of the Corn Production Act in 1921 was regarded by the farming community as a 'great betrayal'. Political pressure for reconstruction after 1918 quickly dissipated in the face of powerful interests wishing to return to pre-war 'business as normal', and in the interests of financial austerity. In contrast, the Second World War brought about a dramatic and to a large extent permanent desire to protect the countryside from urban development and reconstruct devastated city centres. Public opinion wanted to see towns and cities rebuilt after the war along modern and efficient lines although opinion did not necessarily agree with the technocratic approaches adopted by architects and town planners.

During the war, public opinion was particularly sensitive to the question of property speculation. The early response of the coalition to pressure for rebuilding blitzed cities was much influenced by adverse public reaction against speculative landlords. Developers were accused of acquiring bombed sites in order to sell or develop them after the war at an inflated profit. The damage caused by bombing created a new public demand for the replanning of city centres, involving the control of land use and compulsory state purchase of development land. The Blitz not only undermined the financial profitability of urban property markets but increased public opposition to land and property speculation in an atmosphere of wartime equality of sacrifice. The war also reinvigorated the town and country planning movement, whose influence had been limited before the war. The dispersal of industry and population away from built-up areas brought about by the Blitz reversed pre-war planning opinion which was concerned about the threat this might have posed to the countryside. The war made public and political opinion more receptive to the arguments of the town planning lobby and recommendations of the Barlow Commission, set up in 1937 to inquire into the problems of the distressed areas.

The publication of the Barlow Report in 1940 had been delayed by the outbreak of the war. It was directly responsible, through a chain reaction brought about by the domestic impact of the war, for the events that led up to the creation of the whole complex post-war planning machine during the years 1945 to 1952. It provided the intellectual justification for the creation of a new Ministry of Town and Country Planning in 1943, and towards the end of the war, government intervention to direct industrial location.[1] The

1 *Distribution of Industry Act, 1945.*

Blitz triggered the implementation of some of the key areas of further work suggested by the Barlow Report. Churchill appointed Sir John Reith, the previous director general of the BBC, as Minister of Works in October 1940, with specific responsibility for repairing and rebuilding bomb-damaged buildings. His appointment led the coalition to embark on the follow-up studies on compensation and betterment (Uthwatt Report in 1941) and on Land Utilisation in Rural Areas (Scott Report in 1942) which proved to be very influential, not unlike, but not as well-publicised as, the Beveridge Report. 'The result was a remarkable concentrated burst of committee work and report writing from 1941 to 1947, which laid the foundations of the post-war urban and regional planning system in Britain.'[2]

It had been widely anticipated before the outbreak of war that London and other major conurbations would be levelled to the ground by bombing. Mass Observation noted widespread fear of air attack and the belief that 'the bomber would always get through'.[3] However, when war finally came, the physical impact of the Blitz, although deeply shocking physically and psychologically, was far less than had been originally feared.[4] For the historians of planning in London, 'the most important effect of the war was not the extent of physical destruction, but rather the degree of economic dislocation'.[5] In Birmingham, the war caused 'more inconvenience than injury, more decay than destruction'.[6] The City escaped lightly: '…as with housing, damage to industrial plant was not heavy. Factories were already geographically dispersed and the important firms further dispersed production to other units'.[7] Compared to mainland Europe, therefore, English cities did not suffer the almost 'biblical annihilation' inflicted by British and American bombers, which were capable of long-range bombing on a large scale in contrast to the limited range and comparative ineffectiveness of the German air force.[8]

The impact of the Blitz on popular attitudes to planning and land-use control was immediate and dramatic, especially during the latter part of 1940 and 1941. The Blitz transformed the town and country planning lobby into an effective if sometimes over-optimistic pressure group for change.[9] The scale of houses destroyed or made uninhabitable created the possibility of major replanning and reconstruction after the war, particularly in the minds of planners, who likened the opportunity to that presented and missed by

2 Hall, *Urban and Regional Planning*, p. 71.
3 Madge and Harrison, *Britain by Mass Observation*, pp. 89–91.
4 Calder, *The People's War* and *The Myth of the Blitz*; Cherry, *Birmingham: A Study in Geography, History and Planning*, pp. 136–9.
5 Young and Garside, *Metropolitan London: Politics and Urban Change, 1837–1981*, p. 223.
6 Cherry, *Birmingham: A Study in Geography, History and Planning*, p. 140.
7 Ibid., p. 139.
8 Diefendorf (ed.), *Rebuilding Europe's Bombed Cities*, pp. 1–14.
9 Hebbert, 'Frederick Osborn, 1885–1978' in Cherry (ed.), *Pioneers in British Planning*, p. 187; Hardy, *From Garden Cities to New Towns*, pp. 240–93.

the Great Fire of London three hundred years before.[10] As in other areas of public policy, the war brought town planning professionals and lobbyists into the outer reaches of government circles and onto the myriad consultative committees that were set up to investigate the different aspects of government policy.[11] A large number of architects and planners were co-opted onto Sir John Reith's panel of experts in the autumn of 1941 to develop proposals for the physical reconstruction of bombed cities.

Architects and town planners also acquired an enhanced role and importance in local government. Cities badly damaged by the Blitz started to make immediate plans for reconstruction. Sir John Reith invited local authorities 'to plan boldly and comprehensively'. This was backed-up by the prospect of central government grants and the promise of legislation to make planning easier, although Reith recognised he was not in a position to deliver these promises straightaway.[12] Fired by this encouragement, all the major cities commissioned ambitious plans for the physical redevelopment of their areas. This led to the publication by the end of the war of a whole series of reports, epitomised by Abercrombie's plan for London.[13]

Support for state control of land use and powers of compulsory acquisition by local authorities increasingly manifested itself, especially amongst planners and engineers, as the only practical means of translating the new city plans into reality. It was hoped that such new powers would help overcome the high cost of urban land and the obstacles created by existing arrangements for compensation and betterment, which made land expensive. Planners argued that state control or ownership of land 'would simplify and cheapen the whole process of re-planning enormously'.[14] Donald E. Gibson, the City Architect of Coventry, argued in December 1940, only a few weeks after the first and devastating air raid on that city, 'that private interests must be subordinated to public ones', and that the only solution to national planning 'now lies in some form of land nationalisation. Will the landowners, with their often short-sighted and acquisitive outlook again be allowed to smash the ideas of our twentieth-century Wrens?'[15] A leading town planner argued that 'Hitler's bombers have transformed (planning) from a Utopian dream to a necessity … the damage wrought by Nazi bombers in many of our cities is on so extensive a scale that large-scale reconstruction will be required'.[16]

While enthusiasm for replanning remained largely the concern of a relatively small circle of planners, local government representatives, legislators

10 *Statistics Relating to the War Effort*, Cmd. 6564, p. 32.
11 Paul Addison, *Road to 1945*, pp. 164–89.
12 John Reith's Scrapbook, 1938–1943 – BBC Written Archives S60/6/10/2, pp. 50–70 and S/60/6/11, pp. 1–31.
13 Osborn (ed.), *Planning and Reconstruction, 1944–45*, pp. 337–52.
14 Boumphrey, *Town and Country Tomorrow*, pp. 136–7.
15 *Daily Herald*, 5 December 1940.
16 Robson, *The War and the Planning Outlook*, p. 7 and p. 12.

and journalists, it was the impact of the war on the market for urban land that raised more public concerns about landownership and the dangers of property speculation. The war seriously affected property markets, particularly those in urban areas. Rateable values underwent dramatic declines, particularly in those central areas of cities directly damaged by the Blitz. It also badly reduced the rate income of local authorities. In Plymouth for example the rateable value of dwelling houses and flats fell by over 20% between 1941 and 1946, a pattern repeated in other war-damaged cities.[17] Property transactions suffered accordingly. In May 1940, Bovis, a major London property company, which had grown during the 1930s housing boom, noted that the war had brought all property development to a standstill. They expected the market to remain depressed for the duration.[18] The *Estates Gazette* reported in February 1940 a severe loss of confidence in urban land markets and a decline in rental values, particularly in the West End of London.[19]

Wartime legislation and requisitioning also undermined confidence in the market for land. The War Damage Act (1939) removed tenant liability for repairs and the Rent Restrictions Act discouraged investment. The early months of the war saw a virtual halt in urban property markets. A number of property speculators and developers were ruined due to the withdrawal of loans and foreclosures of mortgages by building societies and insurance companies. Soon after the start of the Blitz, many London property companies were 'experiencing financial difficulties as a result of the war' and were seeking a moratorium on the payment of dividends. One commentator noted that 'Investment in London properties in the last ten years has reached something of the proportions of the railways boom', but these companies had not had time to build up reserves to protect themselves against the depression in urban land values created by the war.[20] However, despite the extreme uncertainty of the market, 'a number of far sighted entrepreneurs began to purchase property' with a view to making a killing after the war. 'Buying property at rock-bottom war-time prices, to benefit from future capital appreciation, was a strategy which formed the foundation of a number of post-war fortunes.'[21] It was in these circumstances that the Blitz gave rise to the allegation of property speculation by secret syndicates.

While urban land declined in value, in contrast to rural areas where government intervention in farming had the effect of increasing land values, the prospects of post-war profits remained good, especially as the wartime Excess Profits Tax did not cover land transactions. The *Economist* referred to property speculators as 'Land Leeches'.[22] Concerns about the dangers of

---

17 Hasegawa, 'The Rise and Fall of Radical Reconstruction in 1940s Britain', pp. 140–1.
18 *The Times*, 15 May 1940.
19 *Estates Gazette*, 3 and 24 February 1940.
20 *The Political Quarterly*, 12 (April–June 1940), pp. 36–7.
21 Scott, *The Property Masters*, p. 101.
22 *The Economist*, 1 February 1941.

profiteering were expressed across the political spectrum. Richard Stokes, Labour MP for Ipswich and ardent single taxer, criticised the 1941 budget for failing to introduce a 100% tax on land sales, favouring 'not the nationalisation of land, but the collection of the economic rent publicly created for the public good'.[23] Sir Kingsley Wood, the Chancellor of the Exchequer, resisted Labour demands for the extension of Excess Profits Tax to land values and questioned whether speculation was in fact taking place.[24] However, the National Conservative MP for Lowestoft, and chairman of Adnams Brewery, wrote to Arthur Greenwood, the Minister of Reconstruction, calling for action against land speculators. 'Are urgent schemes of reconstruction of our devastated areas', he asked, 'to be suddenly checked and held up and twisted and stunted by a great increase in site values due to land speculators having brought up the areas of devastation?'[25] He pleaded with Greenwood to 'stabilise all land values on their pre-war basis so that the (local) authorities are free to carry on rebuilding and re-planning without being bled by the land speculator'.[26] The *Daily Herald* ran a campaign calling for the secret property syndicates (the 'Blitz Brigands' and 'Crater Snatchers') to be brought to public account.[27]

Popular attitudes to town and country planning

Until the publication of the Beveridge Report in 1942, the government had actively discouraged debate on post-war reconstruction for fear of undermining civilian morale. But the Ministry of Information had been criticised for its timidity in promoting discussion on post-war aims. When it did encourage debate, for example persuading *Picture Post* to issue a special edition in 1941 devoted to 'the Britain we hope to build when the war is over', it evoked an enormous public response. The Ministry of Information's Home Morale reports indicated a growing interest in the shape of post-war Britain as the prospect of immediate defeat receded during 1941, with particular concern being expressed about unemployment and housing.[28]

The Mass Observation reports show a slightly different and more complex picture. In a London survey carried out in 1941 it was found that half the people asked about reconstruction thought it meant purely 'physical' rebuilding, and only a quarter gave it any social, economic, political or international connotation. There was also a very sharp division of opinion between those who thought reconstruction should start now and those who wanted to wait.[29] Other reports indicated that reconstruction and town planning was

23 Papers of Richard Stokes – Box 1, 'Four Years Work, 1938–42: A Retrospect, 9 April 1941'.
24 *Parliamentary Debates*, Vol. 360, 28 January 1941, cols. 420–1; *The Times*, 21 December 1940.
25 Papers of Arthur Greenwood (MS ENG c. 6244, f. 305–10).
26 Ibid.
27 *Daily Herald*, 29 January 1941.
28 McLaine, *Ministry of Morale*, pp. 171–85.
29 Mass Observation File 913 – Notes on Some Reconstruction Problems, 13 October 1941.

predominantly a middle-class interest. For example, at a Reconstruction Conference held in Bath in September 1941, the enthusiastic audience of nearly 400 was at least 80% middle class: 'there was not one really working-class person there as far as could be seen, except the Liverpool postman who gave such a very eloquent speech on the slums'. The audience was described as being 'very idealistic, progressive and on the whole socialistic'. The session on town planning strongly advocated that building should be taken over by the municipal authorities and not left in the hands of jerry-building private men whose sole motive was profit.[30] This class theme was explored by Mass Observation in more detail in a report on 'Propaganda for Town Planning', in which the planning profession was attacked for elitism and failing to communicate with ordinary people.[31]

The class-based nature of town planning also was apparent in film and radio propaganda, especially in terms of the projection of peace aims. Films like *New Towns for Old* and *When We Build Again*, issued in 1942, portrayed planners as 'serious, bespectacled, pipe smoking gentlemen … surrounded by assistants in white coats sitting at drawing boards'.[32] In 1941 the BBC ran a series of talks on physical reconstruction called 'Making Plans', but although listening figures had started well, particularly for those talks dealing with the experience of ordinary people bombed out by the Blitz, by the autumn they had dropped to less than 20% of the total potential audience. The BBC decided to continue with a second series of talks in 1942 on regional government, national planning and landownership, but the discussions were dominated by expert witnesses, and as a result they did not have a wide popular appeal.[33]

Of more popular concern were issues relating to poorly designed interiors of houses and flats, lack of social amenities and the controversy about the merits of living in a house with a garden as opposed to living in flats. Architects came in for a great deal of criticism. The flats v. houses debate had severely divided town planners and architects during the 1930s and 1940s. It was found that the majority of people surveyed wished to live in a cottage with a garden. If asked about their attitudes to the countryside they expressed a general inclination to go 'back-to-the-land'. But this was tempered by more specific and realistic concerns about rural isolation, lack of employment, travelling distances to work and poor social networking in rural areas.[34]

The subject of town planning was more popular in the army as a result of the activities of the Army Bureau of Current Affairs, although the emphasis

30 Ibid., File 865–66 – Bath Reconstruction Conference, September 1941.
31 Ibid., File 1162 – Report on Propaganda for Planning, 18 March 1942; Mannin, 'Town Planning and the Common Man'.
32 Pronay, 'The Land of Promise: The Projection of Peace Aims in Britain' in Short (ed.), *Film and Radio Propaganda in World War Two*, pp. 69–75.
33 BBC Written Archives R51/445/2–3 (Making Plans).
34 Mass Observation File 983 – Tom Harrison, 'Houses or Flats' article written for *Town and Country Planning*.

was still on practical housing reform. A considerable amount of space was devoted to the issues of town and country, physical planning, neighbourhood units and the design of houses in the booklets issued by the Directorate of Army Education in 1944.[35] The novelist and wartime diarist James Lansdale Hodson noted in his journeys in England during 1942 that in a lecture on planning attended by about thirty men from different regiments that 'all were united in wanting the government to control where factories and houses must go – and nobody wanted to live in a flat. They want semi-detached houses and, in some cases, subsidised rents that vary with income. No slums for them, and no leaving areas derelict'.[36]

However, Mass Observation did detect some long-term changes in attitudes to town planning, particularly relating to shifts in hopes and expectations during the period 1941 to 1943. In September 1942, before the military fortunes of the war had begun to change in favour of the Allies, only 12% expected any government intervention and less than 20% hoped for any. This reflected the growing sense of frustration and disillusionment with the role of government in the third year of the war, and the ebbing of support for replanning after the end of the first phase of the Blitz. In August 1943, after the military course of the war had turned decisively, and seven months after the publication of the Beveridge Report which had raised expectations about post-war reform, 30% expected increased government town planning while less than 30% hoped for any.[37] This hardening of expectations in 1943 can be accounted for partly by the creation of the new Ministry of Town and Country Planning in that year and partly by growing enthusiasm for post-war reconstruction.

Popular support for town and country planning was high during the early part of the war, especially during the Blitz when ideas for the replanning of city centres received a great deal of public attention in the press. It is not clear, however, what meaning the general public attached to the term town planning and reconstruction apart from a general desire for physical rebuilding. Public enthusiasm for replanning declined after the worst effects of the Blitz were over and as disillusionment with leaders and government increased. In 1943 public expectations strengthened significantly as discussion of post-war reconstruction took on a more realistic aspect, as the fortunes of the war changed. However, the growing enthusiasm for town planning in general translated itself into specific support for related policies such as land nationalisation, taxation of land values and the relocation of industry. Many of the planning issues were highly technical and bureaucratic, such as the enormously complex field of compensation and betterment. Internal government arguments concerning the role of a central planning authority, and the reform of local government, were subjects that did not find a resonance with

---

35 Directorate of Army Education, *The British Way and Purpose. BWP Booklets 1–18.*
36 Hodson, *Home Front*, p. 190.
37 Mass Observation, *The Journey Home* (London, 1944), p. 16.

popular public opinion at a time when the immediate concerns of personal survival and rationing occupied the minds of the mass of the population.

The coalition response to property speculation

In January 1941 the government set up an expert committee of inquiry, chaired by Mr Justice Uthwatt, to advise on what steps should be taken to prevent the work of reconstruction from being prejudiced by property speculation.[38] In the long term the Committee was asked to investigate three highly difficult, technical and controversial issues: (1) the payment of compensation and the recovery of betterment in respect of the public control of the use of land; (2) the possible means of stabilising the value of land registered for development or redevelopment; and (3) the extension of powers to enable land to be acquired for the public on an equitable basis. Sir John Reith's announcement of the Committee's terms of reference was met with considerable enthusiasm. Labour's *Daily Herald* confidently asserted that the 'Blitz Buzzards' have been knocked off their perch by Reith's warning to speculators and anticipated support for both land nationalisation and taxation of land values.[39] *The Times* earnestly hoped that some way would be found for stabilising the value of land for development and establishing an equitable basis for the public purchase of land.[40] Even professional groups involved in the management of land, such as the Land Agents Society, pressed the Committee to give local authorities power to compulsorily acquire land on an equitable basis, although they rejected any further intervention in the market for land.[41]

The Uthwatt Committee issued an interim report in April 1941.[42] It recommended that no inflation of property values, which would increase the cost of reconstruction to the public purse, should be allowed. It invited the government to announce, as a general principle, that compensation for publicly acquired land should not exceed March 1939 values. This was to prove very controversial later in the war as landlord interests put pressure on the coalition government to water down this recommendation (see chapter 6). The report also took seriously the various public announcements of Sir John Reith for the need for a central planning authority, and for legislation to prevent work being undertaken which might prejudice reconstruction. Sir John Reith had been busy during 1941 trying to persuade the War Cabinet to set up a Ministry of Town and Country Planning, with wide powers to control development. But the ineffectiveness of the Cabinet Committee of Reconstruction, chaired by Labour's Arthur Greenwood, and the opposition of the Ministry of Health to losing its planning powers, slowed

---

38 Cullingworth, *Environmental Planning, 1939–1969, Vol. 4.*
39 *Daily Herald*, 30 January 1941.
40 *The Times*, 3 February 1941.
41 *The Economist*, 14 June 1941; PRO: CAB 117/130 – Letter, 24 December 1942.
42 *Interim Report on Compensation and Betterment*, Cmd. 6291.

the pace of reform, to the disappointment of the planning lobby and its supporters in the press and Parliament.[43] The Department of Health, which was responsible for town planning, as well as the smaller urban, and district local authorities, feared losing their planning powers to larger regional authorities.[44]

Uthwatt also recommended that areas suffering from extensive bomb damage should be identified and developed as a whole, with local authorities given the power to acquire land compulsorily. The government accepted the principle of using March 1939 land values as a means of determining compensation and supported the need for planning authorities to have greater powers to purchase land for development. In July 1941, Reith announced that legislation would be forthcoming to implement such proposals.[45] This was a commitment that the government later lived to regret when landlords and backbench Conservatives mounted a vociferous campaign against Uthwatt. However, Reith's attempt to create a separate and powerful Ministry of Town and Country Planning was successfully resisted by the Ministry of Health and others in the Cabinet opposed to the setting up of a new government department. Instead a Council of Ministers was established with weak terms of reference to coordinate long-term planning policy. It took Reith until February 1942 to broker a compromise with the Cabinet to transfer the town planning responsibilities of the Ministry of Health to a renamed Ministry of Works and Planning. But his unorthodox approaches and unpopularity with civil servants led to his sacking. He was replaced by Wyndham Portal, a Conservative more closely allied to Churchill, who wished to slow down the pace of reform.[46]

The second and final Uthwatt Report, published in September 1942, recommended a complex system of compensation and betterment and greater powers to planning authorities to purchase land compulsorily. The Committee had clearly been sympathetic to the question of land nationalisation but rejected it on the grounds of practicability.[47] It distinguished between urban and rural areas, or 'Developed Land' and 'Undeveloped Land'. In terms of rural areas, it argued that it was in the national interest to prevent building, particularly close to urban centres with high building value, especially if the soil is highly fertile and suitable for agriculture, or if it needed to be preserved as a beauty spot or for recreational purposes, such as coastal regions. It reflected a strong wartime concern to protect farming and the countryside. It also recognised that it was desirable to restrict existing large cities from expanding further, reflecting the powerful influence of the Town

43 Cullingworth, *Environmental Planning, 1939–1969, Vol. 1*, pp. 2–18.
44 PRO: CAB 87/20, 58 and 59.
45 *Hansard – House of Lords*, Vol. 119, 17 July 1941, cols. 849–54.
46 PRO: CAB 65–9, February 1942 (18(42)1); Paul Addison, *Road to 1945*, p. 177.
47 *Report of the Expert Committee on Compensation and Betterment (Uthwatt Report)* – Final, Cmd. 6386, p. 27.

and Country Planning Association, which lobbied vigorously for a policy of dispersal and satellite towns.

Uthwatt laid the foundations, given its rejection of land nationalisation, for a major increase in state control over the use of land. For urban land it recommended much wider and simpler powers of purchase for local authorities at pre-war prices (31 March 1939 values) and a periodic 75% levy on increases in annual site value, with the object of securing such betterment for the community. This levy would then be used to pay compensation to those landowners unable to realise the potential value of their land as a result of being denied planning permission. Uthwatt regarded such a levy as a practical method of recouping betterment similar to the many albeit unsuccessful attempts to introduce land value taxation before the war.

For rural land Uthwatt recommended the state purchase of all development rights for the whole country for a single lump sum. Any development on such land would have to have the consent of the planning authority.[48]

Uthwatt was widely welcomed by the planning lobby as a major contribution to resolving the problems of planning and reconstruction.[49] However, for the interests of private property, the report represented a major attack on the principle of ownership and a backdoor attempt at nationalisation. The nationalisation of development rights was 'in itself a powerful blow against private property, and the Conservative Party was thoroughly hostile to the principle'.[50] But the organisations that represented the landed interest were divided. They had been put on the defensive by the adverse wartime public opinion towards landlords as speculators. The Country Landowners' Association (CLA) condemned the acquisition of development rights by the state as expensive and unnecessary. It thought that existing town and country planning legislation was adequate to deal with compulsory purchase, where land was acquired at market value and not artificially fixed. However, it did acknowledge that an increased level of state intervention was inevitable as a result of wartime developments and it conceded the need for a central planning authority as an acceptable alternative to the potential threat of land nationalisation.[51] The CLA, which represented the interests of the agricultural landowner, was reluctant to get involved with the land question in urban areas. But it was under pressure from the Land Union, which represented the urban landowner, to work more closely together to oppose attacks on the landed interest. However, such overtures were rejected by the CLA partly because they recognised the strength of public feeling against the property speculator.[52] It was left to the National Federation of Property Owners to

48 Cullingworth, *Environmental Planning, 1939–1969, Vol 1*.

49 *Town and Country Planning*, Vol. X, No. 39 (Autumn, 1942), pp. 84–5.

50 Paul Addison, *Road to 1945*, p. 178.

51 PRO: CAB 117/128 – Letter 2, November 1942; Country Landowners' Association AD1/32: Minute Book of the Executive Committee, 7 March 1941 and 2 November 1942.

52 Country Landowners' Association AD1/33: Minute Book of the Executive Committee, 10 February 1944.

attack Uthwatt with more vigour. They equated state acquisition of land with nationalisation and campaigned to ensure that landowners effected by war-time depreciation be adequately compensated at market rates after the war.[53]

The response of the coalition government was more cautious. The War Cabinet agreed that it would not commit itself to legislation implementing the report 'given that some of the proposals seemed likely to give rise to controversy'. But it did agree that there would be no harm in pledging to put the machinery for central planning on a sound basis.[54] Later that month the Cabinet decided to introduce legislation creating a Minister of Town and Country Planning responsible to Parliament and a Commission to assist the Minister with the ownership and management of development rights.[55] The new ministry was finally established in 1943, but it had weak and limited terms of reference. Responsibility for industrial location remained with the Board of Trade, and the Ministry of Health held on to their housing and local government functions. The first Minister of Town and Country Planning also attracted criticism, not least because of his close association with the National Federation of Property Owners, which was opposed in general to the extension of town planning legislation.[56]

In contrast to the property lobby, support for land nationalisation was widespread within academic and professional circles and in the press during 1941 and 1942. For example, the *Economist* argued that it was impossible not to be impressed by the case for land nationalisation, which it maintained should be supported in principle.[57] *Political and Economic Planning*, an influential think tank formed in 1931, noted with enthusiasm in November 1941 that before the war 'the ownership and management of land is a subject which excited very little interest, except among a minority of specialists', and that it needed

> Nazi submarines to drive home to the nation the stupidity of neglecting its farm and forest land, and Nazi bombers to compel Parliament to consider extricating our cities from the straitjacket of an anachronistic system which should have been recast years ago.[58]

This enthusiasm for land reform applied equally, but less controversially to the future of agriculture and the protection of the countryside. But unlike the urban land question, there developed a degree of political consensus on the question of the future of agriculture and the countryside.

---

53 PRO: PREM 4/92/9 – Memorandum, 11 February 1943; *Estates Gazette*, 3 July 1943.
54 PRO: CAB 65 (WM 150 (42) 3), 4 November 1942.
55 PRO: CAB 65 (WM 155 (42) 7), 19 November 1942; WP (42) 528 – Memorandum 17 November 1942; and (WM 162(42) 9), 30 November 1942.
56 *Property Owners' Gazette*, December 1945.
57 *The Economist*, 10 January 1942.
58 *Political and Economic Planning*, No. 180, 4 November 1941.

Impact of the war on agriculture and the countryside

In rural areas, the impact of the war was dramatic (such as the evacuation of children) but proved to be less politically divisive. The war brought about irreversible government intervention (temporary at first) to increase domestic agricultural production and to maintain farm prices. The government also requisitioned large stretches of the countryside and took over country houses for the war effort, amounting to over 11 million acres of land or nearly 20% of the total area of the country.[59] By the end of the war, the government estimated that since 1939 over 800,000 acres of agricultural land – 'most of it the best land' – had been 'taken for airfields, factories, defence works, and other purposes arising out of the war'.[60] In fact, the official figure for requisitioned land was over 900,000 acres, at a cost to the Treasury of £733 million.[61]

The historians of planning have maintained that unlike the Great War, the controls of the Second World War created a formal land-use planning system and a close and continuous government involvement in farming which continued after the war. They noted in particular the special way in which rural areas figured in official comment. 'It was rural England (and not any other parts of the Kingdom) which was seen as the quintessential essence of what was being defended.'[62] It is now widely argued that this appeal to what has come to be called 'Deep England' continued after the war in the way that it was seen as important to support the farmers, who had fed the nation during the economic blockade, and to entrust them with the job of protecting the rural landscape from urban growth. 'Deep England' is defined as a literary, pictorial and cultural construction denoting a 'Green and Pleasant heartland' stretching from Wessex to Lincolnshire, and Sussex to Worcestershire, but excluding the north and those parts of the Home Counties disfigured by suburban intrusion. This mirrored and extended the idealised image of the countryside ('Constable Country') as represented by the southern counties that was prevalent in popular culture during the interwar period. The remarkable revival of agriculture during the war, combined with this patriotic interest in the countryside, created a closer relationship between town and country based on a forging of common interests to increase food production and protect the countryside and landscape.[63]

The economic aspects of wartime agriculture have been well covered by historians.[64] Farming and the countryside recovered from its severely depressed

---

59 Defence Lands, Report of the Defence Lands Committee, 1971–1973 (Nugent Report 1973).

60 *The Times*, 20 December 1944, p. 2.

61 *Third Report from the Select Committee on National Expenditure (1944–45). Release of Requisitioned Land and Building*, 29 March 1945.

62 Cherry and Rogers, *Rural Change and Planning*, pp. 71–2.

63 Calder, *The People's War*, p. 496 and *The Myth of the Blitz*, pp. 180–208; Howkins, 'A Country at War: Mass Observation and Rural England, 1939–45', pp. 75–97.

64 Brown, *Agriculture in England: A Survey of Farming, 1870–1947*; Holderness, *British Agriculture since 1945*; Britton, 'Agriculture' in Worswick and Ady (eds.), *The British Economy, 1945–1950*; Hammond, *Food and Agriculture in Britain, 1939–45*; Milward, *War,*

pre-war condition and developed into one of the key wartime 'social services'. 'The response of the farming community to the need to feed the nation in the face of German blockade is part of the rural folklore of the twentieth century.'[65] Arable acreage increased from under nine million to over fourteen million as a result of the 'Ploughing Up Campaign', the main objective of which was to produce crops for direct human consumption. The decline in meat production was compensated by the keeping of pigs and chickens on smallholdings and in domestic gardens. A Gallup Opinion Poll in March 1941 indicated that since the beginning of the war, over 30% of families had started growing foodstuffs and keeping livestock, and by August 1943, over 60% had access to a garden or allotment.[66] The results of this campaign were remarkably successful. By the end of the war, British farms had doubled the value of home-produced food from 14 to 28 billion calories.[67]

The Wartime Agricultural Executive Committees, which had been quietly re-established in embryonic form as early as 1936, were largely responsible for achieving these increases in arable production.[68] There were sixty-one county committees made up of local farmers, landowners and farmworkers. They represented the Ministry of Agriculture at a local level and exercised draconian powers of intervention and requisition. Inefficient farms that did not meet strict efficiency and production targets were taken over. During the war, over four hundred and forty thousand acres were requisitioned and the tenancies of nearly a quarter of a million further acres were terminated. In practice, they operated a strict system of land-use control, directing farmers to grow particular crops, and could order farmers to accept credit to buy fertilisers and tractors. As a result, British farming saw a striking increase in mechanisation and a more limited use of phosphates (in comparison to after 1945). The landscape of large areas of the country began to change as lush pastures were ploughed up for wheat and barley. While the picture of the horse-drawn plough remained the predominant if not idealised image of farming during the war, the appearance of the tractor represented the reality of wartime production and brought about a transformation of the landscape.

Both farmers and workers benefited from the introduction of guaranteed prices and regulated minimum wages. The coalition government announced in November 1940 that markets would be maintained for the duration of the war and for at least one year after the end of hostilities.[69] As a result farmers'

Economy and Society, 1939–1945, pp. 245–93; K. A. H. Murray, *Agriculture*; Whetham, *British Farming, 1939–1949.*

65 Cherry and Rogers, *Rural Change and Planning*, p. 74.

66 Gallup (ed.), *The Gallup International Public Opinion Polls: Great Britain, 1937–1975, Vol. 1, 1937–1964*, p. 42 and p. 80.

67 K. A. H. Murray, *Agriculture*, p. 242.

68 Whetham, *British Farming*; K. A. H. Murray, *Agriculture*, pp. 278–310; Armstrong, *Farmworkers*, pp. 202–4; Hurd, *A Farmer in Whitehall.*

69 Middleton, *The Formulation and Implementation of British Agricultural Policy, 1945–1951*, p. 30.

income rose by 300% in the period from 1937 to 1943, a level which was significantly higher than wages in general.[70] The prosperity of farmers was much
remarked upon, especially the extent to which in popular mythology they
appeared to be able to circumvent rationing and ensure themselves a plentiful
and healthy diet, and not least, supplies of petrol.[71] The social position of
farmers improved not only as a result of their important role in carrying out
essential war work, but in the way that farming became seen as a partnership
with government and more specifically as a 'Social Service'. This idea was
advocated by both the National Farmers Union (NFU) and the agricultural
trade unions.[72]

The war saw a reversal of rural depopulation. The regular agricultural
workforce increased from 500,000 in 1940 to 613,000 in 1945. This was
supplemented by the Women's Land Army, which reached a membership of
87,000 by 1943 and was made up of mainly recruits from the towns, and the
use of prisoners of war and school children for harvest work.[73] The membership of the National Union of Agricultural Workers tripled in size between
1939 and 1945, and the introduction of a minimum wage narrowed but did
not bridge the gap between urban and rural wage rates.[74] Wage rates rose
faster than the cost of living, and agricultural labourers experienced for the
first time in living memory an improvement in their standard of living and
status.

By 1945 a limited consensus had been reached concerning agricultural
policy, with an acceptance that the state should play a greater role in guaranteeing prices of agricultural produce. But the extent of this intervention
was still the subject of argument. The Treasury was opposed to subsidising
agriculture. But by the time the World Food Conference at Hot Springs in the
USA in June 1943 recommended an urgent expansion of food production
after the war, a policy confirmed by the British government in 1944, the earlier
anxieties about a flood of cheap food imports after the war had been replaced
by the spectre of post-war food shortages and poor nutrition. This change in
perception provided the rationale for the introduction of price guarantees for
a limited period to cover the transition from war to peacetime conditions. As
a result, the Annual Price Review was introduced in 1944 guaranteeing the
price of sheep, cattle and milk until 1948. This was a mechanism involving the
government negotiating with the NFU-agreed prices for the following year.[75]
This became a corner stone of post-war agricultural policy, consolidating the
role of the NFU at the heart of government decision making.[76]

70 K. A. H. Murray, *Agriculture*, p. 379.
71 Armstrong, *Farmworkers*, pp. 202–20.
72 *The Land Worker*, June 1944.
73 Armstrong, *Farmworkers*, p. 211. See also Verdon, *Working the Land*.
74 Groves, *Sharpen the Sickle*, pp. 225–9.
75 K. A. H. Murray, *Agriculture*, p. 351.
76 Martiin, Pan-Montojo and Brassley, *Agriculture in Capitalist Europe, 1945–1960*.

The war also had a significant impact on the wider state of rural society. The gap between urban and rural amenities remained and probably widened during the war. But the arrival of large numbers of evacuees from urban areas, not just those fleeing from the Blitz, but members of the Women's Land Army and prisoners of war, and the billeting of American troops, widened social horizons. However, it is not clear how far this either broke down social barriers or strengthened the existing rigid social relationships that sociologists have argued characterised rural society.[77] Wartime changes in the social structure of the countryside may have reinforced social distinctions by putting more power and influence into the hands of farmers and local elites. Elements of the surviving traditional landed establishment were figureheads on the county council War Agricultural Executive Committees. But the war accelerated the continuing decline in the fortunes of the traditional landed establishment. As Cannadine has pointed out, although the war saw a 'triumphant aristocratic resurgence' in the corridors of power, in the longer run, it accelerated the decay and disintegration of the landed establishment.[78] This was brought about not only by loss of income, but loss of servants, houses, life and not least faith in themselves as a class in the face of wartime collectivism, planning and ridicule, epitomised by popular attacks on Colonel Blimp.

The country houses of the remaining aristocracy were ruthlessly requisitioned for government service as hospitals, schools and barracks and consequently suffered physical damage and plebeian invasion. The one million domestic servants still employed in 1939 had almost disappeared two years later. Rent controls saw income from land and farming fall dramatically in real terms for landowners, while the income of farmers rose considerably through the expansion of subsidies. Increases in direct taxation and death duties (up to 65%) dealt further considerable blows to aristocratic fortunes and prestige. The sale of country houses and works of fine art dried up almost completely, and the National Trust benefited from donations of houses and land.[79]

These changed circumstances witnessed the creation of a new realism on the part of landowners 'that allowed the country house to be considered as part of the planned countryside'.[80] An influential strand of landed opinion, led by Lord Salisbury and the historian G. M. Young, responded warmly to wartime demands for strengthened rural planning. This sought to prevent uncontrolled development and suburbanisation, and to preserve an idealised version of the traditional landscape and the role of the landowner in agriculture. 'This group accepted the inevitability of central planning as preferable to nationalisation, and wished only to gain maximum control over agriculture for farmer-landowners.'[81] Young saw the rededication to agriculture

77 Newby, Bell, Rose and Saunders, *Property, Paternalism and Power*.
78 Cannadine, *The Decline and Fall of the British Aristocracy*, pp. 606–35.
79 Milne (ed.), *The National Trust: A Record of Fifty Years' Achievement*.
80 Mandler, *The Fall and Rise of the Stately Home*, p. 312.
81 Ibid., p. 321.

as the salvation of the landed gentry and embraced the Scott and Uthwatt Reports wholeheartedly.[82] The control of land use by the state placed the landed establishment on the defensive during the early period of the war, as it saw its traditional role of leadership undermined by the example set by the county council War Agricultural Executive Committees as a progressive and improving landlord. The editor of *The Field*, Brian Vesey-Fitzgerald, admitted in 1941 that 'in principle the arguments in favour of land national-isation are overwhelming. And conditions in the future, even in the immediate future, are likely to strengthen them much further'. His only defence against nationalisation was the practical question of administration.[83]

The CLA was thrown onto the back foot by the wartime 'indictment of landowners'. Lord Bledisloe, a past president of the Association, confided to his Executive Committee 'that in view of the growing demand for national-isation, would it not be advisable to suggest a middle course, such as taking over the land by the state to be leased to the present owners for 999 years'.[84] In public, the CLA sought to preserve 'the landlord tenant system under pri-vate ownership'. It argued that it was only the burden of death duties and Excess Profits Tax which prevented landlords from making the necessary cap-ital improvements.[85] However, it was forced to accept the principle of national control of planning by a central authority.[86] It recognised 'that this involves the application of compulsory powers in the national interest', but it rejected the proposal in the Uthwatt Report that the state should acquire the devel-opment rights in undeveloped rural land as a step too far in the direction of land nationalisation.[87]

In the face of such state intervention, landlords fought an up-hill battle to preserve the 'farmer-owner' as a 'person who is wedded to the soil and cannot escape his responsibilities'. But it was the perceived failure of landlords as a class that put them most on the defensive, particularly the accusation that they had sacrificed the upkeep of their estates to the upkeep of their mansions and their standard of life. In reply, the landlords argued that 'they are per-fectly ready and willing to carry on with their task and that to urge that in common fairness the necessary state aid should be given as a corollary to the centralised control which they are prepared to accept'.[88] However, their case for a 'restoration of leadership and an aristocratic conception of responsi-bility' found little public support in the atmosphere of wartime collectivism.[89]

---

82 Young, *Country and Town*.

83 Vesey-Fitzgerald (ed.), *Programme for Agriculture*, p. 190.

84 Country Landowners' Association AD1/31: Minutes of the Executive Committee, 30 May 1940.

85 Country Landowners' Association P2/A7: 'Agricultural Policy After the War', 6 May 1942.

86 PRO: HLG 80/50 – Evidence of the Country Landowners' Association to the Scott Committee.

87 Ibid., 'Memorandum on the Final Report of the Uthwatt Committee', 2 November 1942.

88 *Estates Gazette*, 18 December 1943.

89 *Country Life*, 17 September 1943.

The war also had the effect of reviving the moribund rural land market. The Incorporated Society of Auctioneers reported that rural areas had not been so adversely affected as urban areas, and that 'there had been considerable buying of agricultural land'.[90] By the end of the first year of the war, the *Estates Gazette* stated that agricultural development had led to a great demand for farming land.[91] The press reported in July 1943 that 'agricultural land values [had risen] rapidly as the demand by big moneyed people for first-class farms outstrips the supply'.[92] Prices for vacant possession of farm real estate rose considerably reaching £47 an acre in 1943, more than 80% above their pre-war level.[93] Such pressures created serious concerns about land speculation. The government introduced new defence regulations in November to restrict the power of the purchaser of rural land to give sitting tenants notice to quit.[94] *The Estates Gazette* considered that these new regulations had only a 'steadying effect on prices of farmland. The trend of money from cities to the land is of considerable importance in that agriculture has been starved of capital for so many years that the present influx is a tonic long overdue to the industry'.[95]

The coalition was as equally responsive to the wartime needs of the countryside as they were to the impact of the Blitz on urban areas. One of the first acts Lord Reith took as Minister of Works in October 1941 was to invite Lord Justice Scott, one of the founding members of the Council for the Preservation of Rural England, to consider the conditions which should govern building and other development in country areas consistent with the maintenance of agriculture.[96] The Committee was dominated by leading members of the pre-war preservationist lobby, particularly those concerned to secure the aesthetics of the English landscape and to protect it through a combination of national planning and 'geographical citizenship'. 'Movements for the planning and preservation of landscape which had emerged in the 1920s and 30s gained positions of considerable political and cultural power during the war as the state assumed an increasing role in the direction of life.'[97] The reconstruction machinery created by Lord Reith gave renewed voice to a group of geographers and planners, such as Dudley Stamp, Vaughan Cornish and John Dower, who exercised a significant influence on the direction of rural policy.[98] Dudley Stamp, who had carried out the first comprehensive mapping of land use in the 1930s, was a member of the Scott Committee and

---

90 *Estates Gazette*, 2 March 1940.
91 Ibid., 28 December 1940.
92 *Daily Express*, 17 May 1943, quoted in *Land and Liberty*, July 1943.
93 Ward, 'Measuring Changes in Farm Sale Prices', *Chartered Surveyor*, December 1957.
94 PRO: CAB 117/38 – 'Speculation in Agricultural Land 1941'.
95 *Estates Gazette*, 10 January 1942.
96 *Land Utilisation in Rural Areas*, Cmd. 6378.
97 Matless, 'Visual Culture and Geographical Citizenship: England in the 1940s', p. 424.
98 Wibberley, 'The Famous Scott Report: A Text for All Time?', *The Planner*, 7 (1985), pp. 13–20.

provided it with detailed information supporting the argument for a system of national planning.[99]

The terms of reference of the Scott Report conflated the issues of rural preservation and agricultural protection. The preamble expressed 'a deep love for our countryside', quoting H. G. Wells who had said that 'there is no countryside like the English countryside ... in its firm yet gentle lines of hill and dale'. The rural elegist and historian G. M. Trevelyan was also cited: 'without vision the people perish, and without natural beauty the English people will perish in the spiritual sense'.[100] The report thus directly addressed the interwar controversy over the urban threat to the countryside and sought to prevent a return to 'the old unregulated sprawl of town into country with all its attendant evils'.[101] At the same time, it made the assumption 'that industry will, to an unknown and perhaps unforeseeable extent, want to come into the countryside'. Scott therefore sought to address a number of different competing demands. His Committee had to balance the state of wartime agriculture and the needs of the urban population for food both during and after the war, and the preservation of the landscape for aesthetic reasons against the need for urban access to rural areas for recreational and spiritual purposes. He also had to decide the extent to which industrial development should be prevented from taking place in the countryside, balanced against the need to improve rural amenities, employment and services.

On its publication in 1942, the report recommended that town and country planning should be made compulsory over the whole country, with the larger county borough vested with planning responsibilities. It supported the creation of national parks and nature reserves. It argued that the well-being of rural communities depended almost exclusively on the maintenance of a healthy and well-balanced agriculture, which should be based on the traditional mixed character of British farming. No diffusion of industry into rural areas was therefore desirable. Rather, industry should be encouraged first to make use of vacant or derelict sites in towns, and where industry is brought into country areas it should be located in existing or new small towns and not in villages or the open country.[102]

Scott was widely welcomed in the press, particularly his view that agriculture had a prior and special claim over other industries in the countryside. He had supported the policy of organisations like the Land Union, for example, which represented the interests of rural landowners and argued that the country owed them a great debt not only for farming in the best interests of the fertility of the soil, 'but who by the careful management of their estates,

99 Rycroft and Cosgrove, 'Mapping the Modern Nation: Dudley Stamp and the Land Utilisation Survey', pp. 91–105.
100 Cmd. 6378; Cannadine, *G. M. Trevelyan*, pp. 141–80.
101 Cmd. 6378; Miller, 'Urban Dreams and Rural Reality', pp. 89–102.
102 This summary is based on *PEP*, No. 198, 22 December 1942. Tichelar, 'The Scott Report and the Labour Party', pp. 167–87.

the planting of trees, and the construction of buildings in keeping with the character of the countryside, made England the beautiful place which it still is'.[103] *The Times* argued that the report's recommendations largely reflected existing government commitments and that there should be no delay in legislation setting up a central planning authority to control all development across the country.[104]

More significantly, the Conservative MP Douglas Hogg congratulated Scott for steering the Committee away from the issue of land nationalisation.[105] Scott had effectively sidelined the issue, support for which had been growing during the early years of the war amongst academics and agriculturists. Astor and Rowntree had argued just before the war for the nationalisation of farmland where it was clear that private ownership was incapable of providing capital investment.[106] This argument was given new relevance by the intervention of the county council War Agricultural Executive Committees. The case for land nationalisation was increasingly supported by academic opinion as the war progressed. In 1941 Daniel Hall, the chief scientific adviser to the Ministry of Agriculture, maintained that private landlords were either unwilling or unable to restructure farming along efficient lines and that ownership should be invested with the state.[107] Sir George Stapledon, professor of agricultural botany at the University College of Wales, pressed for 'the State to purchase the land outright ... to bring the land into good heart'.[108] C. S. Orwin, director of the Agricultural Economics Research Institute at Oxford, also argued that the position of the private landlord had become untenable. Like Hall he believed that the answer was the unified control of land use and a policy of rural reconstruction under public ownership.[109] He pressed strongly for the state to acquire the freehold of the land at valuations based on its present use, not upon its prospective value, and this must be accepted as a prerequisite of planning control.[110] Populist commentators, like the farmer A. G. Street proposed national ownership as the only remedy for the shameful condition that the farming industry found itself in, a view that was also reflected in the anti-property views of the popular broadcaster, J. B. Priestley.[111] However, opinion was divided over whether land nationalisation could be justified in rural areas, given the sacrifice which landowners and farmers were making in fighting the war on the home front. The Archbishop of York supported urban land nationalisation on the grounds that the value of town land was created through community intervention but argued for the

103 *Estates Gazette*, 14 February 1942, p. 138.
104 *The Times*, 15 August 1942, p. 5.
105 Ibid., MSS/119/3/S/55, Letter to Scott, 19 August 1942.
106 Astor and Rowntree, *British Agriculture: The Principles of Future Policy*, p. 270.
107 Hall, *Reconstruction and the Land*, p. 257.
108 Stapledon, *Make Fruitful the Land*.
109 Orwin, *Speed the Plough*, pp. 25–39; Orwin, *The Problems of the Countryside*, p. 41.
110 Orwin, 'Rural Land Ownership and Planning', p. 94.
111 Street, *Farm Cottages and Post-War Farming*; Nicholas, *The Echo of War*, pp. 241–5.

retention of private ownership of rural land for fear of depriving the country-side of its natural leadership.[112]

The coalition referred the detail of the Scott Report to the complex inter-departmental reconstruction machinery for further consideration. This is where it remained without resolution for the rest of the war. In November 1943, over a year after the report's publication, the government gave its much delayed and general support, publicly announcing that many of Scott's recommendations were already existing policy.[113] It reaffirmed the view that agricultural considerations be given full weight in planning. 'Emphasis will be laid on the successful cultivation of the soil as the foundation of all rural economy.'[114] The other area where progress was made on the Scott Report was the recommendation for the creation of national parks. The Dower Report on National Parks in England and Wales proposed the establishment of a commission. Unlike the recommendations of the Uthwatt Report, which proved to be highly controversial as the war neared its end, the Scott Report achieved a relatively high level of consensus, but little legislative activity. It would take the post-war Labour government to legislate.

Summary

The domestic impact of the war transformed the land question in both town and country. It raised the profile of the town planning lobby and increased its influence in government circles. The Blitz brought about a new public demand for replanning city centres, involving the control of land use and compulsory state purchase of development land by local authorities. More importantly, it reinforced public opposition to land and property speculation and this in turn gave weight to the demand for some sort of state control, ownership or taxation of land to prevent reconstruction from being prejudiced by wartime profiteering.

But the promise of government action was not fulfilled. Although the recommendations of Uthwatt were widely publicised and supported in the atmosphere of wartime enthusiasm for replanning, and directly led to the cre-ation of a Ministry of Town and Country Planning in 1943, they became enmeshed in a Whitehall machine that was distrustful of the creation of a new ministry. The Scott Report did not require any new legislative action by the coalition and therefore did not generate any acute political controversy. But the long-awaited legislation to implement the Uthwatt Report proved to be a serious disappointment and a source of political controversy in 1944. In this atmosphere of political conflict there was no basis for introducing radical land reform that directly threatened the rights of private property. Chapter 6

---

112 *Estates Gazette*, 27 September 1942, p. 299.
113 *The Times*, 1 December 1943, p. 5.
114 PRO: CAB 66 WP (43) 485 – 'Land Utilisation in Rural Areas' Memorandum by Minister without Portfolio, 29 October 1943; *The Times*, 1 December 1943, p. 2 and p. 5.

will discuss the way in which this led to a political crisis in the coalition government in 1944, and a change in Labour Party policy from one of land nationalisation back to a renewed emphasis on taxation of land to be achieved through town and country planning. The traditional land reform policy of the rating of site values was therefore dropped in favour of recovering the 'unearned increment' through legislation to control the use of land.

6 Tensions in the wartime coalition government

The war witnessed growing tensions within the coalition government over the rights to landed property. It also saw the Labour Party retreat from a policy of land nationalisation in favour of seeking to recover the 'unearned increment' by nationalising the development rights in land, rather than the land itself. This chapter starts by reviewing the political response to the recommendations of the Uthwatt and Scott Reports. While Uthwatt led to an acute political crisis within the government, nearly breaking up the coalition less than a year before the 1945 general election, Scott produced a wider level of agreement, although no legislative proposals as such, apart from a decision to continue on a temporary basis with guaranteed prices for agriculture after the war and a general commitment in principle to create national parks.

It was the Labour Party that championed land reform during the war in the face of severe opposition from landowners in the Conservative Party. But its support for land nationalisation was questioned particularly by its parliamentary leaders holding ministerial office in the coalition. By 1945, the party had abandoned its policy of land nationalisation and replaced it with an intention to introduce stronger town and country planning legislation. Land-use control was regarded thereafter as the vehicle for recouping betterment (the unearned increment) and determining the level of compensation for land compulsorily purchased by the state. This new approach to the taxation of land values, or seeking to capture the increased value of land from development activity, replaced the traditional policy of land reform based on the rating of site values.[1] The party also began to gradually retreat from a policy of rural land nationalisation as it came to recognise that it was irrelevant to the immediate problem of post-war food shortages and could have compromised its relationship with the farmers in the drive for increased productivity.[2]

---

1 Tichelar, 'The Conflict over Property Rights during the Second World War' and 'Central-Local Tensions'.
2 Tichelar, 'The Labour Party, Agricultural Policy and the Retreat from Rural Land Nationalisation'; Chase, 'Nothing Less Than a Revolution?', pp. 79–95.

The conflict over property rights in urban areas

The wartime controversy over land reform reached a climax during the second half of 1944, following the publication in June of the government's Town and Country Planning Bill and the accompanying White Paper on the Control of Land Use.[3] This proposed legislation was the government's belated response to the Uthwatt Report. It demonstrated the failure of the coalition to reach any acceptable compromise after protracted and unresolved debate within the various committees set up to consider post-war reconstruction. The coalition was accused of breaking its promise to restrict the price of land acquired compulsorily to a 1939 standard value and acceding to pressure from landowners to extract more and more concessions on the question of compensation.

The period up to November, when the bill was enacted, witnessed bitter political controversy over the rights of landowners with Labour members of the government refusing to compromise over the principle of the 1939 price of land. This controversy split the Labour Party and threatened to undermine the basis of the coalition itself at the time when traditional party-political strife was reasserting itself during the latter half of 1944. By the time a deal had been agreed in October, which preserved the principle of the 1939 price ceiling, relationships within the coalition had reached a point of no return. Opinion within the party had hardened against any continuing alliance with the Conservatives. The issue of land reform directly contributed to the eventual decision of the Labour Party to leave the coalition.

In October 1943, the Deputy Prime Minister, Clement Attlee, was advised that progress on implementing post-war reconstruction was very uneven. Most headway had been made in the areas of international economic cooperation, social services and agriculture. Attlee's personal assistant identified lack of speed in implementing the Uthwatt Report as a 'major black spot ... and a serious impediment to local authorities housing and industrial relocation'.[4] In his New Year broadcast as deputy prime minister, Attlee acknowledged that while there was a large measure of agreement on reconstruction, 'issues are bound to arise on which strongly conflicting views are held'.[5] This proved to be an accurate forecast of future controversy over land reform. Disagreements within the Cabinet delayed the publication of legislation until June when it was no longer politically possible to keep the blitzed cities waiting for specific measures to start the difficult process of replanning. Pressure from within the party, particularly during the course of 1943 when the military fortunes of the war turned decisively in favour of the allies, forced Labour ministers in the coalition to take a more proactive stand.

3 *The Control of Land Use*, Cmd. 6537 (1944).
4 Papers of William Piercy 8/4 – Note by Durbin to Attlee on Post-War Reconstruction, 21 October 1943.
5 Attlee Papers, Dept. 11, f. 170 and 195.

The 'retreat from coalition' had started earlier in the year as it became clear that Conservative opinion was lukewarm about Beveridge and other post-war reforms.[6] Churchill's commitment to the immediate 'replanning and rebuilding of our cities and towns' in his broadcast in March was heavily qualified by the need to win the war first.[7] In November 1943 the government responded favourably to the Scott Report on Land Utilisation in Rural Areas, although this did not require any fresh legislation.[8] In the same month the pace of progress noticeably quickened when Attlee persuaded Churchill to create a more powerful Reconstruction Committee, and appointed Lord Woolton (over Lord Beaverbrook) as the new Minister of Reconstruction with a seat in Cabinet, charged with responsibility for planning the transition to peace.[9]

However, despite this progress, the Minister of Town and Country Planning, the Conservative W. S. Morrison had been trying to persuade Churchill to agree to a comprehensive alternative to the Uthwatt Report that was more favourable to landlord interests.[10] As the war progressed these policy difficulties could not be resolved by the coalition's reconstruction policymaking machinery.[11] In such circumstances only limited legislation was possible. Local authorities were not required to prepare planning schemes.[12] Most controversy centred on the issue of the price to be paid for land. Uthwatt had recommended that compensation should not exceed pre-war values (as at 31 March 1939). This principle had been publicly accepted by the government, and subsequently used for assessing war damage under the War Damage Act of 1941. But the effect of the war on the value of land made the implementation of this principle a complex minefield. While the war had depressed the cost of land in blitzed areas, particularly in the southern coastal towns, the value of agricultural land had increased as farming became more profitable. As the price of land fell in urban areas, along with dramatic falls in rateable values following evacuation and war damage, landowners argued that they would certainly want to wait for prices to recover after the war before selling.

Conservative opinion within the coalition argued that if local authorities were to be allowed to purchase land compulsorily at 1939 values, this would lead to serious inequality between those owners whose land was publicly acquired and owners who sold privately.[13] John Anderson, the Conservative

6 Jefferys, *The Churchill Coalition and Wartime Politics*, pp. 166–87.

7 Churchill, *War Speeches, Vol. 2*, p. 434.

8 PRO: CAB 65 WM (43)152 – 10 November 1943; CAB 66 WP (43) 485 – 'Land Utilisation in Rural Areas', 29 October 1943.

9 Harris, *Attlee*, p. 226.

10 PRO: PREM 4/92/2 – 'Memorandum on Control of Land Use by Minister of Town and Country Planning', 15 July 1943; CAB 117/134 – Letter from W. S. Morrison to Lord Woolton, 17 November 1943.

11 PRO: PREM 4/92/3 (Land Planning) and 92/6 (Central Planning Authority).

12 Garside, *Town Planning in London, 1930–1960*, p. 254.

13 PRO: CAB 66 WP (44)122 – 'Housing in the Transition Period', Memorandum by the Minister of Economic Warfare (Earl of Selborne), 18 February 1944.

Chancellor of the Exchequer, pressed for a departure from the Uthwatt principle by allowing adjustments to be made in the level of compensation for any increases or decreases in the value of land since 1939. As Chancellor, he was also anxious to prevent local authorities in general from either buying up land cheaply or benefiting from any open-ended commitments from central government to borrow to finance redevelopment, the cost of which was estimated to be over £575 million.[14]

The early commitments given by Lord Reith to the local authorities thus proved to be a serious embarrassment to a government unable to agree the basis of compensation to landlords. The appointment of Lord Woolton as the new Minister of Reconstruction in November 1943 had raised expectations that a comprehensive planning bill would be published in early 1944. By March 1944, the coalition was being severely criticised for the continuing delay. The Tory Reform Committee issued a bulletin stating that post-war housing would be compromised if local authorities did not know their financial liabilities for compensation.[15] Lord Astor, the Mayor of Plymouth, complained bitterly about the failure of the government. He forecast that 'the future of the Coalition may well depend upon the adequacy of the land policy it is about to propose, since that policy will govern the whole prospect for decent homes and well-planned cities after the war'.[16]

In these circumstances, the Cabinet agreed a compromise. It was decided that a bill would be introduced to provide powers and exchequer assistance for reconstruction areas, while the wider questions of compensation, betterment and land use would be dealt with by way of a White Paper. The scope of the proposed legislation was restricted to providing limited and short-term support to local authorities in only those areas directly affected by the Blitz. Most controversially, the bill replaced the 1939 price ceiling with the proposal that the amount to be paid in compensation should not fall below 1939 values, thereby ignoring any fall in the value of urban land since the start of the war. This was a major change with significant political and financial implications.[17]

The proposed bill proved to be deeply disappointing to the local authorities. They had used wartime conditions to campaign for increased planning powers and a resolution of the difficult and complex question of compensation and betterment. The blitzed cities had quickly appointed consultants and architects to start the ambitious process of replanning.[18] The Labour-controlled London County Council (LCC), in particular, used Lord Reith's request 'as the starting point in a campaign for new planning powers which

14 Cullingworth, *Environmental Planning, 1939–1969: Vol. 1*, pp. 113–19. *The Times*, 25 October 1944.
15 *The Times*, 11 March 1944.
16 *The Times*, 24 March 1944. See Astor to Reith, 16 March 1944, BBC Written Archives, S60/6/11, p. 71.
17 Cullingworth, *Environmental Planning, 1939–1969*, p. 112; *The Times*, 24 June 1944.
18 Cherry, *Town Planning in Britain since 1900*, pp. 95–100.

lasted throughout the war'.[19] However, after the immediate impact of the Blitz had lessened after 1942, the question of local authority planning, and especially compensation and betterment, came up against a number of powerful vested interests, including landed and property interests which mobilised with some success against the Uthwatt Report.[20]

Three issues dominated the strained and difficult consultations between the local authorities and the government: (1) the powers and procedures to compulsorily acquire land for development; (2) financial aid from the Treasury to carry out reconstruction and housebuilding; and (3) the basis of compensation to landowners who had been compulsorily bought out. In their evidence to Uthwatt, the Association of Municipal Corporations (AMC), which represented the larger urban authorities, emphasised local control and determination.[21] They looked to central government to give local authorities enhanced planning powers to prevent uncontrolled building. In addition, they sought simplified and speedy powers of compulsory acquisition at a price which should not exceed the value of the property at the time of purchase or the value at 31 March 1939, whichever was the lowest. They expected redevelopment to be financed by the granting of loans from the Treasury. But they were opposed to a national system of compensation and betterment, whereby the government would collect and distribute payments from a central pool. 'If you are collecting money from local betterment you must keep it for local compensation. You must not take money from Hertfordshire and spend it in Cornwall.'[22]

Labour-controlled councils were equally jealous of their independence and fearful of any proposals that might consolidate wartime government centralisation or introduce regional government.[23] Municipal landownership was considered to be a viable alternative to the complete nationalisation of land. Some in the party argued that a policy of complete nationalisation would create administrative and legal problems, leaving aside the political controversy.[24] An alternative to nationalisation was the establishment of a National Land Compensation Fund, the main source of which would be a levy of 90% of any increase in the capital value of land. For some, this was 'a return to the principle of the Snowden Land Tax – with this difference: that the whole of the increment tax thus raised should be earmarked for planning compensation'.[25] The proposal found its way into the party's official policy statement

19 Garside, 'The Failure of Regionalism in 1940s Britain' p. 106.
20 PRO: CAB 117/128 and 130.
21 Nuffield College Social Reconstruction Papers, C5/6: Evidence of the Association of Municipal Corporations to the Uthwatt Committee, 4 April and 19 June 1941.
22 Ibid.
23 LPA: RDR 55/January 1942 – 'Suggested Short-term Programme for Housing and Town Planning in the Immediate Post-War Years'.
24 LPA: RDR 106/July 1942, 'The Machinery of Planning by F J Osborn'; RDR 120/July 1942, 'The Machinery of Planning'.
25 Ibid., p. 5.

on *Housing and Planning after the War*, disappointing those who had been campaigning for a policy of complete land nationalisation.

In 1942, at a conference of blitzed cities, Labour local authorities made it clear to the central party that their first priority was post-war housing, with the need to overcome shortages of building materials and manpower, and for central subsidies to finance reconstruction. Although land nationalisation was seen as the only long-term satisfactory solution, it was certainly felt that local authorities should in the interim 'be given wide powers of acquisition and control over the use of land in their areas'.[26] The conference was more concerned about the vexed question of compensation rather than the mechanics of state ownership.[27] Of equal concern to Labour councils was the deteriorating financial position of urban local authorities brought about by the severe loss of rate income created by the war. This was compounded by anxieties about 'whether those industries which had evacuated from blitzed areas would return at the end of the war to provide employment for local residents and rate revenue for the authority. It was feared that if the old system of rates and subsidies remained unaltered local authorities would plan large but act small'.[28]

On a pragmatic level, therefore, Labour local authorities were more interested in the cost of specific sites and their precarious financial position arising from the inadequacies of the rating system than in the more general and highly controversial question of land nationalisation. They also reacted angrily to the proposals of the National Executive Committee (NEC) of the party to introduce regional government and to transfer to these new bodies responsibility for town and country planning. The war had raised the prospect of major local government reform and had accelerated the tendency towards centralisation. But this issue proved to be a deeper problem, raising fundamental questions about the size, function and financing of local government. As a result, it remained largely unresolved during and after the war. The debate on local government proved to be one of the most divisive and contentious of the 1943 annual conference.[29]

The views of Labour local authorities proved to be highly influential in the way that the National Party responded to the Town and Country Planning Bill in 1944. The Labour-controlled LCC provided a major focus of opposition to the bill through the access which its leaders Lord Latham and Lewis Silkin had to party policymaking. The local authority associations had been invited by the Ministry of Town and Country Planning to take part in a series of lengthy consultations on the bill at the end of 1943.[30] Matters came

---

26 LPA: Policy Committee, 24 July 1942, 'Summarised Report of the Conference of Representatives from Blitzed Areas held on 29 and 30 August 1942'.

27 Ibid., p. 3.

28 Ibid., p. 3.

29 Tichelar, 'Central-Local Tensions', pp. 187–206.

30 Minutes of the County Councils Association, 15 December 1943; Minutes of the Association of Municipal Corporations, 2 December 1943.

to a head in May 1944, when they and the LCC met the Ministry of Town and Country Planning. The local authorities objected most strongly to the financial aspects, in particular the compensation clauses and the restrictions imposed on the level of Treasury grants for redevelopment.[31] The outcome of these consultations was reported to the War Cabinet a few weeks later. The Cabinet recognised that the adoption of the March 1939 value as a standard, rather than a ceiling, would be highly contentious. It knew that this would result in local authorities having to pay 1939 prices in all cases of compulsory acquisition, whereas they believed that they could buy at a lower figure. The Minister of Town Planning was given two weeks to prepare an amended bill which would reduce criticism and embarrassment. Churchill hoped that political attention would be preoccupied with the Normandy landings.[32]

However, such hopes proved unfounded. The Earl of Selborne, the Minister of Economic Warfare, who had championed the landlords' cause in the Cabinet, threatened to resign from the government. 'I do not see how anyone who values property as an institution can countenance these proposals.'[33] Before the final Cabinet meeting in June to agree the bill, Attlee was advised to remind Churchill that his previous public commitment to adequate powers for rebuilding blitzed cities had been highly explicit in his reconstruction broadcast to the nation. 'We cannot help thinking that the credit of the government as a whole may suffer a set back after the admirable impression created by the White Paper on Full (sic) Employment.'[34] But in the end Labour ministers in the coalition were forced to accept the draft bill as the best they could hope for in the circumstances. They had managed to safeguard the principle of the 1939 price basis, even though they had retreated on the issue of the price ceiling by accepting a price standard that ensured that some landowners would be paid more in compensation than originally intended. The Minister of Reconstruction told Churchill that the bill was 'the best compromise we can get and we cannot any longer delay giving local authorities the power they need. The Bill will be knocked about in the House, from both sides and for different reasons'.[35] For these reasons it was not possible to avoid political controversy when the bill was finally published along with the White Paper on the Control of Land Use on 20 June 1944.

Labour local authorities called for its immediate rejection on the grounds that the financial assistance to be given to councils 'was ludicrous and miserably inadequate'.[36] The *Daily Herald* condemned the failure of 'the

---

31 A joint memorandum issued by the local authority associations (AMC, CCA, UDC, Non-County Boroughs, RDCs) and the LCC – Minutes of the Urban District Councils Association, 30 June 1944; see also Cullingworth, *Environmental Planning, 1939–1969*, pp. 121–2.
32 PRO: CAB 68 (44), 7–24 May 1944; Dalton Papers, Diary, 24 May 1944.
33 PRO: PREM 4/92/8, Letter from Selborne to Churchill, 24 May 1944.
34 William Piercy Papers, 8/16 – Note by Durbin to Attlee, 6 June 1944.
35 PRO: PREM 4/92/7 – Woolton to Churchill, 15 June 1944.
36 *Daily Herald*, 24 June 1944.

Government to reach a bold conclusion on one of the most urgent reconstruction problems'.[37] Lord Latham led the campaign for the bill's total withdrawal describing it as a 'Triumph of the Rights of Property'.[38] He likened
the story of the bill to a great betrayal, three years after local authorities had
been encouraged to plan boldly: 'If this bill becomes law the prospect of any
really worthwhile large-scale, comprehensive planning in this country will be
dark in deed…. Where local authorities must buy land for housing they will
be forced in many cases to pay a price which may be higher than its market
value.'[39] The London Labour Party convened a special conference to consider
the bill, condemning it as 'totally inadequate, wholly insufficient and a gross
distortion of Uthwatt'.[40] Silkin called it 'a miserable and mean measure and
a victory by the landowning interests. If the Labour Party accepts it, even in
principle, it will be guilty of having betrayed the hopes of all who have placed
their trust in our Movement'.[41] The Parliamentary Labour Party (PLP) was
pressed to reject the bill at its second reading.[42] Greatest criticism was reserved
for the replacing of the 1939 ceiling with a 1939 standard.[43] But the unity
of the local government position did not hold. On 30 June the *Daily Herald*
reported that despite the initial rejection of the bill by the local authority associations acting collectively, the different associations had met separately. 'The
associations were anxious to avoid a direct challenge to the Government.'[44]

The response of the PLP was more cautious. It had weathered the storm of
the backbench rebellion over the Beveridge Report and it now faced a revolt
on land reform. On this occasion the timing was more difficult, coinciding
with the preparations for the Second Front, a point that the *Tribune* argued
had added to its dilemma.[45] However, it was the views of the local authorities that exerted the most pressure on the PLP to stay within the coalition.[46]
The crisis came to a head in July when the PLP held an emergency meeting
to discuss what action should be taken on the second reading. It was decided
that the party would abstain.[47] In the event only five Labour MPs defied the
Whip and voted against the bill.[48] The bulk of the PLP decided that despite
its inadequacies, it was better than nothing at all, and that it was politically
impossible to ignore the urgent needs of local councils.

37 *Daily Herald*, 24 June 1944.
38 *The Times*, 24 June 1944.
39 *Daily Herald*, 26 June 1944.
40 *Daily Herald*, 29 June and 12 July 1944; Ernest Bevin Papers, 2/8/1, Letter from London
    Labour Party to Ernest Bevin, 10 July 1944.
41 *Tribune*, 7 July 1944.
42 LPA: Minutes of the Parliamentary Labour Party, Special Meeting, 6 July 1944.
43 *The Times*, 6 July 1944; *Estates Gazette*, 8 July 1944.
44 *Daily Herald*, 30 June 1944.
45 *Tribune*, 24 March 1944.
46 *Daily Herald*, 1 July 1944.
47 LPA: Minutes of the Parliamentary Labour Party, 12 July 1944.
48 *Daily Herald*, 13 July 1944.

The struggle over the bill was renewed in the autumn when it entered its final stages. The summer recess and the Normandy landings pushed the controversy into the background. But during this period the organisations representing landed interests increased their campaign to obtain more concessions on compensation and to restrict the scope of local government planning powers. The discomfort that the publication of the bill and the White Paper had caused within the coalition, and the small size of the revolt against the bill at its second reading, had increased their confidence. They began to exert considerable influence in both Houses of Parliament through the lobby agents of the Land and Property Coordination Committee that had been set up in 1943 by the Country Landowners' Association (CLA) and the Land Union to attack Uthwatt.[49] The CLA welcomed the White Paper in July 1944 as 'better than Uthwatt' and went so far as to question 'the whole principle of planning in its effect on the liberty of the subject'.[50] Along with a number of other landed and professional bodies, it intensified the demand for 1939 prices to be adjusted for inflation and added, for good measure, that owner-occupiers bought out by the state should also be compensated for disturbance.[51]

Fifty pages of amendments were tabled by Conservative backbenchers when the third reading of the bill was commenced in October. These sought to increase the payment of compensation to all owners of property (including investment properties) in line with the War Damage Act of 1943. It had been agreed earlier that owner-occupiers needing to buy a replacement home following compulsory acquisition should receive a 30% addition to 1939 prices, to take into account increases in building costs. Conservative amendments wished to extend this provision to all property owners, whether occupiers or absentees, including shopkeepers and factory owners. The PLP refused to make this further concession.[52] The Labour Minister Ernest Bevin responded that if the clauses were dropped 'the whole question of the basis of compensation would have to be considered a-fresh'.[53] Two days earlier he had circulated a note to his colleagues in the coalition stating categorically that he could not accept any compromise to the 'rough justice' agreement reached by the War Cabinet in June that had accepted a price standard instead of a 1939 ceiling. He was, however, prepared to accept that owner-occupiers should be paid an additional amount for the cost of replacement but as long as this did not benefit speculators.[54]

49 *Property Owners' Journal*, May 1943.
50 Papers of the Country Landowners' Association, AD1/12: Minutes of the Executive Committee, 13 July 1944.
51 Ibid., AD1/33: Minutes of the Council, 29 June 1944; *Estates Gazette*, 9 September 1944; *The Times*, 5 September 1944; Labour Research Department, *Land and Landowners*.
52 LPA: Minutes of the Parliamentary Labour Party, 10 October 1944; *Daily Herald*, 7 October 1944.
53 PRO: CAB 65 WM 133(44), 1–6 October 1944.
54 Ernest Bevin Papers, 2/5: 'Note on the Town and Country Planning Bill', 4 October 1944.

But Conservative backbenchers were not prepared to make any compromises. Churchill was forced to make a dramatic intervention in the House of Commons on 6 October to try and broker a deal.[55] He succeeded in persuading the House to drop the controversial clauses that linked compensation to 1939 prices. 'Unless an eleventh-hour compromise can be reached,' *The Times* noted 'only that part of the Bill which empowers local authorities to acquire land will reach the statute book. The quite crucial questions of price and cost will remain unanswered.'[56] This proved to be too much for the PLP that considered it had already made enough concessions. However, like earlier in the summer, the crisis was soon averted. This time it was the Conservative rebels who were forced to vote against the government, which remained committed to the principle of compensation based on 1939 prices, subject to fair treatment to owner-occupiers. Ernest Bevin took a strong line against further concessions making it clear to the right wing of the Conservative Party that this was a possible resignation issue.[57]

A settlement was finally reached on 12 October, when the principle of the 1939 price for land was agreed as the basis of compensation subject to owner-occupiers of buildings or agricultural holdings being able to claim up to 30% for increases in wartime costs.[58] This was in line with the solution proposed by Ernest Bevin.[59] 'Nobody wishes to see any profits guaranteed under this Bill to speculators who bought land or houses at less than 1939 prices.'[60] *The Times* suggested that the solution 'marked an appreciable change in the Labour Party's attitude … and that it should not be difficult to achieve an agreement in Cabinet which will be acceptable to the majority of the House'.[61] This proved to be the case. Despite further opposition from Conservative MPs who wanted the 30% provision extended to investment property, the War Cabinet confirmed the Attlee compromise on 23 October.[62] Fifty-eight Conservative rebels voted against the bill on 25 October.[63]

But Churchill faced more problems in the House of Lords. Viscount Cranborne, the Conservative Leader in the Upper House, threatened to resign over the failure of the bill to extend the 30% additional compensation to owner-investors 'who [are] in many cases no better off than the owner-occupier'. Churchill found this too much to stomach:

55   Hansard, 6 October 1944, cols. 1369–99.
56   *The Times*, 7 October 1944.
57   *Daily Herald*, 9 October 1944.
58   PRO: CAB 65 WM 136(44), 2–12 October 1944; *The Times*, 14 October 1944.
59   Bevin Papers, 2/5 – 'Proposals for a Solution on the Town and Country Planning Bill', 10 October 1944.
60   *The Times*, 12 October 1944.
61   *The Times*, 9 October 1944.
62   PRO: CAB 65 WM 140(44), 13–23 October 1944.
63   Jefferys (ed.), *Labour and the Wartime Coalition*, p. 193.

Personally I think that if anyone gets out of the present war with the same property values as he had in 1939, his case is not one to cause particular compassion in the state of the world today. With the world in chaos and every human being's fortunes governed by the cruel hazards of war, it is altogether unsuitable to endeavour to establish these exact mathematical and meticulous standards of justice, if it be justice, in one particular class of real estate. A broader view must be taken. The Leader of the House of Lords cannot resign.[64]

In the end, the views of the majority of the War Cabinet prevailed and the bill was enacted in November. Labour's position in the coalition was therefore safeguarded for the time being. Tactical considerations outweighed the merits of individual policy issues. But the conflict had demonstrated the public revival of political differences within the heart of the coalition over the question of urban land reform. The leadership of the Labour Party persuaded its MPs that it was desirable to 'finish the war before Labour left the coalition and a general election was held, and that prior to such an election Labour should not press for major changes in policy or legislation which would involve a showdown with their Conservative colleagues'.[65]

In October the Labour Party announced that it would continue in the government 'just so long as, in the opinion of the Party conference it is necessary in the national interest and for fulfilling the purposes for which the Government was called into being'.[66] Despite the inadequacy of the legislation on town planning, the party tried to salvage some pride from the stand it had made over the compensation clauses. The *Daily Herald* pointed out that if this had not been made, local authorities would have had to fall back on the Land Act of 1919 for determining compensation for land acquired compulsorily. 'This would have fixed values at scarcity prices. This alternative procedure, it is reliably estimated, would have enriched the landowners by hundreds of millions of pounds at the expense of the tax payer.'[67] *The Times* noted that the original estimate of £575,000,000 for local authorities buying up their war-damaged areas would now be increased by the more generous formula for compensation.[68] The CLA welcomed the changes that had been made to the bill. It regarded it as an ad hoc settlement that did not set any precedents on the question of compensation.[69] In practice, the Act provided sweeping powers to local authorities to engage in reconstruction and development after the war. But the policy of land nationalisation was sacrificed in the process largely as a consequence of the way in which Labour local authorities

64 PRO: PREM 4/92/8 – Cranborne to Churchill and His Reply, 24 October 1944.
65 Harris, *Attlee*, p. 236.
66 LPA: Minutes of the NEC, 29 October 1944.
67 *Daily Herald*, 11 October 1944.
68 *The Times*, 25 October 1944.
69 Country Landowners' Association, Minutes of the Council, 9 November 1944.

had put pressure on the central party to downplay the policy of land national-isation in favour of more immediate and pragmatic reform of town planning. A similar process of policy dilution took place with regard to the policy of land nationalisation in rural areas.

The political response to the Scott Report

The Labour Party supported the recommendations of the Scott Report and accepted without question its primary recommendation that agriculture as an industry had a prior claim to land in rural areas.[70] There was a cross-party understanding that the government elected after the war would introduce legislation to achieve this aim. Both Labour and Conservative came to believe that the best way of preserving the countryside and the aesthetics of the land-scape was to see the land kept productive through farming. The Labour Party rejected the possibility of introducing manufacturing into rural areas because it supported the view that the purpose of town planning was to control urban sprawl and contain it within existing urban areas or carefully planned new or satellite towns.[71] This would help preserve the position of Labour local authorities and protect their vulnerable rate bases from an overemphasis on dispersal of population and industry away from traditional areas of Labour electoral support.[72] The need to promote a civic urban consciousness and restore urban life after the war was as equally important as fostering rural idealism and accepting the anti-metropolitan tendencies of the Town and Country Planning Association.[73] The Labour Party in particular was keen to emphasise the need for community building in its urban strongholds, as well as the need to bring rural life up to the level of the economic and social conditions of the towns. It was not prepared, however, to sacrifice one for the other. In line with public opinion, it wanted to see the countryside protected as part of a wider programme of reconstruction in both urban and rural areas.

This level of wartime agreement between the parties removed the pressure on the coalition to introduce legislation on Scott before the end of the war. The only area where real policy progress was made on the Scott Report before 1945 was the recommendation for the creation of national parks, although the Treasury was opposed to the setting up of an independent National Parks Authority. The Ministry of Town Planning had appointed John Dower, a planner, self-taught architect and Friend of the Lake District, to prepare a report identifying possible suitable areas of outstanding natural beauty. The White Paper on the Control of Land Use, published in 1944, also reaffirmed the government's commitment to national parks.[74] Dower's report, which

---

70 Tichelar, 'The Scott Report and the Labour Party'.
71 Tichelar, 'The Scott Report and the Labour Party'.
72 Tichelar, 'Central-Local Tensions'.
73 Matless, *Landscape and Englishness*, pp. 173–284.
74 *The Control of Land Use*, Cmd. 6537 (1944).

was finally issued in the closing months of the war, was accepted as personal advice to the Minister of Town and Country Planning, and it was left to the post-war government to implement its findings. It identified 8,000 square miles of wild country as potential national park areas and argued that no development other than farming or forestry should be allowed to take place. It also argued that it was not necessary for the land to be acquired by the state, supporting instead a strengthened system of land-use control exercised through a National Parks Commission.[75]

The war had raised the profile and influence of recreational and amenity groups. The Scott Committee had received detailed evidence from the Ramblers' Association in favour of centralised planning and the creation of a National Parks Commission.[76] A joint manifesto issued in June 1945 by the Ramblers' Association and the Youth Hostels Association (YHA), which between them represented a membership of a quarter of a million, pressed for wide-ranging legislation. It supported 'effective control of land use and development in the national interest'; unlimited public access to all unculti-vated mountains, moors, heaths and downs; the setting up of a Footpaths Commission to compel local authorities to fulfil their responsibilities to keep paths open; the creation of long-distance footpaths, such as the proposed Pennine Way; and lastly a National Parks Commission.[77] The National Trust pressed Scott for a national planning authority strong enough to deal with the claims of government departments and the vested interests of local authorities.[78]

The role of the National Trust in preserving the countryside had under-gone some important changes in public perception during the war. The area owned by the Trust had grown from 46,500 acres in 1938 to 110,000 acres at the end of 1944 with the expansion of the Country Houses Scheme. 'Largely invisible before the war, the Country House Scheme came under scrutiny in popular newspapers as more houses entered it and public sensitivity to the disposition of property increased.'[79] The war had transformed the role of the National Trust. Its secretary recognised in 1945 that the control of land use and the location of industry can only be done effectively by the state.[80] Within the Trust, its continued purpose began to be questioned in the face of the prospect of increased state intervention. By the end of the war the Trust had assumed a new role of 'country-house-museum-keeper' to socialist Britain.[81]

---

75 National Parks in England and Wales, Cmd. 6628, May 1945; Sheail, 'John Dower, National Parks and Town and Country Planning in Britain', pp. 1–16.
76 PRO: HLG 80/97 – Evidence of the Ramblers' Association to the Scott Committee.
77 'Draft Joint Manifesto of the YHA and the Ramblers' Association, May 1945', LPA: Papers of the General Secretary GS/ENT/2&4.
78 PRO: HLG 80/42 – Evidence of the National Trust to the Scott Committee.
79 Mandler, *The Fall and Rise of the Stately Home*, p. 323.
80 Milne (ed.), *The National Trust: A Record of Fifty Years' Achievement*, pp. 122–4.
81 Mandler, *The Fall and Rise of the Stately Home*, p. 329.

The Scott Report did not therefore prove to be as controversial as Uthwatt. The Land Union welcomed the Scott Report as a constructive document while condemning Uthwatt as destructive of the rights of property and freedom of enterprise.[82] Scott avoided the issue of landownership and sided with popular public opinion in support of preserving the traditional landscape and function of the countryside despite the economic lessons of the war that demonstrated the need for larger-scale mechanised farming. The strength of popular attitudes to the countryside, and the use of the countryside for patriotic purposes during the war years, taken together with the increased popularity of the farmers, effectively depoliticised the rural land question. This was in sharp contrast to the situation in urban areas. However, in terms of both rural and urban land nationalisation, the experience of the war had pushed the Labour Party to abandon its earlier commitment to a policy of outright state ownership. The reasons were different for each area, but both developments left the party's left wing betrayed.

The Labour Party's retreat from land nationalisation

In terms of urban land reform, the compromise that the Labour Party had made on the Uthwatt Report in 1943 was extremely disappointing to the wider Labour movement. In October 1944, the TUC annual conference condemned the legislation calling for its drastic amendment to peg compensation to 1939 prices or present values, whichever was the lower, pending full land nationalisation.[83] However, the main concerns of Labour local authorities throughout the controversy had been to gain further planning powers and financial assistance from central government while preserving their independence. They continued to criticise the inadequacies of the Act over the question of compensation and poor financial support, particularly as the housing crisis became more acute towards the end of the war. But some Labour councillors in London welcomed the limited progress that the legislation had given them in order to start rebuilding after the end of hostilities.[84]

Internal differences about land nationalisation re-emerged at the delayed annual party conference in December 1944. In the build up to the conference, its policy committee had sought to finalise its views on land, housing and town and country planning, issues which had by this stage become inextricably inter-related. Included within the party's short-term programme for the forthcoming election was a belief 'that nationalisation of all urban and agricultural land is the only effective means of exercising the full control of land-use'. But in line with previous decisions it suggested 'as an interim measure the introduction of a Bill to enable the Government and other public authorities

---

82 *The Times*, 15 April 1943, p. 2.
83 *Annual Report of the Trades Union Congress*, October 1944, pp. 233–4.
84 Hadfield and MacColl, *Pilot Guide to Political London*, pp. 82–92.

to acquire any land they may need for any purposes'.[85] The draft conference resolution on housing and town planning agreed that the procedure for the compulsory acquisition of the land for housing purposes should be speeded up and simplified. Interestingly, it went on to add that the housing programme must be linked up with and form part of a National Plan for the redevelopment of cities and towns, industrial relocation, new and satellite towns and control of development on good agricultural land.[86] The way these policies became interlinked represented a dilution of the demand for outright land nationalisation, which by the time the manifesto was drawn up in 1945, was relegated to a long-term aim.

The influence of Hugh Dalton, who was Labour's President of the Board of Trade in the coalition, was important in this respect. He had introduced a Distribution of Industry Bill as one of the final measures of the outgoing coalition government. This Act, which received Royal assent on the day Parliament was dissolved on 15 June 1945 after Labour had left the coalition, gave the Board of Trade powers to acquire land for creating trading estates in defined Development Areas, previously known as Special Areas.[87] Despite opposition from Conservative hard-liners, Dalton's regional policy proposals became 'an accepted part of the Coalition Government's reconstruction programme'.[88] But in order to get the bill through, important concessions were made which sacrificed the coordinated planning of land use between the Board of Trade and the Ministry of Town and Country Planning.[89] The limited powers given to the Board of Trade to set up trading estates proved to be a severe disappointment to those reformers who had sought to create a powerful central planning authority to coordinate the planned dispersal of population and industry as recommended by the Barlow Commission in 1940. Despite this narrowing of horizons, Dalton used his position as chairman of the party's policy committee to get agreement to a conference resolution in November 1944 specifically linking housing, town planning and the balanced distribution of industry.[90]

Pressure from Labour local councils also led to a dilution of the policy of land nationalisation. The annual conference in 1944 approved a resolution on housing and town planning, but it was amended in a number of important respects, reflecting the party's wish to see local government strengthened in the face of possible state centralisation. The conference approved of national planning, but only if all land purchased by compulsory order (using central

85 LPA: RDR 271/October 1944 – 'Headings for Consideration in the Discussion of a Short-Term Programme'.
86 LPA: RDR 276/November 1944 – Draft Resolution on Housing and Town Planning.
87 Pimlott, *Hugh Dalton*, pp. 400–7; PRO: CAB 66/WP (44) 640 – 'Legislation on Balanced Distribution of Industry', Memorandum by the President of the Board of Trade, 10 November 1944.
88 Scott, 'British Regional Policy, 1945–52', pp. 358–82.
89 *The Times*, 9 June 1945.
90 LPA: Minutes of the NEC, 22 November 1944.

funds) would become the property of local authorities. The cause of central planning therefore came up against the interests of local authorities to protect their independence.[91] Labour local authorities rejected centralised solutions to the problems of town and country planning, such as wholesale land nationalisation or central control over development rights, preferring to acquire more limited powers of compulsory acquisition to purchase specific land for redevelopment without having to pay inflated compensation to private landlords. They looked to central government to provide the necessary resources to finance redevelopment. Labour councils wanted more independence as well as more central financial support to implement local improvements without having to raise local rates or lose their rate bases to neighbouring local authorities. The war offered no solution to this contradiction. The Labour Party nationally was forced to accept the more limited demands of their own fiercely independent local councils in the absence of the failure of the coalition government to either reform local government in general or to increase the power of the central government to nationalise or control land use. The views of Labour local authorities on town and country planning was a major influence on the way the party had by 1945 diluted its earlier commitment to wholesale land nationalisation.

But this did not meet the expectations of the left wing of the party which fought a re-guard action to reinstate a commitment to nationalisation in general at the annual conference in December 1944. The left-wing MP Ian Mikado successfully moved an amendment criticising the National Executive's lukewarm attitude to nationalisation in their report on Employment and Financial Policy. This committed the party to the transfer of land, building, heavy industry, all forms of banking, transport, fuel and power to public ownership.[92] However, in practice, the debate had little to do with the merits of specific proposals for nationalisation and more to do with the impending return to party politics and the end of the truce. The resolution was carried despite opposition from the leaders and it caused some irritation from those ministers who thought this might prejudice Labour's electoral chances in the impending general election. The key significance of the vote was that when Herbert Morrison came to draft the party's manifesto *Let Us Face the Future* in 1945, 'he found to his annoyance that as a result of the 1944 party conference he had to include a pledge to nationalise iron and steel as soon as Labour came to power'.[93]

However, this consideration did not apply to the question of land reform. The trend of party policy was too well established by early 1945, regardless of the experience of the Town and Country Planning Bill and the recalcitrance shown by landlord interests during its stormy passage. Herbert Morrison could argue at the Blackpool conference in May 1945 that

91 Tichelar, 'Central-Local Tensions'.
92 *The Report of the 43rd Annual Conference of the Labour Party*, December 1944 p. 163.
93 Harris, *Attlee*, p. 240; Donoughue and Jones, *Herbert Morrison*, pp. 330–1.

if we try at one blow to nationalise the land we shall be faced with vast problems of universal valuation of every plot of land in the country. We shall be in a vast financial transaction. Surely during this period – a period of first things first – as long as we have the power to purchase land at a fair price and expeditiously, as long as we can buy up the inefficient landowner in agricultural areas, that is enough for the time being and the bigger project can follow later.[94]

This view prevailed and the conference approved those sections of the manifesto dealing with agriculture and housing. Land was not included in the programme of those areas for transferring to public ownership, such as coal, gas, electricity, transport, iron and steel. In terms of housing and town planning, the manifesto was less radical:

> Labour believes in land nationalisation and will work towards it, but as a first step the State and the local authorities must have wider and speedier powers to acquire land for public purposes whenever the public interest so requires. In this regard and for the purposes of controlling land-use under town and country planning, we will provide for fair compensation; but we will also provide for a revenue for public funds from 'betterment'.[95]

The same more limited approach applied to agricultural policy. The state would only take over agricultural land if the landlord was unable or refused to provide proper facilities for his tenant farmers.[96]

Although pre-war demands for state intervention, centralised land-use planning, land nationalisation and the preservation of the countryside were given renewed meaning and weight by the impact of the war and a powerful lobby of town planners, in practice a policy of state acquisition of agricultural land proved too controversial. It threatened Labour's relationship with the farmers, whose prestige had improved enormously during the war. The party remained committed to a policy of land nationalisation in rural areas up to the last year of the war. The influence of the National Union of Agricultural Workers was important in this respect. It had remained firm in its support of land nationalisation even after Labour had diluted its policy in 1945.[97]

A number of factors contributed to the abandonment of Labour's traditional commitment to rural land nationalisation. Not least of these was the added emphasis that the war had given to matters of nutrition linked to the question of cheap food. By the end of the war the primary objective of Labour's rural land policy was to guarantee a supply of reasonably priced

---

94 *The Report of the 44th Labour Party Conference 1945*, p. 91.
95 *Let Us Face the Future* (1945).
96 Tichelar, 'The Labour Party, Agricultural Policy and the Retreat from Rural Land Nationalisation' and 'The Scott Report and the Labour Party'.
97 National Union of Agricultural Workers, Minutes of the Executive Committee, 27 April 1945.

health-giving foods for a predominantly urban electorate, and to negotiate international post-war agreements to ensure a supply of cheap imports of basic foodstuffs. Pre-war fears about a flood of cheap imports after the war had been replaced by concerns about food shortages and potential famine. In these changed economic circumstances, a traditional adherence to land nationalisation became a secondary consideration and eventually an irrelevancy and a liability. It was the experience of the county council War Agricultural Executive Committees in directing land use which led Labour to consider the possibility of alternatives to land nationalisation. The war had made agriculture efficient for the first time in a generation. The cooperation of the farmers in increasing production and in running the county council War Agricultural Executive Committees was essential. By the end of the war, Labour was not prepared to jeopardise this relationship by remaining committed to a policy which many had come to see as a relic from the past and irrelevant to the needs of agriculture.

Labour ministers in the coalition were only too well aware that the post-war economy required the continuation of a prosperous agriculture to supply the domestic demand for food and to relieve the country's precarious balance of payments crisis by reducing imports of basic foodstuffs. In these circumstances when it came to drawing up the manifesto in 1945, the party was only prepared to intervene in a limited way in controlling rural land use in the national interest. It was no longer necessary to nationalise all rural land to resolve the problem of the inefficient landlord. The traditional rural landlord was so badly affected by the war that the evils of 'landlordism' no longer posed political or economic questions that needed to be redressed. Indeed, the really inefficient landlord needed to be rescued by state action or by the National Trust. Land nationalisation as a universal panacea had therefore lost its political resonance in resolving the economic problems of British agriculture. It no longer proved to be a realistic option given the administrative problems of the state becoming the freeholder of all land. The difficulties associated with this course of action became more apparent during the course of the war. It was further compounded by the shortage of skilled staff in both central and local government at a time when the state was requisitioning and managing more land for the war effort.

Summary

Only limited land reform was possible in the context of wartime coalition politics. The coalition partners could not resolve a fundamental conflict over the rights of property. In practice, only holding legislation was enacted during the war, giving local authorities limited powers to start the process of rebuilding. The high expectations of 1941 for comprehensive and centralised planning generated by Lord Reith had been dissipated by 1944 in the face of the power and influence of a number of different interests, not least those of the property lobby defending the rights of private owners.

After 1943, the Labour Party retreated from a policy of land nationalisation in urban areas, not because it feared the creation of internal differences or damaging its electoral chances (support for land nationalisation was anyway running high at over 50% in the opinion polls),[98] but because it responded to pressure from Labour local government for more immediate housing and town planning reform. Labour-controlled councils were suspicious of plans by central government to own or control land use for redevelopment. Similarly, the party abandoned its long-held policy of land nationalisation in rural areas because it became irrelevant to the problems of post-war reconstruction and did not provide an immediate solution to food shortages or the need to increase agricultural production and improve nutrition. Labour recognised that the war had made agriculture efficient for the first time in a generation. It looked to the continuation of the Annual Price Review as a permanent feature of post-war policy, despite earlier reservations about subsidies benefiting inefficient farms and swelling the rent rolls of landlords. In these circumstances Labour was not prepared to jeopardise its relationship with the farmers by pursuing a policy threatening the property rights of farmers.[99]

Land nationalisation was only ever wholeheartedly supported by the Labour Party during the 1930s when it coincided with a growing political enthusiasm for centralised economic and physical planning. Hugh Dalton was very influential in taking Labour down this path.[100] However, after 1945 historians have argued that support for public ownership in general declined as the party came to doubt whether nationalisation was the most efficient economic weapon at Labour's disposal.[101] Others have maintained that the ideological dimension of this retreat from nationalisation reflected the inability of the party to agree what the ultimate purpose of public ownership should be: 'was it intended to facilitate greater economic efficiency and modernisation, or was it designed to secure social justice and redistribution of power, both within a given industry and in society as a whole'.[102]

Support for rural land nationalisation before the 1920s was clearly based on the desire to redistribute political power away from the traditional landed aristocracy to small-scale local ownership. Radical land reform before 1914 was dominated by the aim of redistributing political power. But after 1930, with changing patterns of landownership and the extension of the franchise, the debate shifted to the question of how to make agriculture more efficient. The experience of the Second World War demonstrated the virtues of state intervention to replace the inefficient landowner. But it also established that it was not politically necessary to threaten owner-occupation (in either town

---

98 Gallup (ed.), *The Gallup International Public Opinion Polls: Great Britain, 1937–1975, Vol. 1, 1937–1964*, p. 108.
99 Chase 'Nothing Less than a Revolution'.
100 Pimlott, *Hugh Dalton*, pp. 203–24.
101 Brook, *Labour's War*, p. 331.
102 Francis, *Ideas and Policies under Labour, 1945–1951*.

or country) nor economically efficient to take over all land to achieve agricultural modernisation, achieve effective town and country planning, stop damaging speculation in land, protect the landscape from despoliation or increase access to the countryside. It would take more limited and targeted land reform measures to achieve these objectives, a programme of legislation introduced by the post-war Labour government, building on their experience in the wartime coalition.

7 The post-war settlement

The Labour government of 1945 laid the foundations of a post-war settlement on land reform as part of a 'mixed economy'. However, this settlement did not include the financial provisions of the Town and Country Planning Act of 1947, which sought to introduce a betterment levy on development values and ensure that land was acquired by the state at non-inflated prices. The first part of this chapter briefly covers agriculture, smallholdings, new towns and national parks, but focuses on the 1947 Town and Country Planning Act. The second half traces the direction of policy from the election of the Conservatives in 1951 up to their defeat by Labour in 1964. During this time there was a return to a free market in the sale of land for development purposes. Its return helped create the circumstances for an unprecedented boom in land and property prices during the late 1950s and early 1960s. While the cause of land reform dropped down the political agenda during the 1950s, the public controversy over property speculators revived interest in taxing development land as a way of returning the unearned increment to the community, rather than as windfall profits to the developers.

The key features of Labour's land reform settlement can be listed under four headings: agriculture and smallholdings; new towns; town and country planning, including compensation and betterment; and national parks and access to the countryside. It will be argued that this legislation significantly increased the power of the state at a local and national level to purchase and control land in the national interest. Together these policies marked a remarkable extension of state intervention in the way that land was managed and planned, if not directly owned by central or local government commissions or agencies. Despite the severe economic difficulties faced by the government after the end of the war – circumstances which might have been expected to defer or delay the introduction of new and radical bills dealing with non-economic issues – most of this legislation was launched with speed and extraordinary reforming enthusiasm, influenced in the main by wartime collectivism and Labour's post-war vision of a 'New Jerusalem'.

Labour's reform programme represented in many respects a significant and permanent restraint on the rights of landed property. It was also held in high public esteem, especially the protection of the countryside by strong town and country planning and in particular the green belt. However, support for farming and the long-term guarantee of prices for agricultural produce was more problematical. It came under attack in the last quarter of the twentieth century as a result of growing frustration with the behaviour of farmers with regard to the environment and opposition to the alleged inequities of the Common Agricultural Policy. But on the whole, this post-war settlement remained largely intact. It did not come under ideological challenge until the election of a Conservative government in 1979 committed to a more explicit policy of free market economics and privatisation. But the original aims of Labour's 1945 programme of land reform, based on positive planning and the recovery of the unearned increment, were diluted and undermined after 1950 as the planning system was reformed over time to suit the needs of a private market in land.

Historians have referred to the creation of a post-war policy consensus forged in large part by the domestic circumstances of the war.[1] Not all have agreed with this approach, arguing that the phenomena known as 'Butskellism' in the 1950s was the result of a range of other factors, not necessarily related to wartime experiences.[2] In terms of land reform, what can be said is that many aspects of Labour's ambitious land reform programme were influenced by the domestic circumstances of the Second World War. They followed or grew out of either legislation passed by the wartime coalition or the new social and economic conditions created by the war itself. But in other respects, this programme was also a radical departure from the constraints and compromises of the war years and cannot necessarily be characterised as forming part of a policy consensus born of wartime experiences. Rather, its origins can be found in post-war concerns about food shortages, the reconstruction needs of blitzed cities or the difficult and strained relationship between central and local government. Only after 1951 did it become apparent that new towns, town and country planning, especially the green belt, agricultural subsidies and national parks had become part of a cross-party policy agreement that was to last beyond the end of the 1970s.

But other more controversial elements, like the betterment levy, did not survive the early 1950s. Similarly, other wartime policies and trends, such as the support for centralised planning, regional government and local government reform were not included in any post-war programmes. Unlike the Beveridge Report, the recommendations of Barlow, Scott and Uthwatt, relating to centralised physical planning, were largely unrealised after the end of the war. Only limited reform was introduced allocating new responsibilities

1 Paul Addison, *Road to 45*.
2 Lowe, 'The Second World War, Consensus and the Foundation of the Welfare State'; Jefferys, *The Churchill Coalition and Wartime Politics*.

to the larger authorities but accepting the existing structure of local government. This laid the foundations of future difficulties and failures in trying to enact complex legislation to tax land values and control land development in the national, regional or local interest.

Agriculture and smallholdings

The agricultural reforms introduced by the post-war Labour government were a significant extension of the limited and temporary measures carried out during the war. The coalition government had reached no lasting agreement on the extent to which farming should be subsidised after the war. It only intended the price-fixing arrangements to last for a transitional period. When the new Minister of Agriculture, Tom Williams, took over in 1945, he forecast that unless the price guarantees were extended beyond 1947, there was a serious prospect of a return to pre-war conditions of a depressed agriculture: 'Whatever thoughts we might be having about the long term, the essential first need was to maintain the momentum of food production achieved during the war.'[3] The Agricultural Act of 1947 had a direct bearing on the economy by consolidating the wartime system of annual price reviews in order to increase home production to save foreign exchange and meet drastic post-war food shortages.[4]

The Act guaranteed markets and fixed prices, forged a lasting relationship between the government and the National Farmers Union, improved landlord–tenant relationships, and confirmed that the county council War Agricultural Executive Committees would continue on a permanent basis in peace time. The farm worker was given a voice on these committees for the first time, but the iniquities of tied cottages were not addressed, to the disappointment of the agricultural trade unions. The policy was highly successful in increasing domestic production and in heralding a period of sustained post-war prosperity for farmers, assisted by the spread of mechanisation (the famous Massey Ferguson tractors) and the increasing use of chemical fertilisers. It took a generation for public opinion to recognise the long-term dangers of this approach to farming. By then the damage to the countryside had become only too apparent to later land reformers opposed to the environmental and social effects of factory farming and agribusiness.[5]

Thus post-war food shortages, signalled by the dramatic and unprecedented decision to ration bread in 1946, was the primary reason for the consolidation of wartime subsidies.[6] The government also wanted to maintain

3 Williams, *Digging for Britain*, p. 154; Morgan, *Labour in Power*, pp. 303–7.
4 *Post-War Contribution of British Agriculture to the Saving of Foreign Exchange*, Cmd. 7072 (1947).
5 Hetherington, *Whose Land Is Our Land?*
6 Chase, 'Nothing Less Than a Revolution', pp. 78–95; Martiin, Pan-Montojo and Brassley, *Agriculture in Capitalist Europe, 1945–1960*.

wartime controls in order to prevent a recurrence of the boom and slump that followed the First World War.[7] The Agricultural Act of 1947 was an urgent measure which the Conservatives would have been forced to introduce if they had been returned to power in 1945. But it is not clear how far they would have continued with other wartime controls and practices. The Act renewed the life of the county Agricultural Executive Committees, which were given powers to promote good estate management and dispossess farmers for failing to improve or invest. An Agricultural Land Commission was set up to control the work of the committees, as was a Land Tribunal to regulate landlord–tenant relationships. By 1951 agricultural output had exceeded pre-war levels by 150%.[8]

The Labour Party considered this level of state intervention sufficient to meet the post-war economic crisis. In 1948, the party's policymaking committees recommended that no proposal for the complete nationalisation of land should be included in the manifesto for 1950, but that the question of whether any further powers of land acquisition should be sought by local or central government was left open. For a second term Labour government it was recommended that compulsory purchase by the state should be used to acquire whole estates which are put up for sale and which are in danger of being split up or divided into lots, as well as marginal land which could be exploited economically.[9] The party's previous support for small-scale farms had been effectively dropped by this date in favour of economic efficiency.

Publicly owned smallholdings were encouraged for experienced agricultural workers wishing to become farmers on their own account, but on small farms of not less than 50 acres and capable of providing a reasonable livelihood.[10] Economies of scale, mechanisation and chemicals were now more important for increasing the efficiency of food production than encouraging workers back to the land. This was a far cry from the desire to create land settlements for the unemployed and smallholdings for discharged sailors and soldiers after the First World War, which had been such a prominent characteristic of land reform movements before 1914. It demonstrated a move away from the long-held agrarian belief that the country should support a large number of smallholders or peasant proprietorships to help revive a depressed agriculture and in turn bring about wider social benefits to the country. Rather, by 1945, and informed by the experience of the war, the government promoted domestic food production though the use of allotments, hoping to build on the remarkable wartime record of over 8 million tons of food grown or raised in private gardens.[11] Urban allotments therefore replaced rural smallholdings

---

7 Paul Addison, *Now the War Is Over*, p. 27.

8 Pollard, *The Development of the British Economy, 1914–1967*, p. 385.

9 LPA: RD 174/October 1948 and RD 239/December 1948.

10 *First Report of the Advisory Council on Smallholdings* – Ministry of Agriculture and Fisheries (1949).

11 *Advisory Committee on Allotments* and *Report of the Committee on Domestic Food Production* – Ministry of Agriculture and Fisheries (1950)

as one feature of a more modern type of land reform after 1945. In terms of future agricultural policy, the Labour Party had largely dropped its demand for rural smallholdings by 1945. One of its leading rural thinkers argued that the trend towards smallholdings should be mitigated, otherwise 'the alternative is peasant agriculture, technically inefficient, subsidised economically and socially a tragic anomaly'.[12] After 1945, the number of smallholdings declined as post-war reconstruction claimed much available land on the outskirts of urban areas. Post-war affluence after 1950 reduced dependency on home-grown food. 'Allotments became outdoor living spaces rather than productive acreage.'[13]

New towns

The 1946 New Towns Act was introduced with great speed following the rapid production of three White Papers by a committee chaired by Lord Reith. It set up the arrangements for the creation of fourteen new towns run by national development agencies on state-owned land. This form of land nationalisation proved to be essential in the creation of new town development after the war. The New Towns Act of 1946 was an entirely new piece of legislation that had not emerged as an urgent issue of wartime coalition politics. Dispersal of population and industry to new satellite towns had been a major aspect of the Barlow Report and figured heavily in the lobbying of the Town and Country Planning Association. The war itself demonstrated some of the advantages of evacuation of people and factories to rural areas, but it did not necessarily point to the creation of new towns after 1945. Some wartime opinion saw them as a possible distraction from the more urgent requirements of rebuilding existing houses and cities.

The Labour Party had been cautious about embracing a radical policy of dispersal for fear of undermining political and community loyalties in traditional Labour areas. The Minister of Town and Country Planning, Lewis Silkin, a key figure in the Labour leadership of the London County Council (LCC) had clashed with Frederick Osborn of the Town and Country Planning Association (TCPA) during the war on the issue of dispersal and the controversy over flats versus houses with gardens. For this reason, new towns did not appear as a manifesto commitment in the party's 1945 manifesto.

But the Act was introduced by Silkin with great speed as the first measure of the Ministry of Town and Country Planning. Lord Reith chaired a New Towns Committee appointed in October 1945 by Joseph Westwood, the Secretary of State for Scotland, and this produced three reports in less than a year.[14] It was not opposed by the Conservatives at second reading, as long as it did not lead to delays in rehousing or create a 'state tenantry' which might

---

12 LPA: RD 177/Oct 1948; Bateson, *Towards a Socialist Agriculture* (1946).
13 Nilson, *The Working Man's Green Space*, p. 157.
14 Cmd. 6759, 6794 and 6876 (1945–46).

become an inevitable feature of their social make up. The policy did raise some difficult questions for Conservative opinion on land-use planning. The party recognised that a satisfactory solution to the problem of compensation and betterment was required after the war, especially if this undermined agitation for land nationalisation, but there was concern about the terms and conditions and in particular the need for proper compensation to landowners bought out by compulsory order to build new towns. It was opposed to the state being able to force a private owner to sell their land at unimproved values.[15]

Silkin insisted that responsibility for new towns be given to powerful development corporations rather than bodies sponsored or under the control of local authorities.[16] This was to be the source of future central-local government frictions, particularly over new towns designated in existing urban areas such as Stevenage where there was local opposition.[17] Silkin's car was vandalised when he attended a consultation meeting. His determination to make new towns a central government responsibility managed by appointed development corporations reflected the bruising wartime battles in the Labour Party over local government reform. Silkin went on to designate fourteen new town areas. Building work started in earnest in the early 1950s after Labour had left office, and apart from Stevenage 'provoked little antagonism and were later accepted by the Conservatives as admirable institutions'.[18] The creation of new towns along garden city lines became a great post-war success story in the building of new homes and led to the spread of owner-occupation.[19]

National parks

The National Parks and Access to the Countryside Act of 1949 was the final instalment of Labour's post-war land reform. Like new towns and town and country planning, this initiative had a long history.[20] The Second World War had seen an increase in popular support for the idea of protecting areas of outstanding natural beauty and wilderness. Some limited progress had been made within the coalition's reconstruction policymaking committees. The Dower Report published in April 1945 recommended a National Parks Commission, with strong executive planning powers.[21] But the Treasury questioned whether the Commission should have an executive rather than an advisory function, as it was worried about the financial commitments that would be created.

15 CPA: CRD 2/25/1 – Town and Country Planning, 1946.
16 *Town and Country Planning, 1943–1951. Progress Report by the Minister of Local Government and Planning,* Cmd. 8204 (April 1951), pp. 120–38.
17 Paul Addison, *Now the War Is Over,* pp. 79–85.
18 Ibid., p. 80; Duff, *Britain's New Towns;* Lord Beveridge, *New Towns and the Case for Them.*
19 Matless, *Landscape and Englishness,* pp. 201–8.
20 Sheail, 'The Concept of National Parks in Great Britain, 1900–1950', pp. 41–56; Cherry, *Environmental Planning, 1939–1969, Vol. 2.*
21 *National Parks in England and Wales.* Report by John Dower, Cmd. 6628 (May 1945).

This was the first of a series of setbacks, leading to the appointment by the outgoing caretaker government in 1945 of a further committee under Sir Arthur Hobhouse, which recommend administrative arrangements and the first areas for selection. His report was not published until the summer of 1947, by which time the Town and Country Planning Act had consolidated the planning powers of the county councils.[22] As a result Silkin was persuaded to give the county councils the dominant role on the local park committees, only a quarter of whose members were to be appointed by the proposed National Parks Commission, which became purely advisory. This was a severe disappointment to those in the party, like Hugh Dalton who became president of the Ramblers' Association in 1947, and keen walkers like Barbara Castle, who pleaded with Silkin to give the National Parks Commission a more powerful role.[23] Ironically, therefore, while Labour gave the New Town Development Corporations strong executive powers to overcome local interests in 1946, it acceded to local pressure in 1949 and gave the National Parks Commission only advisory powers. The weakness of the Commission no doubt contributed to its survival after 1951 balancing as it did the role of central and local government and the interests of town and country. Its scope for executive action was also constrained by the Treasury.

The National Land Fund, set up by Hugh Dalton in his budget of 1946 to encourage land and property to be donated to the nation or the National Trust in lieu of death duties, suffered similar bureaucratic opposition from the Treasury. Quite remarkably in the economic circumstances, a sum of £50 million was allocated from war surplus supplies for this purpose. But, in practice, during the 24 years of its existence, it spent little more than the interest accumulated on capital due to the reluctance of the Treasury to spend the money in line with Dalton's original intention.[24] Despite these constraints, the National Parks and Access to the Countryside Act 1949 created the Lake District, the Peak District and Snowdonia as areas of outstanding natural beauty to be managed by a Countryside Commission and gave responsibility to the county councils for guaranteeing access to footpaths and right of ways. Lewis Silkin likened the Act to a 'People's Charter for the open air'. Its administrative arrangements encouraged responsible citizenship by ensuring that popular access to areas of outstanding natural beauty were carefully controlled to avoid the urban despoliation and invasion of the countryside that were of such concern to interwar preservationists and planners.[25]

---

22 *Report of the National Parks Committee (England & Wales)*, Cmd. 7121 (July 1947).

23 Castle, *Fighting All the Way*, p. 172; Tom Stephenson, secretary of the Ramblers' Association, was also disappointed with the Act. See *Fabian Journal*, May 1955 – 'Parks for the Nation'.

24 *The Times*, 10, 17 April and 17 May 1946; Rickwood, 'The National Land Fund, 1946–80: The Failure of a Policy Initiative', pp. 15–23; Mandler, *The Fall and Rise of the Stately Home*, pp. 335–42.

25 Matless, *Landscape and Englishness*, pp. 234–64.

Town and country planning and the nationalisation of development rights

Before the Second World War town planning was permissive and only a small area of the country was covered by planning schemes. These proved to be ineffective in preventing urban sprawl and the despoliation of the countryside. Physical planning had been a highly controversial aspect of wartime politics. The White Paper on the Control of Land Use (1944) was not a serious blueprint for post-war reform, but a half-empty compromise 'designed to keep the Coalition together for the duration of the war'.[26] Although only limited legislation dealing with blitzed and blighted areas was enacted in 1944, the war did establish a consensus on the need for more positive planning powers to overcome the refusal of landowners to sell land for development. Landowning interests recognised the inevitability of greater state planning. Together, the Barlow, Scott and Uthwatt Reports established the political case for more state intervention in physical planning, but it took the election of a Labour government to put theory into practice.

The post-war Labour government looked to local authorities to implement its ambitious public housebuilding programme. Housing was the first and most urgent preoccupation of the new government, given the extent of wartime damage and the return of ex-servicemen facing an extreme shortage of accommodation. The coalition had given very little attention to housing as a reconstruction issue, unlike social welfare, education and town planning. This situation was not helped by a desperate shortage of building materials and workers employed in the construction industry. In the absence of any blueprint for housing, or network of voluntary organisations meeting the housing needs of the poor, the government financed local councils to build housing for rent and retained the rent controls introduced at the beginning of the war. Factories were instructed to build prefabricated houses. Housebuilding standards were generally improved. The very limited number of building licences was rationed, with the majority of them allocated to local authorities, which managed to build about 200,000 houses per year after 1945. In doing so the government severely restricted the amount of building works undertaken by the private market, which remained depressed until the upturn in the early 1950s.[27]

But the Labour government also looked to physical planning as an essential part of its programme to rebuild bombed city centres and build more houses for rent. The government saw a limited role for private developers but wanted to purchase their land-holdings for public sector building at a cost which local authorities could afford. Housebuilding and slum clearance had been badly hampered before the war by the high cost of development land,

---

26 Lowe, 'The Second World War, Consensus and the Foundation of the Welfare State', p. 163; Jefferys, *The Churchill Coalition and Wartime Politics*, pp. 176–80.

27 Glennerster, *British Social Policy since 1945*, pp. 66–8.

with compensation paid at market values. The party looked to a combination of positive town planning and taxation of land values to realise its dream of rebuilding blitzed cities. But planners were not seen in a positive light. While academic and professional opinion, including many progressive politicians were very supportive of more state intervention to replan destroyed city centres and clear the slums, 'most people felt it to be either irrelevant or in some way irritating. The great popular desire was for housing and a quiet life. Only a minority was excited by the prospect of participating in their communities ... and thought that planners were standing in the way of new housing'.[28] This view of planning stored up problems for the future. But in the immediate post-war period, Labour looked to strengthen town and country planning as the solution for a number of outstanding land reform issues, including the urgent need to build more homes. For Lewis Silkin, Labour's Minister of Town and Country Planning, the land question was now the responsibility of town planners. In the absence of a policy of immediate land nationalisation, he argued that 'it must be the responsibility of the planner to reconcile competing demands and to secure the best use of the land'.[29]

The Town and Country Planning Act of 1947 created the modern system of development control, based on the preparation of positive plans by all local authorities covering the whole country and greater powers of compulsory purchase, replacing the permissive regime of the 1930s. The local authorities were also permitted to carry out development themselves, being no longer confined as they were under the 1944 Act to development, which only private enterprise was unwilling to undertake.[30] Most of the 1947 Act was to prove an uncontroversial aspect of post-war reform. It has remained largely unchanged to this day, although weakened by privatisation and the economic power of private developers. The Conservative Party welcomed the development control aspects of the Act but rejected the financial clauses as discriminatory against private enterprise.[31] But over time, the concept and practice of planning has undergone many modifications in response to changing public attitudes to participation and to support owner-occupation and free market approaches to land use control.[32]

The war also highlighted the inadequacies of the existing structure of local government to carry out effective planning on a regional basis. No reform of local government was possible during the war. The 1945 Labour government avoided tackling the difficult question of central–local government relationships head-on, although the creation of a National Health Service

28 Beach and Tiratsoo, 'The Planners and the Public', p. 546; Kynaston, *Austerity Britain, 1945–51*, pp. 154–70.
29 Silkin, 'Town and Country Planning', p. 120.
30 *Explanatory Memorandum to the Town and Country Planning Bill*, Cmd. 7006 (1947).
31 CPA: CRD 2/25/2 – Town and Country Planning Bill (1946).
32 Ball, *Housing Policy and Economic Power*, pp. 193–271; Cullingworth and Nadin, *Town and Country Planning in the UK*, pp. 170–95.

represented a major defeat for local authorities.[33] However it was highly selective in the allocation of greater planning powers. The role of central agencies, such as the New Town Development Corporations eroded local government power, while the Act gave the larger local authorities enhanced planning powers over and above the smaller urban and rural district councils.

While development control and powers of compulsory purchase by the larger local authorities became an important part of a policy consensus after 1945, the question of compensation and betterment remained a matter of bitter political controversy. It also became an administratively complex area of policy. By 1949, the Conservatives had rejected the financial clauses seeking to tax development land 'as grossly unfair to owners of interests in land and as restrictive of private enterprise', and as 'nothing less than nationalisation of land on confiscatory terms'.[34] It called for either an increase in compensation set at market levels, a reduction in the level of the development charge, or for total repeal.

The starting point for the legislation was the Uthwatt Report which had rejected the nationalisation of land as an answer to the problem of compensation and betterment, although it agreed it was a logical solution, but not practical politics. The Committee instead recommended the nationalisation of rights rather than title. It proposed that

> The rights of development in all land lying outside built up areas should be vested immediately in the state, subject to payment of fair compensation. For already developed areas local authorities should have broader compulsory purchase powers, ... There should be an annual site value rating as a continuing means of taxing increases in land values.[35]

The Uthwatt proposals were adopted by the Labour Party as an interim measure during the war in order to keep the coalition together. But they were only partially accepted by the post-war Labour government when it came to legislation. It rejected entirely the traditional land reform policy of annual site value rating. As a result, this policy never really recovered as a viable proposition to the dismay of many reformers influenced by Henry George. Labour did, however, accept its advice on compensation but sought to impose a 100% betterment levy for the recovery of the unearned increment. Uthwatt had recommended a lower level of recoupment reflecting the difficulty of actually measuring what contributed to increases in the value of land.

The Act nationalised development rights in land and not the land itself. The county councils and county boroughs were given the power to grant planning permission. If permission was refused no compensation would be paid. This was a vitally important principle of development control which

33 Young and Rao, *Local Government since 1945.*
34 CPA: CRD 2/25/3 – Memorandum on TCP (1949).
35 Grant, 'Compensation and Betterment', in Cullingworth, *British Planning*, p. 62.

survives to this day unchallenged. The denial of compensation for the refusal of planning permission represents a significant erosion of property rights. If permission was granted, any resulting increase in land value was to be subject to a development charge. This was to be secured from the developer before development took place. The Act stated that all betterment was created by the community and would be recovered by the state at the rate of 100%. This started an ongoing debate amongst planners and politicians about what was the most appropriate and efficient level of taxing development without restricting or even destroying the market for land.[36] Therefore taxation of land values became part of the control of land use by local government. In a private market for land where the state was not the owner, this marriage between taxation and town planning laid the foundation for future complexities and difficulties not necessarily anticipated at the time by the politicians.[37]

The Act thus sought to ensure through town planning that land could in practice only be purchased at its existing use value (echoing wartime controversies over the behaviour of speculative landowners). Where land was required for development, it sought to secure for the community the increase in its value attributable to the grant of planning permission. It did this by the imposition of a 100% development charge to be collected by a Central Land Board. It was recognised that the timing of this legislation would result in considerable hardship in individual cases when 'owners could successfully claim that their land had some development value on the appointed day'.[38]

A sum of £300 million was therefore set aside to pay compensation to owners whose land had depreciated in value by the refusal of planning permission. If actual development then took place and the value of the land increased as a result, the landowner would pay back the compensation they had received by way of a 100% betterment levy. It was envisaged that this complex, but one-off, process would be completed in a set period of time of about five years and at least by 1953. After this date, no further payments would be paid out and all development rights would thereafter be owned by the state.

However, in practice, the Act transformed the market for land in adverse and unpredicted ways. 'In place of a free market with land being bought and sold at market prices', the new arrangement was based on transactions taking place 'at existing use value but with the developer paying to the Central Land Board an amount representing the difference between existing use and development values'.[39] It was also assumed that compulsory purchase of land by the state or local authorities would be on the basis of existing use value. 'Thus, in theory, the owner of land should receive the same price for his land whether it was purchased by a public authority or a private developer. Of course, this

36 Lichfield and Darin-Drabkin, *Land Policy in Planning*, pp. 132–6.
37 Ratcliffe, *Land Policy*.
38 Cullingworth and Nadin, *Town and Country Planning in the UK*, p. 161.
39 Cullingworth, *Environmental Planning, Vol. 4*, p. 12.

left owners with little or no inducement to sell their land.'[40] This was probably the most pressing problem, if not direct contradiction, when it came to the implementation of what had developed into a highly complex and difficult piece of legislation.

At the time of its enactment on 1 July 1948, the Labour Party congratulated itself that together with the New Towns Act and the proposed National Parks Bill, there was no need for any further legislation on the question of ownership unless it was thought desirable to seek a mandate for the nationalisation of all land, a policy which some in the party thought more preferable and certainly less complex. An internal policy report argued that the central state and local authorities now had powers of control which were revolutionary when compared with those which previously existed. 'It is not easy now for a landowner to use his land in an anti-social manner and should he do so it is attributable more to lax administration of the law than to defective powers. A major war is being conducted by the Central Land Board to ensure that land is conveyed at existing use value.'[41]

But despite this initial enthusiasm, the report admitted that the outcome of this war was uncertain. It acknowledged that this new way of controlling land use and recovering the unearned increment was evolving at the cost of some birth pangs and occasional hardship. 'Whilst a happy issue cannot at this stage be assured, there are' it hoped 'powerful arguments against nationalisation until the existing system has been given a fair trial ... Nationalisation as an issue is not dead ... It might well become an election issue in 1955'.[42]

Unfortunately for the party, these forebodings had become a reality by as early as 1949, as the Central Land Board struggled to deal with a number of complicated problems. The scheme proved to be unpopular and complex, leading to legal challenges and administrative concessions having to be made, with the Central Land Board adopting a highly combative approach to those speculative landowners who had bought undeveloped land during and after the war (including derelict and bombed sites) in the hope of making substantial capital gains by selling it thereafter at inflated prices. 'Buying property at rock-bottom war-time prices, to benefit from future capital appreciation, was a strategy which formed the foundation of a number of post-war fortunes.'[43] Some landowners subsequently withdrew their land from the market when they realised that they would only be paid existing use value.[44] The hoarding of land was to become one of the most controversial features after 1950; of particular interest was the way that some private landlords and property companies responded to government attempts to control land use in the national interest. The planner Wyndham Thomas has recalled the way the level of the

40 Ibid., p. 13.
41 LPA: RD 220/December 1948.
42 Ibid.
43 Scott, *The Property Masters*, p. 101.
44 Cullingworth, *Environmental Planning, Vol. 4*, pp. 14–42.

betterment charge, and its effects on the market for land, created tensions within the government. As soon as the charge was enacted

> There was a clash between Lewis Silkin, the Minister of Town and Country Planning, and Trustram Eve, the Central Land Board's chairman. Silkin told me of this in his room in the House of Lords in the 1960s. He wanted the charge to be 70%, to give landowners a sweetener, an incentive to sell. Trustram Eve said it had to be 100% to achieve perfect equality of treatment between all landowners, and because of an abstruse argument about hypothetical shifts in development value. The matter went to cabinet, with Trustram Eve's threat to resign if he lost. He won.[45]

But of more immediate concern to the Central Land Board at the time was the extent to which land was being sold at above existing use value.[46] Land changed hands at prices which included the full development value, and 'this was largely due to the severe restrictions which were imposed on building. Building licences were very scarce, and developers who were able to obtain them were willing to pay a high price for land upon which to build'.[47] Furthermore, the way in which the level of development charges were calculated also created alleged hardships which were well-publicised and became the subject of a heated political debate and adverse press comment. In the House of Lords on 16 November 1949, the Conservative Peer Lord Llewellin alleged that the Act had

> descended on a bewildered public and left it gasping at the financial losses it imposes on ordinary private owners and industrial concerns alike, and gasping also at the delays and vexations it sets in the path of all who, four years after the end of the war, still wish to start building.[48]

By way of example Lord Llewellin cited the case of a chemist and sub-postmaster in Liverpool who wanted to move next door to bigger premises and open a new post office, only to be asked by the Central Land Board for £100 levy for the change of use of the premises. Lord Llewellin complained that 'the imposition of this extra charge on people who want to build their own houses may suggest that some persons do not like a man to build and own his house'.[49]

The government was only too well aware of the difficulties the legislation was creating for the small landowner. The Conservatives lost no time in presenting themselves as the defender of property rights. This bad

45 Wyndham Thomas, 'A Review of Development Land Taxes in Britain since 1947', pp. 9–10.
46 Cullingworth, *Environmental Planning, Vol. 4*, p. 29.
47 Cullingworth and Nadin, *Town and Country Planning in the UK*, p. 162.
48 House of Lords Debate, 16 November 1949, col. 165, cc. 713–14.
49 Ibid., col. 716.

publicity brought the scheme into disrepute at a time when public opinion was becoming more frustrated with post-war austerity and interventionist policies in general.[50] Following the debate in the House of Lords, the prime minister appointed a small committee of ministers to 'examine the principles and the application of the principles, on which the Central Land Board are working in determining the amount of development charges'.[51] The Labour government had already made a number of concessions and was still reviewing the operation of the scheme, with the possibility of reducing the betterment levy from 100% to a level with less of a deterrent effect on the market, when it lost the 1951 general election. The Conservative Party pledged to retain the development control part of the Act, but they sought to simplify the procedure for obtaining planning permission. At this stage it was not opposed to a development charge but argued that its level needed to be reduced so as not to discourage proper development. Above all, it wanted landowners paid compensation 'for the full amount of his loss'.[52]

Historians have been divided in their reasons for the failure of this first serious legislative attempt to recover the unearned increment through the vehicle of town and country planning at a national level. For the historians of town planning, the fact that land changed hands at prices higher than use value was due to the severe restrictions which were imposed on building after the war arising from the acute shortages of labour and materials. 'Building licences were very scarce, and developers who were able to obtain them were willing to pay a high price for land upon which to build.'[53] For other historians, the scheme 'proved difficult to administer and was unfair and unpopular, so that it contributed not a little to the eventual return to power of the Conservatives'.[54] For those who have studied the matter in more detail, the Act was 'neither socialist enough nor sufficiently simulative of the private sector'.[55] Leaving aside the nature of adversarial politics over property rights, it faced numerous problems, including the mistrust of local authorities who feared the potential threat posed by an interventionist Central Land Board with wide-ranging powers. This was a concern raised by Labour local authorities during the war. But the real problem was the way in which the Act was drafted:

> It took profit and incentive out of the market without ending the operation of the market in land. In doing this the Act placed landowners in a crucial and pivotal role for the viability of the whole scheme. It ensured that if landowners did not sell their land willingly then the supply of land

50 Morgan, *Labour in Power*, pp. 359–408.
51 Cullingworth, *Environmental Planning, Vol. 4*, p. 42.
52 CPA: CRD 2/25/8 – TCP policy.
53 Cullingworth and Nadin, *Town and Country Planning in the UK*, p. 162.
54 Ravetz, 'Housing the People' in Fyrth, *Labour's Promised Land: Culture and Society in Labour Britain, 1945–51*, p. 154.
55 Cox, *Adversary Politics and Land*, p. 83.

would dry up and, in the peculiar rationing environment of the immediate post-war period, it followed that land would change hands at inflated prices and frustrate the development charge proposals in the Act.[56]

This conclusion is confirmed by those who have examined the scheme as an aspect of land management.[57] For others who have examined the scheme from a left-wing perspective, the Act constituted a barrier to investment.[58] A Marxist critique of post-war planning has drawn attention to a contradiction between a dynamic free market in land, deregulated by the Conservatives after 1951, and a system of negative land-use control which sought to contain urban development through the green belt. In a mixed economy, market forces were more powerful than the limited role of the state to control physical development. In a situation where the supply of land was restricted, market forces were therefore responsible for the inflationary effect on land and property prices rather than the planning system itself.[59] But for those historians supporting a mixed-market approach, the development charge removed all profit from the land aspect of development. It was therefore impossible to rely on the market mechanism for the supply of building land. In any case, the legislation had little effect since only limited private housebuilding was permitted by the Labour government. 'Most housing was council housing on land acquired by compulsory purchase. But as private housebuilding began to revive in the 1950s, the deterrent effect of a 100% tax on development value began to be clear.'[60]

But for others more sympathetic to the design of the post-war planning system, the development charge never had a chance to be fully introduced, given the public commitment by the Conservative Party that it would abolish the development charge as soon as it regained power. The two years from 1949 to 1951 'was less than the five-year period that may be regarded as the normal and necessary minimum for a statute to take full effect'.[61] Ideological considerations played a more important role than concerns about the restricted post-war market for land. Labour's Minister of Town and Country Planning, Lewis Silkin, insisted that he was working towards land nationalisation, and that the party should be 'prepared to exercise compulsory powers against any owner who adopted blackmailing tactics in order to secure for himself a profit which should go to the community'.[62] This position is supported by the official historian of compensation and betterment.[63] As one reviewer of his work has

56 Ibid., p. 101.
57 Leung, *Redistribution of Land Values*, p. 77.
58 Massey and Catalano, *Capital and Land*, p. 18.
59 Taylor, *Urban Planning Theory since 1945*, pp. 99–110.
60 Hallett and Williams, 'Great Britain' in Hallett (ed.), *Land and Housing Policies in Europe and the USA*, p. 119.
61 Ravetz, *Remaking Cities*, p. 67.
62 Ibid., p. 65–6.
63 Cullingworth, *Environmental Planning*, *Vol. 4.*

pointed out, 'the evidence shows that in spite of the widespread criticism of the Act, and of the development charge in particular, in the opinion of some of the officials at the Central Land Board at least, the 1947 arrangements were viable and were beginning to work reasonably satisfactorily'.[64]

The Conservatives and the return of a free market in land

On its return to government, the Conservative Party wanted to increase the role of private housebuilding for a property-owning democracy, although it was not averse to also supporting local authorities in building houses for rent.[65] In the period 1950 to 1960, owner-occupation increased from 29% to 42% while local authority rented housing also increased from 18% to 27%. Grassroot opinion within the Conservative Party was strongly in favour of private ownership on ideological grounds: 'The ownership of property provides the citizen with the only sure shield against trespass on his freedom either by his neighbour or by the state.'[66] But it would take the increasing affluence of working-class council tenants during the 1960s and 1970s wanting to purchase their houses, before a policy of 'Right to Buy' became official party policy in 1985, overcoming the reluctance of its leadership to force local authorities to sell.[67]

Such constraints did not apply to the same extent with regard to town and country planning. The party saw the 'Socialist Town and Country Planning Act' as a barrier to development of all kinds and pledged to repeal its financial provisions. It proceeded on the principle that 'for certain classes of property there should be no development charge and no compensation. For others there should be full compensation and a corresponding charge'.[68] The party's election manifestos for 1950 and 1951 contained a promise to abolish the Central Land Board and to give the private sector a larger role in housing development, 'but it was unclear whether or not it would end, or merely reduce, Labour's 100% development charge'.[69] This ambivalence continued until 1959 when the party returned to a policy of full market value for land sold or purchased for development.

Cullingworth's official history of environmental planning, and Andrew Cox's definitive account, have covered in detail the way policy developed after 1951.[70] Uncertainty about what to do with the development charge was played out between two powerful ministers – Butler, the Chancellor of the Exchequer,

64 Parker, 'Land Values, Compensation and Betterment', p. 316.
65 Weiler, 'The Rise and Fall of the Conservatives' Grand Design for Housing', 1951–64'.
66 CPA: CRD 2/23/7 – Property-Owning Democracy, 1948–49.
67 Davies, '"Right to Buy": The Development of a Conservative Party Housing Policy'.
68 CPA: CRD 2/23/28 – Socialist Attitude to Property, 1952.
69 Conservative Party Manifesto, *Britain Strong and Free* (1951).
70 Cullingworth, *Environmental Planning, Vol. 4*, pp. 59–271; Cox, *Adversary Politics and Land*, pp. 103–24.

and Macmillan, the new Minister of Housing and Local Government. Butler epitomised one-nation conservatism. He confided in his memoirs that 'resistance to predatory attacks upon property will always form important items in the Tory programme', but he went on to argue that such a doctrine 'loses all that is ennobling in its appeal, if it confines itself to these and fails to get down to the principles which lie beneath all such resistance'.[71] The town planner Wyndham Thomas has recalled how Butler

> wanted to keep the development charge, but at 70% or even 60%. At this level, he believed, a market in development land could be restored, and a substantial revenue flow secured. But Harold Macmillan ... (who was) much more sympathetic to the landowner lobby, wanted the charge abolished; though he argued strongly to retain existing use value as fair compensation for publicly acquired land.[72]

The government had to choose between two very difficult policy options – 'was it to return to a totally free market in land, which would question the state's ameliorative and facilitative role; or was it to collect betterment in part, in an attempt to be equitable to the public when state actions created land values?'[73] The outcome of this conflict was to lead to the repeal of the financial provisions of the 1947 Act, the abolition of the Central Land Board and a presumption in favour of the private sector in land-use planning (Town and Country Planning Acts 1953 and 1954).

The 1953 Act abolished the £300 million global fund and 100% development charge. It also ended the role of the Central Land Board as a compulsory purchaser of land. This allowed landowners to recoup all betterment in private land and took town planning back to the permissive approach of the 1930s when local authorities had to pay market rates for development land. In these circumstances, Macmillan sought to protect local government by limiting the price authorities paid for land for planning purposes. He achieved this in the 1954 Town and Country Planning Act, which gave power to 'local authorities and other agencies to purchase land compulsorily at existing use values ... This was also to be the basis of compensation for landowners who were refused planning permission for development'.[74] This legislation created a dual land market. Two values were adopted according to whether land was sold in the open market or acquired by a public authority. Owners selling privately received full market value while owners selling to public authorities received only existing use value. Such complexity created an iniquitous and later untenable position. As land prices increased, partly owing to the influence of planning controls and other social and demographic changes, the gap

71 Lord Butler, *The Art of the Possible*, p. 28.
72 Wyndham Thomas, 'A Review of Development Land Taxes in Britain since 1947', p. 10.
73 Ibid., p. 107.
74 Cox, *Adversary Politics and Land*, p. 110.

between existing use and market values widened, particularly in suburban areas near green belt land.[75]

The inequity of this situation received national attention as a result of the case of Mr Pilgrim, who having purchased land for £400 in 1950, and having failed to make an application for compensation, was compulsorily purchased at an existing use value of only £65. He subsequently committed suicide.[76] A private members bill calling for a return to a free market in land to avoid this iniquity received a second reading, but it was withdrawn following a promise that the government would introduce similar legislation to achieve the same end.[77] This was finally enacted in the 1959 Town and Country Planning Act. 'Owners now obtained the same price for their land irrespective of whether they sold it to a private individual or to a public authority.'[78] Thus 'the Act, while allowing for the continuation of local authority planning of development and urban renewal, ensured that there would be no dual market in land. In future, public land purchase would take place at full market values'.[79]

But at the same time, the government recognised the need to make a number of concessions towards the public sector in the interests of good town planning. It was also aware that it needed to respond in some way to the beginnings of a speculative property boom which had started to become very apparent after 1957. The 1959 Act gave further stimulus to this boom, which was starting to attract adverse public attention and increasing political controversy. The Conservative 'think tank', the Bow Group, representing one-nation conservatism, argued in 1960 that a new planning climate was required to rebuild our cities and to combine the resources of private and public sectors.[80] The new Minister of Housing, Henry Brooke, considered the option of a limited betterment tax or levy, but set at a much lower level than 100%. He even looked at the possibility of a capital gains tax to end the dual market and as an initial response to the early signs of increasing property and land prices. Such a tax was not to be introduced until 1965 by Labour and marked a new development in land reform that sought to disengage the taxation of land values from land-use control and development. This would have pleased the supporters of the rating of site values, who 'would have suggested taxing away all of the landowner's rental income, not just that attributable to betterment'.[81]

In summary, therefore, the 1959 Act sought to mitigate the impact of rising land prices by allowing 'New Towns and local authorities undertaking comprehensive redevelopment and Town Expansion schemes, to discount the

---

75 Cullingworth and Nadin, *Town and Country Planning in the UK*, p. 162.
76 Davis, 'Macmillan's Martyr: The Pilgrim Case', pp. 125–8.
77 Cox, *Adversary Politics and Land*, p. 110.
78 Cullingworth and Nadin, *Town and Country Planning in the UK*, p. 163.
79 Cox, *Adversary Politics and Land*, p. 111.
80 Bow Group, *Let Our Cities Live – A Pamphlet on Town Planning*.
81 Ball, *Housing Policy and Economic* Power, p. 225.

increase in values that their own land plans created for contiguous private land'.[82] In retrospect, the explosion in land prices during the late 1950s and early 1960s was not anticipated by politicians of both main parties or by the planners. Nathaniel Lichfield, a leading town planner who had played a key role in the development of new towns, commented in 1980 that few people would have predicted the rapid rise in land and property values: 'Financial indifference to betterment was soon to be replaced by deep public concern for it.... In the event the building boom ... created large fortunes for some land-owners and gave rise to public concern on the equity issues and also about the effects on the economy as a whole'.[83] Another leading town planner drew a similar conclusion:

> Owners of land allocated for development were now in an enviable pos-
> ition, gathering in large and rising capital gains, free of tax. The specu-
> lative pursuit of planning consents became a rewarding pastime, as the
> planning system distributed fortunes with all the inconsequence of a fruit
> machine. What Labour chose to call 'the scandal of rocketing land prices'
> became a feature of its indictment of 13 years of Conservative rule.[84]

The political response to the property boom

The return to the free market in land coincided with a massive boom in land and house prices. This did much to undermine public sector attempts to bring about urban renewal. After 1957 there was an exponential increase in house and land prices. 'The price of land for public and private housing rose by 223% and 204% respectively between 1961 and 1966; and agricultural land by 195%.'[85] A collapse followed in the 1960s, but the upward trend continued into the 1970s, when 'it has been estimated that between 1972 and 1974 the value of land rose by more than £50,000 million – the equivalent of the entire gross domestic product'.[86] Investment in land and property had become much more attractive and certainly more profitable during a period when British manufacturing was experiencing a period of declining profitability and productivity.[87]

The property boom was the result of a number of demographic pressures as well as being a response to government legislation. Increasing popula-tion and prosperity after 1950 certainly contributed to a growing demand for land for housing and employment. Rising birth rates, earlier marriages

82 Cox, *Adversary Politics and Land*, p. 112.
83 Lichfield and Darin-Drabkin, *Land Policy in Planning*, p. 144.
84 Wyndham Thomas, 'A Review of Development Land Taxes in Britain since 1947', p. 11.
85 O'Hara, *Governing Post-War Britain*, p. 135.
86 Massey and Catalano, *Capital and Land*, pp. 1–3; Cox, *Adversary Politics and Land*, pp. 112–13.
87 Scott, *The Property Masters*, pp. 132–65.

and a growth in owner-occupation were also factors, as was the increase in car ownership, which allowed for longer commuting journeys between home and work, opening up the suburbs for development. The market position of the landowner was therefore strengthened. Some withheld land to maximise profits. The lack of supply of land for development was a particular problem for small builders. Furthermore, as the price of land rose, and local authorities had to pay market prices rather than existing use values, planning blight emerged as an issue, exacerbated by the demands of central government for slum clearance. After the enactment of the 1959 Town and Country Planning Act, the political perception was that the only people to benefit from the boom were big landowners and property developers.[88]

The abolition of building licences in November 1954, as well as the dilution of town and country planning legislation, were two of the primary drivers of this boom, which was to last for ten years until legislation to restrict office development, especially in London (the 'Brown Ban' on office building), was enacted in 1964 (although ironically creating the circumstances for a further boom later on as restrictions were lifted). In the early 1950s institutional investors, especially insurance companies, became aware of the dangers of inflation and began to transform property assets into equity participation schemes as a hedge against rising prices. Moreover, the introduction of rent reviews into commercial property leases allowed rents to be increased at regular intervals making them much more profitable investments. The Church Commissioners, for example, took full advantage of these new innovations in property management and made substantial profits.

Also, property speculators could borrow money from the banks to fund entire projects without committing any of their own funds, unlike in other European countries where closer regulation prevented such practices, removing any financial constraints on the growth of their activities. This made fortunes for a large number of individuals, such as Harry Hyams who built Centre Point and kept it empty to maximise its value, but also led to such developers being cast in the popular mind as arch villains of capitalism.[89] The demolition of historic buildings in order to erect faceless and ugly office blocks to minimum standards also did nothing for the reputation of the new class of property developers whose extravagant lifestyles were increasingly reported in the press. This gave rise to organisations like the Civic Trust and campaigns led by the poet John Betjeman, for example, to protect urban England from despoliation. The criminal activities of Peter Rachman, a speculator in the residential property sector in London, only made matters worse and created a political climate for reform and a demand for greater regulation of the 'property sharks'.[90]

88 Cox, *Adversary Politics and Land*, pp. 112–18.
89 Marriott, *The Property Boom*.
90 Scott, *The Property Masters*, pp. 132–65; Marriott, *The Property Boom*.

The response to these developments was 'a mushrooming of tenants and community action against the direct and indirect effects of this boom, and attempts by all three parliamentary parties to formulate legislation concerning the economic use of land and the definition of the rights of private landownership'.[91] The Conservative Party under Macmillan's leadership started to consider fiscal measures after 1962 in the face of growing evidence of property speculation, although publicly it argued that 'rising land prices were due to the inadequacy of land supply and not land speculation or the freeing of the market'.[92] A short-term speculative gains tax was introduced in 1962 to catch 'the man who buys land in the hope of a quick speculative profit through a sale to a genuine developer'.[93] Behind the scenes, Macmillan revisited the question of a betterment levy, argued for greater support for beleaguered local authorities, and even considered the possibility of taxes on land hoarding speculative profits, but he was defeated by strong opposition from within in his own party.[94]

In a confidential report, the Country Landowners' Association argued that planning was not solely responsible for high prices 'although the grant of planning permission may inflate prices already high'.[95] But it had to acknowledge the widespread view 'that something ought to be done about it'. Its solution was not more state intervention to control the price of land (which would be disastrous) but building in slum clearance areas to higher densities. However Conservative opinion concluded that the 'land question' had cost them the 1964 general election and was more sympathetic to the state recovering some betterment.[96] Although it rejected the financial provisions of the 1947 Act as 'unworkable', it remained supportive of the need for town and country planning to adjudicate between competing claims on land use and it was committed to the green belt.[97]

The Liberal Party advocated its traditional policy of site value rating, which sought to rate land on its site or position value, whether it was developed or not, rather than on the value of the property on the site. This it was argued would raise similar amounts of revenue for local authorities, but it would be an incentive for landowners to develop their sites to the full while a tax on development had the opposite effect.[98] But this policy, which had been so

---

91 Massey and Catalano, *Capital and Land*, p. 1.
92 Cox, *Adversary Politics and Land*, p. 119; CPA: CRD 2/25/11 – Town and Country Planning 1953–64.
93 Hansard: Vol. 657, HC Debates, Col. 979 (9 April 1962); O'Hara, *Governing Post-War Britain*, pp. 135–9.
94 Cox, *Adversary Politics and Land*, pp. 118–24.
95 CLA: Executive Committee, 2 May 1964 (SR 3CLA/A/1/5).
96 CPA: CRD 3/23/1 – Betterment.
97 CPA: CRD L/2/5/10–11 – Town and Country Planning.
98 Hallett (ed.), *Land and Housing Policies in Europe and the USA*, pp. 201–2; Peter Hall et al., *The Containment of Urban England, Vol. 2*, pp. 434–6; Prest, *The Taxation of Urban Land*, pp. 163–70.

influential in the earlier history of land reform under Lloyd George, failed to attract sufficient public or political support after the Second World War. In 1952 the Conservatives had set up a committee of inquiry, under the chairmanship of Erskine Simes to explore its potential. But its membership was split, with the majority raising the very practical issue of how the value of unimproved sites was to be assessed in practice, especially in the absence of a comprehensive and accurate system of land registration. 'The 1947 legislation had provided new, and as the majority thought, overwhelming arguments against the whole idea.'[99] The issue was revived again in the 1970s when the Layfield Report on local government finance considered site value rating, but came out against it, although the Liberal Party continued to support its benefits.[100]

In response to the property boom, the Labour Party revived its demands for the nationalisation of development land. But it tried to learn some of the lessons of the failure of the financial provisions of the 1947 Act. The party also started to consider more direct taxes on wealth and property such as a capital gains tax, but these were not to be taken up until later. Its initial response to the repeal of the financial provisions of the 1947 Act was to advocate the municipalisation of all rent-controlled dwellings in the private sector, amounting to some six million houses and flats, as well as fighting to maintain wartime rent controls in the face of the Conservative government's policy of deregulation. Although such policies had a unifying effect within a divided party, they proved to be electorally unattractive and even more difficult to administer in a decade which saw the increasing popularity and spread of owner-occupation.[101] By the end of the 1950s the party had returned to the idea of a revamped Central Land Board (The Land Commission) and the reintroduction of a betterment charge linked to development, but at a lower level than 100%.

The party's revived interest in land reform in the early 1960s was driven by the scandal of property speculation and the escalating cost of land for development, especially for public housing. During the 1950s, the party had experienced a prolonged period of disunity between the Bevanites, who remained loyal to a policy of nationalisation, including land, and the revisionists, influenced by Anthony Crosland's book, *The Future of Socialism*, published in 1956, who wished to drop Clause Four in favour of a move towards a more Keynesian version of socialism. The revisionists, led by Hugh Gaitskell (who was elected leader in 1956), supported state planning without state ownership and the 'promotion of equality via education and social welfare rather than through large-scale changes in the structure of private property'.[102] Thus the question of land reform, falling short of nationalisation, provided the grounds for a degree of unity between the opposing factions.

99 Ibid., p. 101.
100 Jones, *The Case for Land Value Taxation*.
101 Weiler, 'Labour and the Land'; O'Hara, *Governing Post-War Britain*, pp. 139–43.
102 Harris, 'Labour's Political and Social Thought', p. 33.

Signposts for the Sixties, a statement on home policy approved by the party's annual conference in October 1961, devoted a large part to land reform and the resurrection of the failed aspects of the 1947 Town and Country Planning Act. This statement firmly placed responsibility for the soaring price of land on the Conservative government's return to a free market in 1959. This it argued had severely delayed slum clearance, made town and country planning an impossibility, and had allowed office building to get out of control to the benefit of only speculators and property sharks. In order to reduce the power of private landlords, the party also maintained that more should be done to make it easier for private tenants to buy their own homes and for leaseholders to acquire their freeholds, replacing its earlier and unpopular policy of municipalisation. It also looked to the creation of more new towns to protect the green belt and avoid having to build blocks of flats.[103]

The party in opposition tried to learn some of the lessons of the previous failure of the Central Land Board, but in many respects, what was proposed was not that different. A key variation was that only land 'ripe for building' should be taken into public ownership. After the approval of *Signpost for the Sixties*, a study group on land problems, chaired by Arthur Skeffington MP, submitted a series of proposals to the NEC of the party seeking to refine the policy and resolve some of the difficulties. The need for clear exemptions and adequate levels of compensation was emphasised, but there was still a high degree of optimism that landowners would cooperate with the new Land Commission in the release of sites and the collection of betterment.[104] Lord Silkin, previous Minister of Town and Country Planning, argued unsuccessfully that the new policy must be 'manifestly fair and involve no element of confiscation' recalling his bruising experience of trying to implement the highly complex financial provisions of the 1947 Act. He thought that land should be purchased at current market values and that despite the expense, 'if these values take the same course in the future as they have done in the past, these should be quite formidable'.[105] Douglas Houghton, MP for Sowerby, and future cabinet minister in Wilson's first government, argued for a capital gains tax that should cover stocks and shares as well as real property, but this was not included in the study groups' final report.[106] By November 1962, the study group, which included T. D. Smith, the Leader of Newcastle City Council and other local government representatives, ratified the policy but with a number of serious reservations. These accurately forecast the difficulties that would arise when the Labour government tried to enact the policy following its re-election in 1964.

These reservations reflected the real problems the Labour government experienced in 1948 to 1951 in trying to agree levels of compensation and

103 Labour Party, *Signposts for the Sixties* (October 1961).
104 LPA: RD 220/March 1962.
105 LPA: RD 224/April 1962; Weiler, 'Labour and the Land', p. 332.
106 LPA: RD 222/March 1962.

betterment by a Central Land Board in the face of fierce opposition from land-owners and local authorities fearful of a centralised policy threatening their local power and planning functions. In this respect the study group argued that the proposed Land Commission should work through regional offices to guarantee local control and accountability. It could not agree, however, on the financial implications, arguing that there were too many imponderables to consider. It estimated that a figure of £250 million a year was required to be met from borrowing.[107] These difficulties resurfaced when Labour took power in 1964 committed to creating a Land Commission.

Summary

The land reform programme of the 1945 Labour government formed part of a post-war settlement covering agriculture, smallholdings, new towns, national parks and town and country planning, including development control but not the attempt to recover the unearned increment by taxing development land. The financial provisions of the 1947 Town and Country Planning Act proved to be too complex and controversial and had unforeseen and negative consequences on the market for land. Uthwatt had argued during the war that land nationalisation was the logical solution to the problem of compensation and betterment, but that it was not practical politics. The Labour Party agreed with this position as a wartime compromise. However, when in government after the war, the party continued to retreat from a policy of land nationalisation. Instead, it adopted certain parts of the Uthwatt Report in developing a system of taxing the unearned increment on development land through town and country planning. It linked a traditional policy of land taxation to a system of land-use control, rather than tax the value of land itself through site value rating.

Unfortunately for the government it did not anticipate the effect a 100% levy would have on the private market for land. It had started to try and resolve a number of theoretical and practical difficulties but lost power in 1951. But the primary motivation of the Labour Party was a long-term commitment to land nationalisation to be achieved by a short-term one-off solution to the difficult issue of compensation and betterment as the best means of recovering 'the unearned increment'. This unhappy compromise highlighted the contradiction contained within a 'mixed economy' where land remained in private ownership, but where the state was not powerful enough to control the market for land in the public interest.

The Conservatives were initially divided on what approach to take to the question of compensation and betterment. They were not necessarily opposed to taxing development land at a level that did not hinder the market in a mixed economy, but eventually acceded to the interests of unfettered private property

---

107 LPA: RD 343 (revised) November 1962; Cox, *Adversary Politics and Land*, p. 128.

by returning to a free market in land by the end of the 1950s. This ideological support for a free market in land helped to create the circumstances for an unforeseen and unprecedented boom in property and land prices during the late 1950s and early 1960s. The Labour Party took advantage of this crisis by campaigning against the effects of property speculation and returned to government in 1964 on a wave of opposition to the detrimental effects of uncontrolled increases in land and property prices. In power, Labour revisited the difficult issue of how to recover betterment through development control and proposed the setting up of a Land Commission with powers of compulsory purchase and by a revised system of taxation.

8   Continuing battles over compensation and betterment

Following the election of Labour in 1964, the period up to 1979 witnessed a continuing political conflict over compensation and betterment. To the general public and politicians, the issue was defined more in terms of the growing scandal over rising house and land prices, the evils of property speculation and the failure to build enough public or private houses. In comparison to the late nineteenth century, the property speculator had to some extent replaced the aristocratic landlord as the focus of radical political opposition. The controversy over land and property speculation revived both political and public interest in a renewed attempt at land reform. For the Labour Party the inability to acquire land at non-inflated prices had a negative impact on the role of the state to build public housing and create more new towns. It effectively prevented positive planning. As a technical issue of concern to town planners and economists, the question remained a complex and confusing area of public policy. It became even more so after 1964 with the emergence of other solutions to the question of land profiteering, such as fiscal measures like capital gains tax and land development tax. Planning measures such as partnership arrangements and the idea of 'planning gain' also emerged as potential solutions to obtaining community benefits from the way land was approved for development.

This chapter covers the period 1964 to 1979, a time when historians have argued there was a continuing post-war consensus on broad economic and planning matters. But as we have seen this consensus certainly did not apply to the matter of compensation and betterment. Three distinct periods can be identified during which Labour sought on two occasions to reintroduce a tax on the unearned increment but each attempt was quickly repealed by incoming Conservative governments. The first period was 1964 to 1970, when Labour set up a Land Commission and introduced a betterment levy known as the Development Gains Tax. The second was 1970 to 1974, when the Conservatives abolished the Land Commission but retained a Development Gains Tax as a fiscal rather than a state-interventionist solution to the crisis of property speculation. The third was 1974 to 1979, when Labour enacted the Community Land Act and introduced a Development Land Tax, at a time when the property market collapsed and there was the build up to the IMF crisis of 1976.

However, these renewed attempts made by Labour to recover the 'unearned increment' each underwent significant modification from their original manifesto commitments. As a result, the aim of radical state intervention was diluted. Moreover, for their supporters, each attempt to embed such legislation ran out of time before they could be effectively introduced. Incoming Conservative governments repealed both attempts in 1970 and then again in 1979, giving notice in advance to placate the market. They argued that the legislation was not only administratively burdensome and bureaucratic, but that it was also an attack on the principles of private property.

The chapter quickly summarises those policies relating to support for agriculture, new towns and development control, including national parks and the green belt, which certainly did form part of a post-war policy consensus. But it must be stressed that after 1950, both parties did not threaten the rights of landed property in the way that land reform potentially did immediately after the war, with the election of a socialist government committed in the long term to a policy of land nationalisation. Some of the initial success of these policies, such as new towns, for example, the first tranche of which after a slow start began to be built on a serious scale in the 1950s, was dependent on the ability of the state to compulsory purchase land at non-inflated prices, in effect carrying out a policy of land nationalisation for very specific public purposes. This was the same for the green belt, when the LCC under Labour control bought large tracts of agricultural land after 1934 to create a green girdle around London.[1] Although the ambitious nature of Labour's postwar vision for a 'New Jerusalem', and in particular new town development, the green belt and the creation of national parks, have survived in their original form, they have not been extended in ways envisaged by the post-war Labour government, informed by a collective and optimistic spirit of positive planning born of wartime experiences. Rather they were restricted, if not neutralised, by the failure of the state at either a local, regional or national level to acquire land at non-inflated prices, effectively preventing more positive planning and government intervention taking place.[2] The survival of a powerful private market in land as part of a mixed economy exercised a very negative influence on the ability of the state to intervene effectively in the redevelopment of land for public purposes.

This chapter will review how different historians and other commentators, especially town planners, have interpreted these developments and the cycle of enactment and repeal that marked the failure of attempts to recover a betterment levy. Leaving aside the official history of environmental planning

---

1 Inwood, *A History of London*, p. 723.
2 Winter, 'Land Use Policy in the UK: The Politics of Control', pp. 3–14.

(Cullingworth deliberately left out the broader economic and political context),[3] the most detailed historical account by Cox locates this failure in the adversarial nature of party politics, based on a fundamental ideological disagreement over the rights of landed property.[4] Cox also identified a range of other secondary factors that made this debate a complex issue of public policy, such as interdepartmental conflict between government departments at ministerial and official level, and the difficult relationship between central and local government. Professional interests, such as the views of town planners and property developers also influenced the direction of policy. Later historians have placed more emphasis on the complexity of the issues involved, and the unrealistic expectations that central government solutions could solve problems such as the rising cost of land without generating a range of perverse and unforeseen outcomes. One such paradox was the withholding of land from the market.[5] Cox makes a similar point that both governing parties after 1945 were to an extent ignorant of the effects of their policies on the market for land, which either 'generated property speculation and inflation on the one hand or a disruption of the development market on the other'.[6]

Changes in the post-war consensus on agriculture, planning and new towns

After 1950 government policies relating to agriculture, the development control aspects of town and country planning, including new towns, were developed along lines that did not threaten the principle of private property. Rather they supported a mixed economy with the state regulating the behaviour of the market, but increasingly in favour of the interests of private ownership. In terms of agricultural policy, state intervention became a permanent feature, unlike the laissez-faire policies of the interwar period, leading to what has been described as a second agricultural revolution. State regulation 'profoundly altered the structure of the agricultural industry, and the day-to-day nature of life and work in the countryside'.[7] The wartime agricultural committees, which the Labour government had continued after 1945 to ensure that agricultural productivity was maintained to meet severe post-war food shortages, were slowly dismantled and the staff absorbed into the civil service. The focus of government policy moved away from intervening or even confiscating the land of inefficient farmers to one of subsiding and supporting famers in a private market to increase output at any cost. Farming became highly efficient through economies of scale, mechanisation and the

---

3 Cullingworth, *Environmental Planning, Vol. 1–4.*
4 Cox, *Adversary Politics and Land.*
5 O'Hara, *Governing Post-War Britain*, pp. 131–50.
6 Cox, *Adversary Politics and Land*, p. 199.
7 Newby, *Country Life*, p. 187 and pp. 180–210; Holderness, *British Agriculture since 1945* (1985); Martiin, Pan-Montojo and Brassley, *Agriculture in Capitalist Europe, 1945–1960.*

use of chemical fertilisers, encouraged by grants and subsidies and fostered by the powerful corporatist alliance between the government and the National Farmers Union. The Country Landowners' Association (CLA) argued that the economic success of agriculture, and its family orientated workforce, was the primary justification for the maintenance of the private ownership of land.[8]

There was a growth of the large farm at the expense of both small and medium sized farms.[9] Farms became more specialised, attracting significant capital investment, influenced by the extent to which the government, and then the European Economic Community (EEC) after 1973, subsidised farming, although this included many smaller and inefficient farms as well. The post-war consensus on agriculture remained largely unquestioned but tensions started to emerge over entry to the EEC. The Labour Party remained committed to a policy of cheap food for the urban working class, a policy which reinforced its tendency to oppose the Common Market. The Conservatives like Labour maintained a corporatist approach to state support for agriculture influenced by the effective lobbying of the National Farmers Union.[10]

The number of tenanted allotment plots experienced a heavy decline from its wartime peak of 1942, marking perhaps the final demise of rural smallholdings as an answer to the agrarian land problem, although the Northfield Report published in 1979 recommended that they should continue to receive state support and encouragement, suggesting that they be renamed 'county holdings' rather than 'smallholdings'.[11] The agricultural workforce fell from 1.4 million in 1911 to only 352,000 in 1981. Rural in-migration replaced the declining population of farm workers and changed the social composition of villages. The damaging environmental effects of agribusiness only started to become apparent after the 1960s, and the public esteem of the farmers began to diminish thereafter, as it became clear that the farming community could no longer be trusted to guarantee the preservation of the countryside as envisaged in 1945.[12] By 1979 the state had moved a long way from threatening inefficient farmers with intervention, potential confiscation and even rural land nationalisation, which had always remained a serious option for many members of the Labour Party, to a position of state support and subsidies for large-scale agribusiness operating in a highly competitive but subsidised private market.[13]

A similar process of accommodation in favour of a private market in land can be seen in the way town and country planning developed after 1964. 'The fundamental principles of the planning system have survived broadly

8 CLA: Executive Committee, 9 December 1976.
9 Grigg, 'Farm Size in England and Wales'.
10 Flynn, 'Agricultural Policy and Party Politics in Post-War Britain'.
11 Departmental Committee of Inquiry into Allotments (Thorpe Report, 1969), Cmnd. 4166.
12 Burchardt, *Paradise Lost*, pp. 168–77.
13 Winter, 'Land Use Policy in the UK: The Politics of Control', pp. 10–11.

unchanged since 1947.'[14] Legislation placed a duty on local planning authorities to prepare a development plan and a legal responsibility on landowners to
seek planning permission for carrying out development involving any change
of use. After 1947, the removal of the liability on local authorities to pay compensation for any denial of planning permission encouraged local authorities
to adopt and prepare plans on a larger scale, although progress was slow.
However, the process reflected local and regional variations, differences in
political control and the growing technical demands on planners coping with
unexpected increases in population forecasts, urban growth and overspill,
especially in the Midlands and the South East, and related transportation
issues. Also, the nature of planning was not adequately defined either in practice or in theory. Many planners saw their role in terms of urban design only.
Political, professional and academic opinion remained disappointed that
the profession neither had the inclination or the skills to become developers
themselves, a positive role that was left to the private market.[15] The unre-
formed structure of local government, and the tension between the different
levels of responsibility (county versus district) only added to this ambiguity.

All the same, the development plan remained the prime instrument of
planning policy 'but their weaknesses were becoming ever more apparent'.[16]
The scope for positive planning was severely restricted and the role of local
authority planning departments remained one of negative control and urban
containment, such as preventing development in the green belt. The introduction of new government guidelines (*The Future of Development Plans*) by
the Labour Minister of Housing and Local Government, Richard Crossman,
in 1964, redefining the nature and purpose of the plans, did not significantly
improve matters. The effects of the abolition of the metropolitan county
councils in the 1970s only delayed the adoption of such plans and created
confusion in political and academic circles about their purpose. One historian
of urban planning commented that 'while planners thought of development
plans as blueprints, as their utopian origins implied, they became in practice
simply another facet of the property market which developers had to "play"
and build into their calculations. To this extent they probably made property development more complicated than it had been before the war, but they
did not fundamentally alter it'.[17] Thus the visionary ambitions for positive
planning introduced by the post-war Labour government had by the 1970s
come up against the reality of a largely unregulated property market, where
land changed hands at inflated prices or was withheld for its scarcity value to
increase.[18]

14 H. W. E. Davies, 'The Planning System and the Development Plan', p. 45.
15 Taylor, *Urban Planning Theory since 1945*; Cherry, *Town Planning in Britain since 1900*.
16 H. W. E. Davies, 'The Planning System and the Development Plan', p. 50; Cullingworth and
     Nadin, *Town and Country Planning in the UK*, pp. 76–97.
17 Ravetz, *Remaking Cities*, p. 78; Ambrose, *Whatever Happened to Planning*, pp. 261–6.
18 Ratcliffe, *Land Policy*.

Similar tensions became apparent in the way new towns developed after 1950. The mainly agricultural land on which these were built was compulsorily purchased at existing use value by publicly owned national corporations using Treasury grants; in other words, at non-inflated prices by a policy of land nationalisation. Without such a radical policy, it is very unlikely that they would have been built at all. The intention was that ownership would then pass to the adjacent local authority in their area once development was complete. Letchworth, for example, first designated in 1946, had started to return a profit to the Treasury by the late 1950s. The Conservative MP for the area, Martin Madden, extolled the virtue of this arrangement in 1961 by arguing that 'ownership of the whole freehold ensures that whoever puts up the money and is the ground landlord will be the beneficiary from the increase in the value of the property and site which is brought about by the very activity of developing the area'.[19]

But this classic statement of recovering the 'unearned increment' was soon subverted when the Conservative government in the same year created the New Towns Commission to take over the assets of all completed new towns, including ownership of the houses, which were either rented or leased. At the time the Labour Party was opposed to this transfer of responsibility. John Silkin, Labour's Minister of Town and Country Planning (1974–1976), argued that the assets of new towns should go to democratically controlled local authorities to benefit local communities. Although he was not opposed to home ownership, he banned the indiscriminate sale of houses in new towns while waiting lists remained long.[20] But the foundations of their purchase by sitting tenants had been laid by the 1970s. Labour's Leasehold Reform Act of 1967 allowed tenants to purchase their freehold, while Mrs Thatcher introduced the 'Right to Buy' policy for council tenants in 1980. The privatisation of the new towns was thus slowly realised by the end of the 1970s.[21] Like development control, the original policy of new towns had by the 1970s become subverted to the interests of private property.

Furthermore, the future of new towns was slowly eclipsed by the growth of regional policy and the expansion of existing smaller towns to cope with population growth and overspill from metropolitan areas. The Treasury favoured the lower costs involved and their better record of housebuilding, despite the Labour government instigating a second wave of new towns between 1964 and 1970.[22] After the designation of Milton Keynes in 1967, government funding was redirected towards the inner cities. At the same time, the courts reinstated the principle that landowners 'should be able to claim "hope value" on any land compulsorily purchased, reducing the ability of the New Towns model to deliver cheap land for new housing'.[23]

19 Duff, *Britain's New Towns*, p. 9.
20 John Silkin Papers 5/3/1 – Discussion Documents on New Towns.
21 Wannop, 'New Towns', p. 220.
22 Cherry, *Town Planning in Britain since 1900*, pp. 153–4.
23 Ryan-Collins et al., *Rethinking the Economics of Land and Housing*, p. 88.

The final plank of Labour's post-war programme of land reform – the creation of national parks in 1949 – did not pose a threat to the interests of private property as most of the land in these areas remained in private hands. But they were subject to planning controls and ministerial approval with regard to large-scale developments, of which there have been a number of controversial examples, such as the construction of Fylingdales ballistic missile early warning system on the North Yorkshire Moors. The county councils had a stronger role in their management in comparison to new towns, where central government agencies from the outset guaranteed a degree of centralised control and financial support. Their development therefore was patchy depending on the varying financial and policy commitments of different local authorities, and they remained administratively weak, especially in the crucial area of planning. 'Ironically the main threat to their landscape integrity came not from the small scale, piecemeal commercial, industrial and residential developments which had been anticipated (but which planning legislation proved sufficiently robust to hold in check), but from national government itself (often acting in conjunction with big business).'[24] Moreover, rural land use policies after the Second World War became 'heavily circumscribed by the principle of voluntarism, whereby the maximum freedom was given to owners and managers of land to interpret regulations. It is a principle intricately linked to notions of property rights and compensation'.[25]

Labour's Land Commission and capital gains tax, 1964–1970

The early 1960s witnessed a speculative property boom of unprecedented proportions. This had serious political repercussions for the party most identified with the defence of private landed interests. Financial institutions moved heavily into property investment as a possible hedge against inflation at a time when the profits of other economic sectors were in decline. 'Between March 1958 and March 1962, the total market value of property shares had increased almost eightfold', with fortunes being made for a large number of individuals. As a consequence, the property developer was 'cast in the popular mind as the arch villain of British capitalism'.[26] The Labour Party benefited in part from this association and narrowly won the general election of 1964 with a manifesto commitment to set up a powerful 'Land Commission to buy, for the community, land on which building or rebuilding is to take place'. This it was believed would both end property speculation and avoid the state having to pay inflated market prices, allowing positive planning to replace ad hoc development by a financially unstable private sector. The idea was that the Commission would buy 'all development land at a price based on its

24 Burchardt, *Paradise Lost*, p. 184.
25 Cox, Lowe and Winter, 'From State Direction to State Regulation', pp. 475–90; Cherry, *Town Planning in Britain since 1900*, pp. 154–6 and p. 209.
26 Scott, *The Property Masters*, p. 143 and p. 158.

existing use value plus an amount sufficient to cover any contingent losses by the owner, and to encourage the willing sale of land'.[27] This did not include agricultural land or the freehold of existing residential houses, the absolute property rights of which the Labour Party was at pains to respect.

Wilson had cleverly used the Rachman scandal, which broke out just before the election, to paint the Conservatives as friends of property speculators. It was hoped by resurrecting a revised version of the 1947 Act and embarking on a renewed attempt to recover the 'unearned increment' by the compulsory purchase of all building and development land, that local authorities would be empowered to replan 'our towns' and build more houses for rent or purchase. As part of his modernising strategy, Wilson created a new Ministry of Land and Natural Resources, not dissimilar to the new Department of Economic Affairs formed as a counterweight to the Treasury. The new ministry was headed up by Fred Willey, the left-wing MP for Sunderland North, with responsibility to oversee the ambitious work programme of the proposed Commission. It was seen very much by Wilson and other ministers as a centralised solution to the land question seeking to reduce the negative power of local authorities to block progress. It was also hoped that the Commission would be able to prevent landowners from withholding land from the market as they had in the past, but the party had little evidence to support such a view.

The party's Study Group on Land Problems had received a number of reports before the election, raising serious reservations. Wyndham Thomas, the Director of the TCPA, had described the proposal for a Land Commission to buy *all* land for development as impracticable given the scale and workload involved.[28] Others warned that the financial provisions of the 1947 Act had not worked well.[29] Lewis Silkin, now leader of the party in the Lords and who had steered the original 1947 Act through Parliament, cautioned against any attempt to pay less than the market value, as it 'would operate unevenly and with great uncertainty and in some cases with hardship'.[30] The CLA reported him saying that he advocated a development charge of only 50%, which for 'surtax payers would be better than paying capital gains tax'.[31]

However, despite these reservations, the study group decided to press ahead. It recommended the creation of a powerful Land Commission, in line with the radical approach outlined in *Signpost for the Sixties*, supported by the party's leader Hugh Gaitskell, who saw it as a practical alternative to those demanding an outright policy of land nationalisation. But the study group did not try to develop the proposal in detail given the reservations expressed.[32] Prophetically, its final report emphasised the importance of working through

27 Labour Party Manifesto, 1964.
28 Wyndham Thomas, 'A Review of Development Land Taxes since 1947', p. 12.
29 LPA: RD 148, May 1961.
30 LPA: RD 244, April 1962.
31 CLA: Executive Committee, 12 November 1964.
32 LPA: RD 220, March 1962.

local government. It pointed out the shortage of district valuers as a real problem in terms of coping with the scale of purchasing *all* development land, and the potential this had for creating delays in Labour's housebuilding programme.[33] A further report, just before the election, drew attention to the very complex planning issues involved and the danger that the Commission would be 'overwhelmed by the great volume of transactions unless it was allowed time to build up its administrative resources'.[34] The failure to address these issues from the outset proved to be a serious mistake. However, little legislative progress was made until after the general election in 1966 gave Labour a larger majority.

The task of setting up the Commission in the difficult political circumstances of 1964 to 1966 (a combination of a very narrow majority and the relative inexperience of many ministerial appointments) turned out to be internally divisive. As a result, the government retreated from a radical land policy which had, up until then, unified many elements in the party split over a continuing commitment to nationalisation. The original and ambitious idea of a powerful central government department buying up all development land to address the housing crisis and the scandal of property speculation was slowly whittled down to be replaced by an agency whose purpose was limited to helping local government and the private sector overcome land supply problems. However, an important and new responsibility was added. This was the revival of the policy of collecting a development charge or betterment levy, set at 45 to 50% to recover the 'unearned increment', when the seller realised the gain on the point of sale.[35]

After the 1966 general election it was agreed by the cabinet that the Commission needed time to gradually accumulate a 'land bank' for development and it should do this in stages over a longer period. In the short term it was generally accepted that its initial purpose was the collection of the levy rather than to intervene in the market for land on a large scale. Thus, a balance was sought between the state and the market in order to give landowners some incentive to bring land forward for development. It was recognised that the 100% betterment charge introduced in the 1947 Act had removed this incentive and that a lower level was required in order to gain at least some return to the community. This compromise was achieved following complex negotiations, leading up to the publication of a White Paper in September 1965. The CLA was opposed 'root and branch' to the proposal in defence of private property rights. However, it considered that a betterment tax was inevitable, which it argued would be more acceptable to landowners than the idea that they should not get full market value for their land on the point of sale.[36] For this reason it regarded the Land Commission Bill 'as the most pernicious

33 LPA: RD 343, November 1962.
34 LPA: RD 751, April 1964.
35 *Land Commission* (September 1965), Cmnd. 2771.
36 CLA: Executive Committee, 11 March and 1 April 1965.

it had ever to deal with', forecasting with some validity that it would have the effect of drying up the supply of land for development.[37] But after the election it welcomed Wilson's decision to liquidate the Ministry of Land and Natural Resources and decided to cooperate with the Land Commission in order to safeguard the interests of agricultural landowners, its primary constituency.[38]

In a similar vein, the Conservatives condemned the bill as an attack on the rights of individual property owners and therefore freedom in general. It regarded the Commission as backdoor nationalisation of building land and a centralised usurpation of the powers of local planning authorities. However, in the light of public opinion, it was not opposed in principle to a moderate levy on the profits from development land. But it focused its attack on the way the Land Commission would in its opinion undermine Labour's ambitious housebuilding programme, an issue which it and the Labour Party both correctly identified as a political vulnerability.[39]

Internal government negotiations have been well documented by Cullingworth and described in detail by Cox.[40] Cox correctly argued that while the Labour Party had given insufficient attention to the effect that their interventionist approach would have on the market for land, the primary reason for its immediate repeal by the Conservatives in 1970, was the adversarial nature of British politics and the ideological differences between the parties on the rights of landed property. He also maintained that the Land Commission might not have been a failure in the long term, and that it did not have the time to prove itself before it became a victim of the wider context of party politics. Later historians have generally supported this conclusion. For Weiler, the Land Commission was beset by the complexity of its task, bureaucratic delay, tensions between government departments and the lack of cooperation from local government, which resisted and was suspicious of centralised control. He argued that the scheme wrongly concluded that rising land prices was the result of speculation rather than a shortage of supply, a view that continues to divide political and professional opinion to this day. 'In short, the Land Commission had not only failed, but had also been misconceived. Labour simply dropped it down an Orwellian memory hole, making no mention of the Land Commission in its 1970 election manifesto.'[41]

A number of reasons contributed to the dilution of the original proposal for a commission and the revival of interest in a betterment levy. Two issues were paramount. First there was a serious conflict at ministerial level about the purpose of the Commission and its effect on the housebuilding programme. Second there emerged fiscal solutions to property speculation and

37 Ibid., Executive Committee, 13 January 1966.
38 Ibid., Executive Committee, 10 March 1966 and 9 February 1967.
39 Lord Hailsham Papers – Land Commission 1966 (HLSM 2/42/4/29).
40 Cullingworth, *Environmental Planning, Vol. 4*, pp. 275–337; Cox, *Adversary Politics and Land*, pp. 125–54.
41 Weiler, 'Labour and the Land: From Municipalisation to the Land Commission', p. 341.

wealth accumulation, such as capital gains tax, which were seen as a possible alternative to a betterment levy which it correctly forecast might have proved difficult to collect. Both reflected an ideological difference of opinion over the role of the state in controlling the market for land, falling short of a policy of outright land nationalisation. Thus, long-term ideology (land nationalisation) came into conflict with short-term pragmatism (e.g. housebuilding programmes), with the latter winning out given the nature and imbalances of a mixed economy, where in practice the private market for land exercised more power than the public role of the state.

There was a protracted battle in the cabinet between Richard Crossman, the Minister of Housing and Local Government, and Fred Willey, the Minister of Land, about the purpose and timing of the commission, based on Crossman's legitimate concern about the effect on his housebuilding targets. Wilson had persuaded him to set a huge housebuilding target of 400,000 by 1966, of which 150,000 was council housing. The proposed Land Commission threatened to delay this programme due to the complex nature of its compulsory purchase arrangements. Soon after his appointment Crossman, who confessed he knew very little about housing, began to lobby Wilson with an alternative proposal:

> Instead of trying to introduce the Land Commission ready-made in this Session, what we should do is to create something you can call a land commission but give it as its sole function at this stage the job of raising the tax on the betterment of land. We could argue that this was the first stage in our progress towards the establishment of a real Land Commission which would have a monopoly power to buy all building land. This would of course be something quite different. Introduced now, it could gum up the whole works and destroy our housing programme.[42]

This was the position which eventually won out after the general election in 1966. The Ministry of Land was wound up and its reduced responsibilities transferred to the more powerful Ministry of Housing and Local Government, pleasing its influential permanent secretary, Dame Evelyn Sharp, who had fought a clever rear-guard campaign to preserve the functions of her department.[43] Support for the Land Commission had also become a test of left-wing opinion within the party. Barbara Castle was lobbied by Fred Willey to 'back the more revolutionary proposal, saying that Harold really wanted it. Dick Crossman however was pressing a minor role'.[44] In the end, more progress was made in building houses in both the public and private sectors than in strengthening planning and recovering betterment. The government 'encouraged owner-occupation with low-cost mortgages by retaining

42 Crossman, *Diaries of a Cabinet Minister, Vol. 1*, p. 78.
43 Sharp, *The Ministry of Housing and Local Government*, p. 23 and p. 144.
44 Castle, *Castle Diaries, 1964–70*, p. 16.

the much criticised, regressive, mortgage tax relief ... and better off workers to vacate council housing to free them for those unable to buy. By the time Labour left office in 1970, for the first time more than 50% of households were owner-occupiers'.[45]

Influential opinion amongst town planners was also critical of the original concept of the commission. Wyndham Thomas, the Director of the TCPA, who had served on Labour's Study Group on Land Problems, argued that the commission was too ambitious. He was instrumental in drafting alternative proposals with the help of officials in the Ministry of Housing and Local Government and the Treasury. He went on to serve as a member of the Commission in 1967, but he condemned the stringent accounting rules imposed by the Treasury on the way it operated. 'The Treasury' he maintained later 'resented having another tax-collecting agency outside its control. There was resentment, too, from Richard Crossman and Evelyn Sharp, that the Land Commission was not under the planning ministry's control'.[46]

The idea for a Land Commission was further undermined by the emergence of new and alternative solutions to the problem of land prices, such as capital gains tax. In a Granada TV programme broadcast in 1965 entitled *State of the Nation: Labour and the Land*, Evelyn Sharp stated that

> Neither Dick Crossman nor I had the slightest interest in the Land Commission ... we never understood what the function was supposed to be. Now collection of betterment levy, yes. Or a capital gains tax ... a fiscal thing, this was important. And this was a good way to deal with what was a major point in the party's manifesto: that a good part of the profit from land transactions should be taken by the state. That was right. That could be done. It didn't need a Land Commission.[47]

Richard Crossman was successful in diluting the idea of the Land Commission. He promoted alternative fiscal approaches more under the control of the Chancellor of the Exchequer, who wanted to avoid controversy by relying 'mainly on his new capital gains tax and to keep the betterment levy low'.[48] The party had been discussing the idea of such a tax while in opposition.[49] The annual conference in 1961 proposed a reform of the tax system in order 'to ensure that the burden of taxation falls less heavily upon those who earn their money the hard way and which ensures that those who get their money the easy way by capital gains, by inheritance, by speculation, pay their fair share'.[50] In 1965 James Callaghan introduced a capital gains tax in his budget

45 Thane, 'Labour and Welfare', p. 108; Glennerster, *British Social Policy Since 1945*, pp. 141–5.
46 Wyndham Thomas, 'A Review of Development Land Taxes since 1947', p. 12.
47 Quoted in Cox, *Adversary Politics and Land*, p. 134.
48 Crossman, *Diaries of a Cabinet Minister, Vol. 1*, p. 260; see also pp. 101–2, p. 126, p. 157, p. 168, p. 174 and p. 239.
49 Daunton, *Just Taxes*, p. 286.
50 *Labour Party Annual Conference, 1961*, p. 152.

applied at the rate of 30% to the sale of land or its transfer at death.[51] For many contemporaries this was a far more straightforward and less complex way of recovering the landowner's 'unearned increment', avoiding the difficult and complex administrative problem of how land was valued.[52]

The Land Commission struggled to achieve its more limited remit by the time Labour lost power in 1970. Its record has split historical and professional opinion. Cox argued that by 1970, after some initial teething problems, the Commission had started 'to collect a substantial amount of levy and had begun to facilitate the supply of land for both the private and public sectors. The scheme appeared to work more successfully than the earlier 1847 Act, as there was little sign of either land withholding or inflated land prices'.[53] But Weiler maintained that the Commission 'failed totally to reach its goals. By the end of its first year, it had acquired only two acres of land and collected only £.5 m in betterment levy. In fact by mid-1968, there were discussions in the government about abolishing it on the grounds that it had become a "political embarrassment"'.[54]

The Conservatives and the land development tax, 1970–1974

The Conservatives fulfilled their promise to abolish the Land Commission on their election in June 1970. This laid the foundations of an unprecedented property boom in the early 1970s and was followed by an equally dramatic crash in housing and land prices in 1974. Investment by financial institutions, and especially the banks, was the main cause of this boom, facilitated by a relaxation of office-development permits. 'During the early 1970s, bank advances to the property sector rose substantially from £362 million in February 1971 to £2584 million in February 1974, an increase of 614%.... [T]he repeal of the Land Commission provided a further stimulus to development, by restoring to owners the whole of the development value of their property.'[55] Before the election in 1970 the Conservative leader, Ted Heath, had condemned the Land Commission as a 'prime example of the doctrinaire socialist belief that state intervention can solve everything. We do not say that there should be no levy, but we do say that the Commission will increase the cost of land and will add to the delays on land development'.[56] During the election in 1970 he advocated the imposition of a moderate levy on land prices.

---

51 HC Debates, 6 April 1965, Vol. 710, c. 245.
52 Harriss, 'Land Value Increment Taxation', pp. 567–72; Prest, *The Taxation of Urban Land*, pp. 176–7.
53 Cox, *Adversary Politics and Land*, p. 141.
54 Weiler, 'Labour and the Land: From Municipalisation to the Land Commission', p. 339.
55 Scott, *The Property Masters*, pp. 183–4.
56 CPA: CRD L/3/2/5 – Notes for Mr Heath on Problems of Urban Congestion (1966); CRD B/17/1 – Land Commission Bill.

Mrs Thatcher had been given shadow responsibility for housing and land in 1965 and attacked what she saw as a socialist obsession with nationalising development gains. Her authorised biographer described how her hatred of arbitrary state power, her interest in the rule of law and her tenderness towards property owners all came together in her attack of the Land Commission.[57] In her own biography, Thatcher admitted that it was during this time that she 'first became fully acquainted with the complexities and anomalies of the rating system, whose fate seemed destined to be inextricably intertwined with mine', forecasting the debacle of the poll tax twenty years later.[58] But like Ted Heath, the CLA recognised that while it needed to defend the retention of an open-market value for all land at the point of sale, it was necessary that there be some taxation of development gains, 'but at a level which would leave some incentive to private enterprise'.[59] But when Thatcher replaced Heath as leader in 1975, leading members of the CLA detected a significant change in the atmosphere – 'things were possible now which had not been possible a month ago in terms of mounting a defence of private enterprise', and it held a series of joint meetings with the Confederation of British Industry with the general aim of combatting the effects of capital taxation.[60]

The abolition of the Land Commission Act of 1967 resulted in the sale of land reverting to the free market, restoring to the private owners the whole of the development value. The Conservatives had no plans to replace the Commission or to collect betterment at any level, especially after Labour had introduced a capital gains tax in 1965, levied at 30% instead of at the higher betterment level of 45%.[61] The government returned very quickly to the adversarial politics of *laissez faire*. It embraced a radical free market agenda described by Harold Wilson as the work of '*Selsdon Man*'. Planning authorities would now have to pay full market prices for any development land purchased, compulsorily or by agreement. The Secretary of State for the Environment, Peter Walker, lost no time in lifting the ban on office development in London, imposed by George Brown in 1964 to stop commercial property speculation. He also relaxed controls on office floor space to anticipate increased demand following Britain's expected entry to the EEC. The total deregulation of the market for land represented by these changes, and the wider economic changes fuelling 'the Barber Boom' of the early 1970s, created the conditions for what turned out to be 'a sustained and economically ruinous boom in property speculation'.[62]

In the meantime, the government adopted a private sector approach to planning and blamed local authorities for hoarding land and forcing up

57 Moore, *Margaret Thatcher: Authorised Biography, Vol. 1*, pp. 180–1.
58 Thatcher, *The Path to Power*, p. 136.
59 CLA: Executive Committee, 9 May 1974.
60 CLA: Executive Committee, 13 February 1975.
61 Cox, *Adversary Politics and Land*, p. 156.
62 Ibid., p. 159; Scott, *The Property Masters*, pp. 166–212.

prices. The Department of the Environment exhorted them to release more land for housing (Circular 10/70), with the promise of extra loan sanctions to help put together banks of land ready for development. In March 1973, in light of anxiety about rising land prices, it promised to introduce a land hoarding charge 'to penalise any unjustifiable delay in developing land which is the subject of planning permission for housing'.[63] The charge was directed at property developers as much as local authorities and was to be secured on the land itself and collected by the Inland Revenue. Like the capital gains tax, it was another example of a fiscal alternative to a betterment levy obtained through the planning system. The proposal was never implemented. It was dropped in favour of more radical fiscal solutions as the general economic crisis deepened by the end of the year, caused by the dramatic increase in the price of oil and deteriorating industrial relations leading up to the political crisis of the 'three-day week' in 1974.

But at the same time, the government made life even more difficult for local planning authorities by passing the Land Compensation Act of 1973 which granted new rights of compensation to landowners who were adversely affected by planning decisions. Legal opinion at the time regarded this statute as redressing the balance between public and private interests in favour of the latter – a 'law grounded solely in the ideology of private property', while at the same time seeking to reduce public participation in planning in order to speed up development.[64] The financial effect of the legislation only added to the land costs of local authorities at a time when they were facing growing demands for measures to reduce homelessness and improve conditions, especially in Labour-controlled inner-city areas.

In the absence of any policies to recover the 'unearned increment', rejected on ideological grounds, the Conservatives looked to more flexible and market-friendly town and country planning to encourage development. In the Town and Country Planning Act in 1971, it introduced the idea of planning gain based on negotiated agreements between councils and private developers to realise community benefits, an approach supported by the CLA.[65] These were formal planning arrangements whereby in exchange for planning permission, which granted huge untaxed capital gains to landowners, developers offered to provide new public amenities or services such as low-cost housing or leisure facilities. This new approach was seen as another alternative way of securing a share in development profits for public benefit that did not involve accepting a more interventionist planning role for the state. Planning gain had become fairly widespread by the mid-1970s. However, it had the effect of giving more control over development to the private developers, who were always able to get the upper hand in any negotiations with local authorities. They continued

63 HC Debates, 6 March 1973, Vol. 852, cc. 26, 7–8; *Widening the Choice – The Next Step in Housing*, Cmnd. 5280.
64 McAuslan, *The Ideologies of Planning Law*, p. 106.
65 CLA: Executive Committee, 9 May 1974.

to make disproportionate profits from their speculative activities, contributing in part to rising land prices and land hoarding.[66]

In this new deregulated environment, and where it proved very difficult to control rising commercial rents, property was viewed as one of the few sectors that could be counted on to produce real capital growth in contrast to the more limited investment opportunities provided by other sectors of the economy. Investment in commercial property was characterised at this time as the 'new alchemy'.[67] As a consequence of this combination of circumstances, not least the relaxation of financial controls as part of the government's general economic strategy ('the Barber boom'), property values rose sharply as the banks invested heavily, if not recklessly in land for commercial development. A sizeable number of property speculators made enormous capital gains, such as Harry Hyams, financed by the banks, insurance companies and pension funds in what turned out to be a highly volatile market. It was widely anticipated that rental income from commercial properties would continue to outperform other investments in industry or government bonds. The Conservatives sought to dampen down speculation by freezing rents in January 1973 but were forced to reverse this policy only a few months later because it threatened to undermine the whole financial viability of the banking system and the wider role of the city.[68]

The party came under attack about the asset-stripping and money-making activities of the international trading group Lonrho, of which Duncan Sandys, a former Conservative cabinet minister was chairman. The Prime Minister Ted Heath coined the phrase 'the unacceptable face of capitalism', to describe such behaviour, although he went on to add 'that should not suggest that the whole of British industry consists of practices of this kind'.[69] However, the term resonated with the public, especially as the government seemed powerless, for example, to respond to scandals like Centre Point in London, which was kept deliberately empty in order to maximise land values. The speculative boom in commercial property led to a dramatic and largely unforeseen property crash starting in the second half of 1973.[70] This was one of a series of financial crises from the 1970s, especially affecting the UK and the USA where financial innovation and deregulation created entrenched economic instability.[71]

By this time public opinion had forced the government into a major policy U-turn. The energy crisis, the coal miners' strike, power cuts and the three-day working week only added to a sense of panic. In December 1973, the Chancellor of the Exchequer announced urgent budget measures to address

66 Keogh, 'The Economics of Planning Gain'.
67 Scott, *The Property Masters*, pp. 185–6.
68 Cox, *Adversary Politics and Land*, p. 176.
69 *The Times*, 16 May 1973, p. 1.
70 Scott, *The Property Masters*, p. 193.
71 Harvey, *A Brief History of Neoliberalism*.

the crisis. In terms of land reform, and the need to dampen the speculative boom in property prices, he dropped the idea of a land hoarding tax. He proposed a much stronger tax on property and development gains, which it was estimated would generate £80 million in a full year. Barber described large windfall profits arising from speculation as 'offensive' but went out of his way to differentiate the proposed land development tax from the previous betterment charge levied by Labour's Land Commission, which he described as bureaucratic and ineffective.[72]

This new fiscal measure eventually formed a significant part of the Finance Bill of 1974, enacted by the newly elected Labour government following the general election in February called by Ted Heath as test of his leadership during the miners' strike. Corporation tax for companies was increased from 30 to 52% and income tax for individuals on sales of land and buildings was set at 75%. In order to take speculation out of the property market, corporation tax for companies of 52% was charged on the first lettings of their developments. It was also agreed that the Department of the Environment would take over and let any property which had been empty for two years.[73] The Labour government supported the continuation of these interventionist policies, including the land development tax as an interim measure pending the introduction of their own Development Land Tax in 1976, which was a further, and what turned out to be a final, attempt to recover the 'unearned increment' for the benefit of the community.

Historians of urban change have described the introduction of a land development tax in the crisis conditions of 1974 as a drastic reversal of the Conservative Party's non-interventionist position of 1970. But they have pointed out that the new tax was a fiscal measure, building on the experience of levying a capital gains tax, in contrast to the state-interventionist approach adopted by previous Labour administrations which had sought without much success to recover betterment through the planning system. They concluded that 'no major interventionist role which would see the state, locally or nationally, intervening in a positive way in the land supply and development market, was ever considered seriously by Conservative politicians during this period or throughout the post-war years'.[74]

The Community Land Act and the Development Land Tax, 1976.

It was in response to property speculation and the unprecedented increases in the cost of land for housing that in 1974 the Labour Party embarked again on an interventionist approach to recover the unearned increment through the planning system.[75] Labour did not reject entirely fiscal solutions such

---

72 *The Times*, 18 December 1973, p. 1 and p. 5.
73 Cox, *Adversary Politics and Land*, p. 174.
74 McKay and Cox, *The Politics of Urban Change*, p. 88.
75 Cox, *Adversary Politics and Land*, pp. 176–92; Weiler, 'Labour and the Land: The Making of the Community Land Act', pp. 391–8.

as a capital gains tax or, for example, more targeted approaches to address the problems of the inner cities through partnership arrangements, but it remained loyal to a body of radical thinking that stretched back to the nineteenth century, influenced by the tax doctrines of John Stuart Mill and Henry George. Despite the practical difficulties of carrying out these different ways of taxing development land in a market where private interests predominated, the cause of land reform continued to resonate within Labour Party ideology at moments of economic crisis. This was particularly the case when the opportunity arose to attack the Conservative Party over their identification with property interests, generally and popularly referred to as 'speculators', 'asset-strippers' and 'land grabbers'.

Indeed, the idea of taxing development land proved to be capable of uniting the party against a common enemy, namely the large-scale commercial landowners, developers and property speculators, linked to an unaccountable system of finance capitalism. For a party which had been divided after 1950 over the left-wing demand for more state regulation and nationalisation, including land, and the more egalitarian and 'revisionist' socialism epitomised by Anthony Crosland, the attempt to nationalise development rights through a betterment levy, and to tax wealth through capital gains, became a subject on which the centre and right wings of the party could unite against those on the left arguing for a further extension of nationalisation. Anthony Crosland supported this approach in his final book *Socialism Now*, published in 1974.[76] But neither he nor Gaitskell had sufficient political support within the party to abolish Clause Four, adopted in 1918 calling for the common ownership of the means of production, distribution and exchange, a policy statement which had traditionally included land as a long-term aim.

But left-wing opinion also saw the nationalisation of development rights as a move in the right direction towards eventual land nationalisation and higher levels of taxation on wealth.[77] In 1974, the party was elected on a more left-wing programme than in 1966. Its manifesto called for a fundamental and irreversible shift in the balance of power and wealth in favour of working people and their families, including further nationalisation, such as land and ship building. It stated categorically that 'Land required for development will be taken into public ownership, so that land is freely and cheaply available for new houses, schools, hospitals and other purposes. Public ownership of land will stop land profiteering. It will emphatically *not* apply to owner-occupiers'.[78]

The problem for the party, however, was translating such a manifesto commitment into legislation that would work in a mixed economy where the option of immediate and outright land nationalisation was not considered to be practical politics. The enormous financial implications of compensating

---

76 Jefferys, *Anthony Crosland*, pp. 172–4.
77 Lipsey, *Labour and the Land*; Barras, Massey and Broadbent, 'Planning and Public Ownership', pp. 748–9.
78 Labour Party Manifesto (February 1974).

landowners and the fact that owner-occupation had become so widespread, made reform very difficult to achieve in practice without having to grant wide-ranging exemptions for different types of land. In opposition after 1970, internal policy papers drew attention to a mix of complex, competing and contradictory pressures. Concern was expressed about the fall in house-building and the reluctance of local authorities to build houses in a period of rising interest rates.[79] A London Labour MP advised against overtaxing owner-occupation on the grounds that it would discourage saving and self-reliance, although at the same time he complained about the regressive nature of mortgage tax relief.[80] The future Minister of Local Government and Planning (1974–1976), the left-wing MP John Silkin, son of Lewis Silkin who had introduced the 1947 Act, identified the ideologically driven Conservative Party as the main reason for the destruction of all of Labour's previous attempts to recover the 'unearned increment'. He argued that any renewed attempt should be based on the encouragement of more positive planning by local authorities. This would take the place of the gambles of the free market and of negative control by local authorities – 'speculation in our scarce resources – the land – will no longer be a way of earning a living'.[81]

Silkin was opposed to capital gains tax on the grounds that 'capital losses could be written off against profits', and argued instead that what was required was 'a scheme that combined the main principles of the 1947 Act with a speedier and simpler method of producing the desired result and one which would be more difficult for any succeeding government to destroy'.[82] Opinion within town planning regarded John Silkin as more doctrinaire and less pragmatic than his father.[83] But with the revival of the left wing of the party during the 1970s, his line was more readily acceptable. However, the party could not foretell the adverse economic circumstances that the Labour government would face after 1974, which put paid to ambitious land reform measures in practice.

What turned out to be the final attempt to tax development land came up against the financial reality of a land market experiencing a major crash in its fortunes after the boom of 1970–1973 and a deteriorating economic situation leading up the IMF crisis in 1976. As a result, it had to tone down its original manifesto commitment to recover the unearned increment in the same way that the radical proposal for a powerful Land Commission in the 1960s had been diluted. But its majority in Parliament was not large enough to bring about radical change. The second election in October 1974 gave it a very slim majority that was eroded over time by by-election losses leading to a minority government. It was in these difficult political circumstances that

---

79 LPA: RD 595 – March 1970.
80 LPA: RD 53 – January 1971.
81 Silkin Papers (5/2/7) – Speeches 1974–76.
82 LPA: RD92 – April 1971.
83 Wyndham Thomas, 'A Review of Development Land Taxes since 1947', p. 14.

the government also faced the severest economic crisis of the post-war years. 'If it did not rescue the City from the property crash then its desire to rebuild manufacturing industry could not be achieved because so much capital was tied up in property.'[84]

The White Paper on land issued in September 1974 proposed a Community Land Bill and a Development Land Tax, which together it was hoped would enable the community to control the development of land in accordance with its needs and priorities, and to restore to the community the increase in value of land arising from its efforts.[85] Labour's manifesto for the second crisis election in October 1974 boldly stated that the

> government will take into public ownership land required for development, redevelopment and improvement. These proposals do not apply to owner-occupiers, whose homes and gardens will be safeguarded. But the public ownership by local authorities of necessary land is essential to sensible and comprehensive planning both in our towns and in the countryside. The land will be paid for at existing use value and the expensive disgrace of land speculation will be ended.[86]

During the 1970s, the Labour Party became equally concerned about the rising cost of agricultural land and the effects of speculation in rural areas. It came out more strongly in favour of the nationalisation of rural land and recommended an all-embracing Rural Land Authority.[87] In 1976, the party published a policy statement called *The Public Ownership of Agricultural Land – Immediate Proposals for Action*, which called for the voluntary transfer of ownership of agricultural land as a means of paying capital taxation and the proposed wealth tax. The publication had sufficiently worried the CLA that it set up a working party to counter the threat of land nationalisation, even though it had been reassured by John Silkin, who had moved from the Ministry of Housing and Local Government in 1976 to become the Minister of Agriculture, Fisheries and Food, that agricultural land was not under threat of public ownership.[88] During 1977, Silkin had been trying to encourage the CLA to cooperate with a survey to identify the extent of investment in rural land by financial institutions and overseas buyers,with the aim of finally producing a complete register of ownership, a long-standing demand of land reformers. Although the CLA was sceptical, wishing to promote the benefits of private ownership over what it saw as the real threat of nationalisation by a future Labour government, it agreed to cooperate with such a survey.[89]

84 Cox, *Adversary Politics and Land*, p. 178.
85 *Land*, Cmnd. 5730 (September 1974); Cox, *Adversary Politics and Land*, pp. 176–92; Weiler, 'Labour and the Land: The Making of the Community Land Act'.
86 Labour Party Manifesto (October 1974).
87 LPA: RD 620 (February 1973).
88 CLA: Executive Committee, 11 May 1978.
89 CLA: Executive Committee, 12 May, 16 June, 14 July, 13 October (1977).

The party believed that the cost of rural land was being artificially increased by the involvement of financial institutions, pension funds and overseas investors, the exact same influence that was affecting development in urban areas, leading to uncontrolled property speculation. Silkin set up a committee of inquiry in July 1977, chaired by Lord Northfield, the previous Labour MP for Birmingham (Donald Chapman) to investigate the way such investment was changing trends in farm structure and ownership, and potentially pricing out of the market young people wishing to enter farming as a career.[90] The party had already passed legislation in 1976 to ensure that tenant farmers inherited their parents farms when they died, thereby reducing the property rights of freeholders.[91] The motive behind the committee was more a political response to the concerns about the behaviour of finance capital rather than with rural land reform in general.[92] It prompted in turn a Marxist analysis of the role of capital in land and polemical calls for the nationalisation of 'the City'.[93] Lord Northfield did not issue his report until after the re-election of the Conservatives in 1979. He rejected demands for rural nationalisation and any changes to the security of tenant farmers.

However, in terms of urban land, the White Paper published in 1976 turned out to be a pale imitation of the original manifesto commitment to bring all development land into state ownership. In a new and interesting departure, it proposed that local planning authorities should be given the power, but not the immediate duty to acquire development land at current use values and not a central government department or agency created for that purpose like the previous Land Commission. (This did not apply in Wales where a regional Welsh Land Authority was proposed.) By devolving power to a local or regional level, it was hoped that the disadvantages of an over-centralised approach could be overcome and local government could be encouraged to intervene in the market for land and plan more positively. However, in terms of the type of land to be acquired, a large number of exemptions were agreed including owner-occupied houses, agricultural land and land which already had planning permission. This latter exemption was designed to prevent the collapse of property companies which had bought land at high prices before the slump in the market at the end of 1973. All other land for development would then be subject to a Development Land Tax of 80%.

There were two circumstances that led to the dilution of the original manifesto promise when Labour took power in 1974. First, the government had to accept that planning authorities did not have the skilled staff and experience to take on the task of full-scale land management and development. Therefore, there had to be a more gradual move towards total land nationalisation not unlike the two stages to land purchase adopted by the Land Commission ten

---

90 *The Times*, 17 September 1977, p. 3 and 24 September 1977, p. 2.
91 Agriculture (Miscellaneous Provisions) Act, 1976.
92 Winter, 'Revisiting Landownership and Property Rights', p. 74.
93 Massey and Catalano, *Capital and Land*.

years before. Local authorities were exhorted to plan for ten years ahead when they could start acquiring banks of land for development. In a second and later stage they would be obliged or even compelled to do so by ministerial order. In the final and third stage, all development land would be taken into public ownership. In reality this meant that in the short term the commercial property market remained unaffected, and only liable to Development Land Tax on land which planning permission had not yet been obtained.

The second circumstance, and the more crucial one, was that the government had to recognise that in the words of Anthony Crosland at the Department of the Environment 'a healthy market in commercial property is necessary for the achievement of the government's social and economic objectives ... and that much savings and pension money, depends on income from commercial property, which also constitutes an important credit base for industry'.[94] John Silkin, who had defended the Community Land Act 'like a tigress with her young', was forced to admit the need for financial realism in a speech to a local government conference in January 1976 – 'We all know the constraints of public expenditure. Indeed one of the advantages of the land scheme' he added weakly 'is that it will help public expenditure by cutting the cost of land purchase for local authorities'.[95] He was attacked from the left, by opponents such as John Tilley, the Labour leader of Wandsworth Borough Council and future Labour MP for Brixton, who considered the legislation 'a bitter disappointment to those who believe in [the] rapid extension of the public ownership of land'.[96] It was these wider economic constraints, and the lack of revenue to fund local authority land purchases as a result of the cuts imposed by the IMF after 1976, that contributed most to the lengthening of the timetable for the state purchase of all development land by local authorities. (The Welsh Land Authority had a better record of success.) The phased introduction of what was once a radical objective was interpreted at the time, and especially by the land market, as almost an indefinite postponement.

Academic opinion at the time was on the whole equally disappointed by the way the scheme had been reduced in scope and effect. For the authors of a left-wing critique of the way the property market operated, the proposed legislation 'left the property market unchanged. Commercial rents will rise to market levels, the rents of existing buildings will continue to flow to a select few, and as before, buildings can be traded as a commodity. In other words, the principal elements of private wealth creation will flourish'.[97] In fact, Ambrose and Colenutt thought that the Community Land Bill could spark a new property bonanza by limiting the number of development sites thus causing rents to rise. Only a policy of comprehensive public ownership, they argued, could lead to positive planning unhindered by the rising cost of land.

94 Quoted in Cox, *Adversary Politics and Land*, p. 181.
95 Silkin Papers – 5/2/5 and 5/2/7 – Speeches 1974–76
96 *Tribune*, 17 October 1975.
97 Ambrose and Colenutt, *The Property Machine*, p. 169

Research carried out after the enactment of the legislation reached similar negative conclusions. The School for Advanced Urban Studies in Bristol noted in an interim report published in 1979 'that the private development industry appears to be continuing much as before and though its own decisions may be very much affected by uncertainty and expectation of repeal there has been minimal intervention from local authorities'.[98] They identified the inadequate level of resources, the lack of incentives to intervene in the market and its depressed state as the main reasons for lack of progress. The Conservatives had promised that they would repeal the 'Communist Land Bill' on the grounds that it amounted to confiscation and a denial of basic human rights, of which property ownership was an essential part.[99] The private market for land therefore waited for the expected return of a Conservative government. Legal opinion also noted how the early pledge to repeal the Community Land Act had undermined the aims of the legislation. 'Political commitment waned, financial resources were cut and many local authorities found that the Act inhibited rather than promoted achievement of their planning objectives.'[100]

The Labour Party itself was forced to acknowledge the constraints although it remained hopeful that the scheme could be rescued if it was better financed. This was unrealistic in the economic circumstances. In a statement from its National Executive Committee, issued in February 1978, it called on the government to resource local authorities to build up land banks and strengthen the Development Land Tax by closing loopholes. It lamented the negative approach of the local authorities towards positive planning and recommended new legislation to free up vacant land and create a public register of all land and its ownership to be made available for public inspection.[101]

But in an interesting afterthought, the report argued that more attention should be targeted at the needs of the inner cities. In fact, the Labour government had started to develop an approach to resolving the decline of the inner cities by adopting a community development and partnership approach between central and local government, focused in particular on the problem of waste land.[102] This new perspective on land reform was increasingly seen by many in the party, as well as professional town planning opinion, as a more viable policy in addressing the needs of particular areas of the country than the blanket and comprehensive remedy represented by the Community Land Act. On their election in 1979 the Conservatives continued with this new policy development by creating enterprise zones and urban development corporations, which placed a much greater emphasis on partnership with the private sector and downplayed the role of local government (Local

98 Barratt, Boddy and Stewart, *Implementation of the Community Land Scheme: Interim Report.*
99 Weiler, 'Labour and the Land: The Making of the Community Land Act', p. 403.
100 Grant, 'Britain's Community Land Act: A Post-Mortem', pp. 359–73; Emms, 'The Community Land Act – A Requiem', pp. 78–86.
101 LPA: *The Community Land Scheme: Some Proposals for Change* (February 1978).
102 White Paper, '*Policy for the Inner Cities*', Cmnd. 6845 (1977); Inner Urban Areas Act (1978).

Government and Planning Act 1980).[103] Like fiscal measures to tax wealth and land, such as capital gains tax, this new way of looking at land reform developed as a possible alternative to the failed policy of seeking to recover the unearned increment for the community. This policy had now failed three times since 1947.

Summary

Ideological considerations played a crucial part in the failure of the Land Commission (1967) and the Community Land Act (1975) to achieve their original political aims. Other factors also contributed to the failure, such as the difficult relationship between central and local government over planning; the inadequate levels of financing; and the underestimation of the workload implications of state acquisition of all development land by either central government departments or local authority planning departments. But the conflict over the rights of landed property was the primary reason for the continuing failure to recover the 'unearned increment' for the community. The complexity of the various acts also contributed to their failure such as the confusion created by the exemptions required to safeguard the rights of owner-occupiers and farmers, and the bureaucratic requirements of land valuation. The lack of understanding by both governing parties of the effect of their policies on the behaviour of the private market for land also played a role in the failure of the state to control or regulate property speculation, especially the tendency of the market to withhold land. However, Conservative promises of early repeal of Labour legislation threatening the rights of private property were not based on any misunderstandings of this nature, but on clear party advantage in the interests of private property.[104]

The emergence of alternative land reform policies after 1964 also contributed to undermining the policy of recovering the unearned increment through the control of development. By far the most influential of these was growing support for fiscal measures designed to tax capital gains or wealth, a policy that did not require the calculation of land values. Moreover, a powerful Treasury was always opposed on principle to any attempts by other government departments to raise taxes like the betterment levy not in the control of the Inland Revenue. Furthermore, the way planning policies developed after 1964 also provided alternative means of trying to obtain for the community some of the benefits accruing to property developers, without threatening property rights through taxation. A partnership arrangement like planning gain was one way this could be achieved. Another was to consider more targeted approaches to specific problems affecting particular geographical areas, such as the inner cities, which were struggling to deal with

---

103 Moor, 'Inner-City Areas and the Private Sector'.
104 McKay and Cox, *The Politics of Urban Change*, pp. 102–3.

vacant derelict land where private development proved to be difficult. On their election in 1979, the Conservatives sought to develop and extend this partnership approach to urban planning. Also, they did not repeal the Development Land Tax immediately, recognising that some form of recouping land values was necessary in controlling the adverse political consequences of uncontrolled property speculation. Chapter 9 will trace the way this approach to land reform developed after 1979 up to the present day.

Part IV

The land question and the housing crisis, 1979 to 2017

9 The triumph of private property and future options for land reform

Land reform underwent a radical change of direction after the election of the Conservatives in 1979 as a result of the privatisation of public assets (including land) and the significant expansion of owner-occupation through the Conservative's 'Right to Buy' policy. By the year 2000, owner-occupation as a proportion of total households had reached a peak of 71%, but by 2011 this had declined to 64% (48% in London and diminishing rapidly) as the rising cost of housing and land started to price first-time buyers out of the market. The deregulation of financial services in the 1980s also encouraged private home ownership through the promotion of land as an investment. Other policy developments reinforced the spread of owner-occupation, such as changes to the tax system (capital gains and mortgage relief), and the deregulation of council rents. As a result, the private rented sector grew and now operates in a largely deregulated market. As a proportion of total households, it is now larger than publicly rented housing.

This chapter starts by reviewing the changes in the structure of landownership after 1979. The land policies of Conservative governments from 1979 to 1997 will then be described, identifying those trends, such as privatisation, deregulation and financialisation, which contributed to the spread and then decline of owner-occupation, but which also led to the housing crisis and the financial crash of 2008. The record of Labour governments from 1997 to 2010 will then be outlined; comparing the various measures they proposed to influence the way land could be made more available for housing to their previous attempts to recover the 'unearned increment'. The chapter will conclude by briefly referring to developments after 2010 and the current options for land reform in the context of the financial crash of 2008 and changes to land tenure. Is the taxation of land values a realistic or viable policy in the twenty-first century, when compared to other alternative planning or tax reforms to control property speculation and address the housing crisis? Do community land trusts provide a way forward? Does 'The Right to the City' and other radical 'occupy' movements represent a serious challenge to the triumph of private property? What scope is there for a revival of political interest in the land question as a response to the failure of neoliberalism? Indeed, has the housing crisis, seen in its widest context, become the new land question of the early twenty-first century?

Changes in landownership during the second half of the twentieth century

A number of historical trends in the structure of landownership during the second half of the twentieth century can be identified. They include: the growth of home ownership accompanied by a trend to smaller homes as family sizes reduce; the decline in tenant farming and the increase of institutional and international investment in agriculture; the survival of concentrated hereditary landownership in the countryside; and the contraction of state landownership and the growth of communal landowners like the National Trust and wildlife trusts.[1] Perhaps the most significant change apart from the spread of owner-occupation in urban areas has been the decline of tenant farming, with important implications for the future of agriculture and the countryside. The trend towards owner-occupation was less pronounced in rural areas (owner-occupied farms reached 57% of all holdings by the 1980s) where aristocratic and institutional landownership survived and financial institutions and overseas investors started to buy agricultural land on a larger scale, and where tenant farmers found it more difficult to purchase their freeholds. The Labour government had commissioned the Northfield Report in 1977 to examine the lack of data about the ownership of farmland and to address concerns about the sale of agricultural land to financial institutions and overseas buyers. This concern was driven in part by anxiety about the property speculation in urban areas being repeated in the countryside, with investment by the pension companies and international interests pricing smaller tenant farmers out of the market. Opinion at the time considered that such developments had serious potential repercussions for agricultural production, environmental protection and public access to countryside.[2] The Labour leader Michael Foot voiced similar anxieties in 1983 about the need to reverse the disappearance of small farms and to combat the destruction of the countryside by the Common Agricultural Policy.[3] This concern continues today in radical criticisms of the way in which 'feeding the nation' has become a 'secondary consideration' to speculators buying up thousands of acres annually to avoid tax.[4]

Lack of transparency and the prevalence of opaque trust arrangements have made identifying ownership and trends in the structure of landownership in rural areas a difficult task. In the absence of a central register of landownership which could identify tenure arrangements more accurately

---

1 Home, 'Land Ownership in the United Kingdom'.
2 *The Times*, 17 September 1977, p. 3.
3 Foot Papers – Speech to the Socialist Countryside Group (L38/7).
4 Hetherington, *Whose Land Is Our Land?*

for planning purposes, Northfield calculated that tenant farming as a proportion of total agricultural acreage had declined. He estimated it to be less
than 40% of the total area of the country by the late 1970s, representing a
significant reduction since the high-water mark of 90% in the 1880s. The traditional nineteenth-century pattern of aristocratic landlord, tenant farmer and
agricultural labour had been almost transformed out of existence by the last
quarter of the twentieth century, replaced by a mixed structure of institutional
ownership, a declining proportion of smaller owner-occupied farms, and a
workforce made up increasingly of 'sweated' immigrant labour organised by
gang masters. Northfield repeated the call for better land registration, but he
rejected the idea that there was large-scale institutional investment in rural
land (ownership was under 2%), although he expected this to increase slowly
over the medium term. He also dismissed radical demands for state intervention, such as changes to inheritance or wealth taxes and the policy of land
nationalisation, a conclusion strongly welcomed by the Country Landowners'
Association (CLA) as a milestone in the debate about landownership.[5] But
he did recommend that the security of tenure for tenant farmers be protected
and that smallholdings, renamed county holdings, should continue to be
encouraged.[6]

These modest measures of land reform, echoing an earlier tradition
of agrarianism that did not threaten the principle of private property,
disappointed those campaigning for more radical solutions. But they did not
surprise those land campaigners who had always maintained that 'neither
financial institutions nor the government own more than a fraction of Britain's
rural land, ... as it has been for a thousand years'.[7] Tenant farmers were to
be equally disappointed when the House of Lords reduced the rules of inheritance in favour of their landlords only a few months after the publication
of the Northfield Report, and later on when the Conservatives completely
abolished statutory succession for tenant farmers in 1984, restoring the control and autonomy of private landowning interests over their leaseholders.[8]
Tenant farming continued to decline to under 30% of rural land acreage by
the end of the century.[9]

The Northfield Report confirmed the survival of large private landownership as a continuing trend in the twentieth century. Like many other
commentators, Northfield supported private ownership, whether by the larger
institutional landlords or by owner-occupiers who ran their own farms, as
the best means for ensuring the environmental and social stability of rural
society. This reflected the continuing influence of the recommendations of
the Scott Report (1943) and post-war rural policy, which had entrusted the

5 CLA: Executive Committee, 11 October 1979.
6 Northfield Report, 1979.
7 Shoard, *This Land Is Our Land*, p. 97.
8 *The Times*, 24 December 1979, p. 3; Marsden, 'Property-State Relations in the 1980s'.
9 Cahill, *Who Owns Britain?* p. 15

protection of the countryside to the farming community.[10] However, confidence in the farmers' ability to safeguard the environment started to be eroded from the 1960s by growing evidence of damage caused by agribusiness, and especially the role of the large landowner funded by EEC subsidies and capital investment.[11] Thus by the beginning of the twenty-first century, notwithstanding the growth of home ownership in urban areas, landed wealth was 'still concentrated in relatively few hands. An estimated 200,000 individuals (mostly comprising the monarchy, aristocracy and gentry) own about two-thirds of the land and it is estimated that some 1,700 individuals own a third of all land'.[12]

In contrast, state landownership declined after reaching a peak during the Second World War, when the state owned almost a sixth of the UK land area, largely but not exclusively for military purposes. By the late 1950s, the Conservatives congratulated themselves on freeing state-owned land and property from wartime emergency requisitioning, although controversially, much land remains in the ownership of the Ministry of Defence (e.g. Salisbury Plain and Lulworth Cove).[13] The 1980s saw a further transfer of over 40,000 hectares of development land from the public to the private sector following a new requirement on public bodies to maintain registers of ownership as a prelude to their sale to private developers. This left the Forestry Commission and the Ministry of Defence as the largest state owners, although local authorities still held substantial land-holdings in many metropolitan as well as rural areas.

While publicly owned land has declined, communal landownership by charitable trusts, like the National Trust and the Royal Society for the Protection of Birds, has increased. At the same time, the rights of public access to large tracts of privately owned common land have been further protected by the Countryside and Rights of Way Act 2000.[14] In this respect the rights of private landed interests over large areas of rural land have been curtailed to some extent by state action. The green belt continues to protect rural land from uncontrolled development, in contrast to the situation in many urban and suburban areas, especially London and increasingly other metropolitan areas, where commercial development remains largely unregulated by a relatively weak system of development control favouring the private developer.

In terms of urban land-holdings, recent analysis of trends has suggested that 'traditional patterns of ownership, which had formerly seen a strong "landed estate" component, have been eroded ... as private wealth and institutional investment have increased ... especially in relation to commercial property'.[15] While residential urban property is now predominantly privately

10 Tichelar, 'The Scott Report and the Labour Party'.
11 Shoard, *The Theft of the Countryside*; Burchardt, *Paradise Lost*, pp. 68–77.
12 Home, 'Land Ownership in the United Kingdom', pp. 104–5.
13 Land Powers (Defence) Act 1958; CPA: CRD L/2/5/4 – Land and Property, 1959.
14 Home, 'Land Ownership in the United Kingdom', p. 105.
15 Dixon, 'Urban Land and Property Ownership Patterns in the UK', p. 551.

owned as a result of 'Right to Buy', ownership of urban development land by 2006 was divided between a declining public sector (38%) and a relatively small group of increasingly powerful builders, property developers and large landowners (62%).[16] The Callcutt Review of Housebuilding Delivery (2007) noted, in particular, how the market for urban land had become dominated by large companies, many formed as a result of acquisitions and mergers, exercising a significant degree of leverage over planning authorities in negotiations over development and planning gain.[17]

But the most significant trend after 1979 has been the spread of residential owner-occupation in urban areas, which makes up only about 14% of total land use in the UK, but within this relatively small area, accounts for about two-thirds of all registered land titles. The main driver of this spread has been a combination of beneficial tax and mortgage subsidy systems, and the 'Right to Buy' policy introduced by the Conservatives in 1980, which created the opportunity of rapid capital gains. By the early 1990s the mortgage market, which up to that time had been controlled by traditional building societies run on mutual principles, had been taken over by the banks following 'the Big Bang' in 1986. The 'accompanying securitisation and internationalisation of mortgage markets' played a major role in the trend towards the growth of home ownership.[18] The encouragement of owner-occupation and the ideological defence of private property has been one of the primary features of the growing influence of neoliberalism in the UK and USA.[19] By 1996 over 2.2 million properties had been sold in the UK at various discounts to sitting tenants by local authorities, new town corporations and housing associations, with about 30% of tenants exercising their 'Right to Buy'. The volume of sales exceeded expectations and led to more affluent tenants moving out of the public sector 'so that those that remain come from a narrower social base and a higher proportion of them are low-income households or are reliant on welfare benefits'.[20] While the proportion of households redefined as social housing therefore declined after 1980, the private rented sector grew rapidly. By 2011, it eventually outstripped public or social housing as a percentage of total households (18.5% to 17.3%).[21] Dependency on the private rented sector also increased as a result of the rising cost of land for housing, which prevented many potential buyers from becoming owner-occupiers. These trends in tenure arrangements are the direct result of the major land reform measures enacted by the Conservatives after 1979.

16 Ibid., p. 549.
17 Callcutt Review of Housebuilding Delivery (November 2007).
18 Dixon, 'Urban Land and Property Ownership Patterns in the UK'; Ryan-Collins et al., *Rethinking the Economics of Land and Housing*, pp. 109–57.
19 Harvey, *A Brief History of Neoliberalism*, p. 2.
20 Wilson, Research Paper 99.36 – The Right to Buy, *House of Commons*, 1999.
21 ONS, *A Century of Home Ownership*.

Land reform and the Conservatives, 1979 to 1997

As promised, the Conservatives immediately repealed Labour's Community Land Act (1975) on their election in 1979. The CLA was delighted that 'there are now no less than six members of the association in the cabinet' and was relieved that land nationalisation was no longer considered to be a serious political threat to property interests.[22] The Conservatives embarked upon a radical departure in land reform policy though the enactment of their flagship Local Government Planning and Land Act 1980. This moved land-use policy away from state intervention through public ownership to one of privatisation through the sale of council houses and of publicly owned vacant land. They also encouraged the greater involvement of the private sector in planning through enterprise zones and development corporations, where planning controls were lifted, and different partnership approaches, such as planning gain introduced in 1990 and the Private Finance Initiative, introduced by John Major in 1991. After 1979, a partnership approach between private and public sectors characterised attempts to recover betterment from development land rather than through direct state intervention or targeted taxation.

The policy of planning gain was consolidated through the Town and Country Planning Act of 1990. This introduced 'Section 106' arrangements, whereby community facilities, such as affordable housing, were provided alongside private developments and paid for out of the increases in land value realised by the granting of planning permission. Such an approach was welcomed by many planners and developers. Malcolm Grant from the Department of Land Economy at Cambridge University saw it as a more practical and possibly more long-lasting answer than the ideological approach adopted by Labour governments in the past.[23] Later commentators argued that it 'became by far the most effective and durable system of "taxing" development and securing contributions to local infrastructure'.[24]

But in reality, while some community facilities were obtained, planning became even more a servant of the private market in land. The abolition of the metropolitan authorities saw their regional planning functions devolved to a smaller tier of less powerful local councils unable necessarily to withstand the economic power of a land market dominated by big landowners and property developers. Other academic opinion noted at the time how the 'private sector ... has a more favourable policy environment within which to operate than during most of the post-war period. Planners in local authorities are less able to dictate, as opposed to supervise and monitor, the pattern of development than at any time over the last 40 years'.[25] The government's

---

22 CLA: Executive Committee, 10 May 1979.
23 Grant, 'Compensation and Betterment', pp. 74–5.
24 Dobson, 'Community Infrastructure Levy: Will It Deliver?', p. 120.
25 Goodchild and Munton, *Development and the Landowner* (preface).

own Property Advisory Group had as early as 1981 argued that 'the practice of bargaining for planning gain was unacceptable and should be firmly discouraged'.[26]

Historians of planning have interpreted this move away from a regulatory to a negotiatory style of development control as partly the result of the failure of previous attempts by the Labour Party to collect betterment through the planning system.[27] The policy was designed to increase the negotiating influence of the private market in development control while avoiding the need to introduce the taxing of development land to control property speculation. It was also seen as a new way of subsidising affordable private housing following the withdrawal of the state from building council housing. The cost of providing affordable housing, therefore, fell on the developer, leading some economists to conclude that

> Section 106 can be seen as a form of development tax, negotiated on a case by case basis, even though it is not framed as such legally, and cash rarely changes hands. It is also a form of direct subsidy for affordable housing via the planning system. Perhaps because it has evolved gradually, and because each obligation is negotiated separately, Section 106 has not suffered the same fate as the various attempts to introduce development taxes since the Second World War.[28]

Thus, by the early 1990s the planning system under the Conservatives was to a large extent redesigned to suit the needs of private developers. After 1990, planning gain became a more established part of the system for obtaining planning permission. Needless to say, the policy has attracted much criticism from contemporary housing reformers who have argued that the planning system has been radically changed over time to suit the financial interests of developers and landowners. They have been able to use their economic power to increase their profits by reducing the level of affordable housing in development schemes to the detriment of local communities.[29]

The Conservatives replaced an emphasis on state intervention and the recovery of betterment through taxation, which up to that time had achieved a limited degree of consensus between the parties, with a more explicit policy of privatisation and measures to 'release' private enterprise. This approach was justified in ideological terms by the objective of 'rolling back the frontiers of the state'. It sought to diffuse wealth and power generally, mainly through the extension of a 'property-owning democracy', but also through, for example, share ownership schemes. However, although the scope of planning under Thatcher was reduced in favour of the private market, the basic principle of

---

26 Planning Gain – Report by the Property Advisory Group, HMSO 1981.
27 Cullingworth and Nadin, *Town and Country Planning in the UK*, p. 166.
28 Ryan-Collins et al., *Rethinking the Economics of Land and Housing*, p. 93.
29 Minton, *Big Capital*, pp. 25–47.

development control was retained; including the fundamental principle that landowners denied planning permission were not entitled to compensation.[30] This continues to be a significant restraint on the rights to landed property in the twenty-first century.

While in opposition, the Conservative Party had undertaken a review of land-use policies. By 1978 it had reached a number of conclusions, many of which were then later translated into legislation. It recommended a modification of planning procedures to ensure an adequate supply of land for development, with more planning appeals being allowed in order to overcome what was seen as local authority obstruction and land hoarding. The party tended to blame local authorities for creating a land shortage by not bringing forward enough land for housing, and thereby contributing to its high cost. Although it noted that there was ongoing disagreement within government about the cause of rising land prices, it took the side of the House Builders Federation, which represented the larger property developers rather than small owners, in arguing that a shortage of development land was holding back housebuilding.[31] In a major change of direction, and in the name of inner-city redevelopment, the government aimed to force local authorities and nationalised industries to sell their land to private developers at market if not lower rates, in particular derelict or waste ground in the inner cities. It called for a 'A Domesday Book of all land in public ownership' to be published within 12 months, with a directive that plots of land be sold off at auction if no planning use could be demonstrated within a set period of time. (The term 'Domesday' was later dropped from final reports.).[32] This policy was enacted in the Local Government Planning and Land Act 1980. As a result, much public land, like school playing fields, was sold to the private sector for development. By 1992 the 'sales of state assets had reached £44.5 billion, together with a further £36 billion from council house sales'.[33]

Initially, the Conservative policy on the recovery of betterment was less radical and more influenced by a spirit of consensus. It accepted the need to retain Labour's Development Land Tax (DLT) 'so as to obtain political consensus with the Labour Party and obviate further changes in the future'.[34] Before the election at least it argued that 'whilst we have reservations concerning the need for this specific tax, we accept that public opinion is disturbed by the prospect of unconscionable gains in land values enjoyed by private individuals upon the grant of planning permission. Therefore, we agree that there

---

30 Thornley, *Urban Planning under Thatcherism*.

31 For a review of this debate see Household Growth: Where Shall We Live? Cm. 3471 (1996) Annex E: The Planning System and House Prices; Bowie, *Radical Solutions to the Housing Supply Crisis*, pp. 25–49.

32 CPA: CRD 4/21/8 – Land Use, 1976–78; B/17/4 – Note on Supply Day Debate on Housing, 5 March 1979.

33 Clarke and Pitelis (eds.), *The Political Economy of Privatisation*, p. 210.

34 CPA: CRD 4/21/8 – Land Use.

should be some form of tax on such gains'.[35] However, it reduced the level of DLT from 100% to 60% as it was considered that this would not be a disincentive to land being bought forward by owners for development nor would it deter developers. This policy was in line with the views of the British Property Federation, which argued that a new tax on betterment should be introduced but at levels which would not discourage landowners from making land available for development.[36]

But after the election, the Conservatives retained the DLT only until 1985 when it was finally abolished in Nigel Lawson's budget as part of the general monetarist policy of cutting taxes on income and capital. It was argued that development gains in the future would be liable to income tax, capital gains or corporation tax, but at much lower levels than 60%. This was strongly welcomed by the property development and construction industries. It was estimated that the government would lose £50 million of revenue in a full year, but this would be offset by the cost of collection of £5 million, a process which the party had always regarded as overcomplex, bureaucratic and an unnecessary interference in the free market.[37]

The party's most radical and influential departure in land reform was 'Right to Buy'. The origins of this policy can be traced back to the late Victorian period when Conservative opinion began to be influenced by the potential benefits of spreading small-scale private ownership through schemes of peasant proprietorship, seen by many as a bulwark against demands for more radical land reform spreading from Ireland.[38] Support continued during the interwar period when the Conservative MP Noel Skelton developed the concept of a 'property-owning democracy' to combat what he saw as the growing threat of the Labour Party if not Bolshevism.[39] The idea was taken up again after 1945 as an alternative to the public ownership principle espoused by the post-war Attlee government.[40]

Following consultation with grassroot members in 1948, the party collected views for a report on 'What We Think about a Property-Owning Democracy'. Influenced by the growth of cold-war thinking, it argued that communism was a threat to both family life and private property. 'The ownership of property' it maintained 'provides the citizen with the only sure shield against trespass on his freedom either by his neighbour or by the state'. The report went on to outline a series of reforms to back up these principles, including 'Let the builders build'; the ending of rent restrictions on council housing; the reduction of Schedule A income tax on rent from land; leaseholders to be given the option of purchasing their freehold; opposition to the Town and Country

35 Ibid.
36 British Property Federation, *Policy for Land* (1976).
37 *The Times*, 20 March 1985, p. 8.
38 Offer, *Property and Politics*, pp. 148–58.
39 Torrance, *Noel Skelton and the Property-Owning Democracy*.
40 Davies, ' "Right to Buy": The Development of a Conservative Housing Policy'.

Planning Act of 1947, with its move towards the nationalisation of development rights if not outright land nationalisation; and the encouragement of owner-occupation and smallholdings.[41]

But the majority of these policy proposals remained on the right-wing fringes of the party and did not form part of the post-war settlement. In particular, the demand for the sale of council houses to their tenants failed to attract the support of the party leadership. It was not until the late 1960s that the policy began to garner wider support, overcoming the argument that central government should respect the autonomy of local councils in providing public housing and the general belief that council tenants would be unwilling to buy anyway. But when campaigning Conservative local councils undertook successful sales schemes in the 1970s, 'party elites reconceived the idea as an attractive and tenable policy option'.[42]

The long-term effects of 'Right to Buy' have been profound in terms of land reform policies. The policy also radically influenced the way in which the economy developed a dependency on investment in property during the last twenty years of the twentieth century. Investment in housing and land for residential purposes now represents over 350% of GDP having increased from under 100% since 1945.[43] The measures introduced to encourage the spread of home ownership led to what has been described by economists as the financialisation of land and housing, with important repercussions for the economy as a whole. By November 2017, UK housing stock was worth £6.015 trillion, or nearly four times the size of the national debt concentrated in London and the South East and with over 60% owned by people aged over 55.[44] The scale of this investment underpins the wider performance if not very survival of the City of London.

'Right to Buy' was also encouraged by the deregulation of council rents and the introduction of assured shorthold tenancies in 1988, supported by changes to the tax system to make it easier to purchase (such as mortgage tax relief), revisions to capital gains and the abolition of Schedule A income tax liability. As a result, housing became an investment opportunity, as well as a new form of credit, rather than representing just a place to live.[45] The ideological consequences have been profound. A neoliberal view of property rights now forms part of a wider set of beliefs based on free markets and free trade.[46]

Apart from the 'Right to Buy', the party also developed before 1979 a range of policies generally attacking the planning system on the grounds that it created barriers to private enterprise, and again many of these ideas were

41 CPA: CRD 2/23/7 – Property-Owning Democracy, 1948–49.
42 Davies, ' "Right to Buy": The Development of a Conservative Housing Policy', p. 422.
43 Ryan-Collins et al., *Rethinking the Economics of Land and Housing*, pp. 9–10.
44 *The Guardian*, 29 November 2017 (source Halifax).
45 Ronald, *The Ideology of Home Ownership*; Murie, *The Right to Buy*.
46 Harvey, *A Brief History of Neoliberalism*, pp. 1–4.

later translated into legislation. By 1978 internal policy reports maintained that the basic presumption of land-use policy is that 'an individual should be allowed to develop his own land if he wishes to do so', unless there are very strong planning grounds for refusing permission. In a final report on land-use planning before the election, it argued that there should be financial sanctions against local authorities who act unreasonably over planning applications with the aim of speeding up the development of land and avoiding stock-piling. The principle of compensation based on market values was strongly defended. This long-held view had been adopted during the Second World War in the party's vociferous opposition to the state paying only 1939 prices for the compulsory purchase of bomb-damaged sites.

After 1980, the Conservative Party also adopted the view that in order to rehabilitate the inner cities, it was necessary for local authority land to be sold off at public auction as cheaply as possible, and that private developers owning the greater part of a proposed development site should be able to buy up adjacent land required to complete the development at 'a fair and realistic price'.[47] While publicly owned land was to be sold off as cheaply as possible under revised valuation procedures, the party defended the principle that land sold by private owners either voluntarily or compulsorily should be fully compensated at market prices, 'otherwise an element of confiscation arises', as confirmed by the Land Compensation Act of 1961 which enshrined the principle of 'hope value'.[48]

The ideological attack on planning and local government (the two were seen as closely inter-related) continued when the party was in office. On the one hand the government abolished a whole layer of metropolitan authorities, including the Greater London Council, as part of a general attack on local government. On the other hand, it sought to bypass local authority planning control by setting up enterprise zones and urban development corporations, including the controversial London Docklands Corporation. Inner-city policy was also driven by the same considerations through the creation of public–private partnerships, a policy supported by the CLA.[49] These corporations and zones had delegated development control functions for dealing with land use and planning decisions. Although they only covered relatively small areas, their influence was significant because they severely restricted attempts at stra-tegic planning over a regional area, tending to neglect wider social consider-ations. They also reduced the opportunity for public participation in decision making, bringing the planning system into further disrepute with a general public which since the war had traditionally distrusted town planners and their methods.[50]

47 CPA: CRD 4/21/13 Land Use and Planning Policy Group (14 July 1978).
48 CPA: CRD 4/21/8 – Land Use 1976–78.
49 CLA: Executive Committee, 9 May 1974.
50 Thornley, *Urban Planning under Thatcherism*, pp. 162–84.

Land reform and Labour, 1997 to 2010

After 1997 the Labour government did not seek to reverse the general direction of Conservative policy on land and housing. Like the Conservatives, it tended to favour planning gain as a means of recovering some level of betterment over its previous approach of directly taxing development land. While in opposition after 1979 the party had gradually modified and eventually dropped a policy of seeking to recover the 'unearned increment' through physical planning and the creation of government bodies designed to intervene in the market for land, such as the Land Commission and the Central Land Board. It had not been opposed to 'Right to Buy' on principle before 1979. But, in practice, by 1983 the party had little choice but to accept the popularity of the policy and the difficulty involved in trying to repeal it. Its manifesto of that year promised to give financial assistance to tenants wishing to buy, although it wanted to phase out mortgage tax relief for higher earners. But remaining faithful to an earlier reforming tradition, the party also stated that it was determined to stop land speculation in order to make comprehensive planning possible (a new way of describing positive planning). It promised to establish land authorities, similar to the more successful Land Authority of Wales (which had avoided abolition), with 'the powers and funds needed to acquire development land – at its current use value – so that local plans can be fulfilled'. It also looked to setting up a new Rural Land Authority, which 'will administer rural land already publicly owned and begin to extend public ownership to tenanted land'.[51] But 1983 was the last time references to physical planning were included by the party in its manifestos dealing with housing, land and the countryside.

By the time of the 1987 general election, its commitment to 'Right to Buy' was reaffirmed as was its policy of maintaining mortgage tax relief. Its land policy was no longer framed in terms of compensation and betterment, but instead was encompassed within general environmental measures designed to protect the countryside and the green belt. It adopted a partnership approach to the inner cities, including restoring powers to local authorities which were encouraged to collaborate with the private sector.[52] Demands for the nationalisation of land were noticeable by their absence after 1983. When Michael Foot addressed the Socialist Countryside Group in 1983, he made no mention of the common ownership of land but was more concerned to condemn membership of the Common Market and its detrimental effect on the environment and small farmers.[53] Left-wing pressure for land nationalisation also failed to attract any significant parliamentary support. In 1985 Tony Benn introduced a private members bill which sought the public ownership of land valued at over £250,000. But he was criticised by the Labour Land Campaign,

51 Labour Party Manifesto, 1983.
52 Labour Party Manifesto, 1987.
53 Michael Foot Papers (L38/7).

led by Dave Wetzel, a councillor for the Greater London Council, of 'going too far' and by a fellow MP for causing electoral damage by publishing his bill just before a by-election. Benn noted that the Labour Land Campaign was more interested in taxation of land values.[54] He was the only Labour MP to give publicity to George Monbiot's 'The Land is Ours' campaign in 1996 in support of the Newbury Bypass protestors and in memory of 'the Diggers'.[55]

By the 1990s, the party had largely dropped any commitments to direct state intervention in the control and management of land. Centralised state control was replaced by a stronger emphasis on 'welfare to work', and income and wealth distribution through the tax system, which included subsidising rents through the benefits system rather than directly investing in housing built by local authorities. It had by this date fully accepted the role of the market.[56] In 1995, following the selection of Tony Blair as leader it 'abandoned its commitment to "common ownership" enshrined in Clause Four of the 1918 constitution and replaced it with policies to help the unemployed into work and the promotion of equality of opportunity through education and training. These policies became the defining features of New Labour.[57]

Thus by the time Labour was re-elected in 1997, the party had no interventionist planning policies in place to restrain the private market in land. Also, in the interests of controlling public expenditure, it did not lift the restrictions on local authority housebuilding, relying instead on subsidising rents through housing benefits. The period before the great crash of 2008 saw the peak of Gordon Brown's confidence in the City of London to end the 'boom and bust' cycle. In pursuing a deregulatory approach to financial services, including any development taxes on land, New Labour did not make any immediate attempts to get developers to share with local communities the enormous profits they made through getting planning permission, certainly not on a par with previous state interventions it had made before 1979.

However, at the end of their first term in office, the Labour government did begin to explore ways of intervening in the market for land in order to control house price inflation and encourage more housebuilding. The housing market had continued to overheat and contribute to a growing housing crisis. Ambitious if not unrealistic housebuilding targets were being consistently missed. Concerns about the negative effects of house price inflation on the economy in general also gave rise to a questioning of the effectiveness of planning gain. Section 106 agreements had always attracted considerable criticism for their inconsistency, unfairness and lengthy negotiating procedures, and for their bias towards private developers negotiating secret deals with local councils without proper democratic scrutiny. They were a major source of friction between developers and local authorities pursuing contradictory

54 Benn, *The End of an Era*, pp. 403–4, p. 416.
55 Benn, *Free at Last*, p. 314 and p. 368.
56 Thane, 'Labour and Welfare', pp. 113–15.
57 Harris, 'Labour's Political and Social Thought', p. 38; Fielding 'New Labour and the Past'.

objectives. In the absence of being able to build houses themselves, councils wanted to maximise the amount of affordable housing through negotiation, while developers sought to maximise their profits by reducing the level of affordable housing provided.

In response to these criticisms, the government published in 2002 a consultation document proposing the replacement of Section 106 agreements with standardised tariffs set by local authorities. This represented a move back to the policy of collecting some betterment at the point of granting planning permission. But this proposal was initially criticised by business interests, which saw the new tariffs as a 'backdoor way' of making developers pay for more local government, and surprisingly by environmentalists who believed the reforms would reinforce inequalities between English regions, hinder regeneration and undermine public trust in the planning system.[58] As a result standardised tariffs were replaced by the idea of an Optional Planning Charge as a partial replacement of planning gain. The Planning and Compulsory Purchase Act of 2004 allowed for the implementation of this compromise, an example perhaps of triangulated policy formation leading to a high degree of complexity. Meanwhile, as the housing crisis deepened, the Chancellor Gordon Brown commissioned Kate Barker, a member of the Bank of England's monetary policy committee, to investigate what was behind the lack of supply of housing. Why was the private sector not building more homes? Do developers limit supply and keep the price of land high, taking maximum advantage of the restrictions in land supply imposed by the planning system?

In her interim report, Barker noted that in order to maximise profits, developers did indeed control the rate of production and 'trickle out' no more than 100–200 houses a year from a large development.[59] She considered it vital that the provision of new houses should not be regarded 'as an opportunity for developers and landowners to make unduly large profits from the rising supply of permissions'.[60] But by the time of her final report in March 2004, her criticisms of property developers had been toned down. They were replaced by recommendations calling on local authorities to identify more land for development in return for a new revenue stream from a planning gain supplement. This tax was to be levied on landowners at the moment planning permission was approved.[61] Barker considered that the planning gain supplement, which was not dissimilar from previous attempts at land taxation, was more straightforward and fairer than the increasingly complex Section 106 negotiations that cause development to be regarded cynically at a local level. The initial response to the report was fairly positive. *The Times*,

---

58 *The Times*, 18 March, p. 46 and 8 July 2002, p. 38.
59 Barker, Review of Housing Supply Interim Report (December 2003).
60 Barker, 'The Political and Economic Case for a Planning Gain Supplement', p. 27.
61 Barker, *Housing Supply: Delivering Stability: Securing Our Future Housing Needs – Final Report.*

for example, remarked that it provided a way forward to soften the 'Nimby' tendency to oppose all forms of new development, which it considered was paralysing the current planning system.[62]

In December 2005 the government published its response to the Barker review. It declared that the opportunity for everyone to live in a decent home – at a price they can afford – is one of the most fundamental goals of government and it promised to extend home ownership to 75% as part of a strategy of delivering sustainable communities. It did not immediately support the proposal for a planning gain supplement ('in order to help finance the infrastructure needed to stimulate and service proposed growth, and ensure that local communities better share in the benefits that growth brings'), but issued a further consultation document to test opinion on the 'case for capturing land value uplift for the benefit of the wider community'.[63] Its main recommendation was that the solution to the housing crisis was to remove restrictions on the planning system and to encourage developers to build in such large numbers that prices would come down.[64]

This approach was very much in line with the view of private developers and their allies in the Conservative Party who had always publicly maintained that the planning system was responsible for delays in housebuilding and that it needed to be radically overhauled to speed up decisions.[65] John Gummer, the former Conservative Secretary of State for the Environment, argued at the time that

> The proper way to proceed is to make the planning process faster and more certain, to actively encourage development. A betterment tax is wrong in principle and like most things that are fundamentally wrong, it will always fail in practice. We should insist on the right to property as one of the fundamental supports of freedom and accept the planning system as an unfortunate necessity. Property must not be stolen from its rightful owners, even by men of goodwill with the best of intentions.[66]

The response to the consultation from private developers was predictably hostile. British Land (a FTSE 100 quoted property company) described the new tax as 'utter madness' and insisted that it would stifle development.[67] The British Property Federation called it unworkable and commissioned research with the Confederation of British Industry, the Home Builders Federation and the Royal Institute of Charted Surveyors which concluded that a windfall property tax would raise less cash than anticipated and was

---

62 *The Times*, 18 March 2004, p. 8.
63 Planning Gain Supplement: A Consultation. HM Treasury and ODPM, December 2005.
64 The Government's Response to Kate Barker's Review of Housing Supply (December 2005).
65 *The Times*, 9 December 2005, p. 2 (S1).
66 Gummer, 'The Moral Argument against a Development Levy', p. 88.
67 *The Times*, 6 October 2005, p. 58.

flawed.[68] The British Property Federation supported what it regarded as the more cost-effective tariff based approach instead of the proposed planning gain supplement, indicating that within the property lobby there was a degree of consensus about recovering some betterment for public benefit.[69] In support of this view, a review of housebuilding delivery, commissioned by the Department of Communities and Local Government in 2006, chaired by John Callcutt, the CEO of the builder Crest Nicholson, concluded that no action should be taken to force builders to act more quickly.[70]

Unable to reach a clear decision, the government issued a fresh consultation in July 2007 comparing the proposed planning gain supplement with tariff-type alternatives. By October the government had dropped the idea of a supplement altogether and replaced it with a new Community Infrastructure Levy as its preferred method of securing generalised contributions from developers. 'The Levy was essentially a halfway house between a formal land tax and a development based "Tariff System", with the essential difference that it was to be set locally through an examination process similar to that for development plans, known as financial viability assessments.'[71] The new levy was enacted through the Planning Act of 2008 and came into force in England and Wales in April 2010.

The Labour Party did look tentatively at other land reform measures, such as the generation of new towns or garden cities to solve the housing crisis. But it did not enact any specific legislation in this respect similar to the groundbreaking measures it introduced in 1945. In 2008, Gordon Brown proposed a series of new 'eco-towns' based on his admiration for the housing innovations he had seen on a visit to Hammarby Sjostad in Stockholm, Sweden. A test development in Bristol was approved to create five 'eco-towns' intended to house up to 100,000 people in homes with zero-carbon emissions.[72] However, these types of developments remained dependent on private sector investment. Although they included some affordable housing, they were in reality a pale imitation of the original concept of garden cities and new towns built on publicly acquired land and sharing in the benefits from a tax on land values.

In the meantime, of course, the unregulated growth in the market for housing and the miss-selling of subprime mortgages led to the financial crash of 2008. In the radically changed economic circumstances after 2008, the question of land reform took second place to bailing out the banks. In February 2010, in a decision to reassure property developers just a few months before the general election, the Conservative Party indicated that if they were elected they would abolish the Community Infrastructure Levy.[73]

---

68 *The Times*, 21 February, p. 44 and 20 September 2006, p. 51.
69 British Property Federation, *Don't Kill the Goose!*
70 Callcutt Review of Housebuilding Delivery (November 2007).
71 Dobson, 'Community Infrastructure Levy: Will It Deliver', p. 125.
72 Hunt, *Yesterday's Tomorrow*, pp. 58–9.
73 Conservative Party Green Paper – Open Source Planning (22 February 2010).

Radical housing reformers have been highly critical of New Labour's approach to housing and land reform. One accused it of 'relinquishing responsibility by removing any mechanism to get developers to share the massive profits they make with local communities'.[74] Others have described their policies as neoliberal and no different in practice to those pursued by the Conservative Party before 1997. 'The Blair and Brown governments believed that all they needed to do was to set higher housing targets, make councils grant more planning permissions and the new homes would be built', and when this did not happen they 'blamed councils for not allocating enough land for housing and not granting enough planning permissions ... despite in London there being "nearly four years" worth of planning consents in the development pipeline'.[75] But more mainstream economic opinion, represented by Kate Barker, continues to identify the availability of land as the fundamental problem. 'We need to have sufficient land released with planning permission, and also reduce landowners' expectations about how much of the benefit of increased values they will get.'[76]

Certainly, by the time it left office, the Labour government had not resolved the problem of how to increase housebuilding in an unregulated market for land, where private developers had, in practice, a very powerful hand in any negotiations with planning authorities over planning gain, including the level of private investment in affordable housing and community infrastructure. A critic of Gordon Brown's economic policy concluded that as prime minister 'he did nothing to apply a brake to the unsustainable property-led and consumer-led boom before the speculative bubble inevitably burst'.[77] Following the crash of 2008, political interest revived again in the taxation of land values as a practical response to the housing crisis. In a well-attended seminar organised by Vince Cable MP on behalf of the recently formed Coalition for Economic Justice, it was argued that

> the private appropriation of community-created site values is lethal in its effect on our economic arrangements, dooming every economic upswing to an ultimate collapse. To end this cycle of boom and bust it is vital that the Government has some control over the level of property prices. Land value taxation would give it that control.[78]

In 2010 the Liberal Democrats included in their manifesto a proposal to levy a tax on homes worth more than £2 million, but this was not included in the coalition programme agreed after the general election, no doubt sacrificed to the policy of austerity and the political difficulty involved in trying to reform

74 Minton, *Big Capital*, p. 39.
75 Bowie, *Radical Solutions to the Housing Supply Crisis*, pp. 54–5.
76 Barker, *Housing: Where's the Plan?* p. 85.
77 Lee, *Boom and Bust*, p. 248.
78 House of Commons Seminar on Land Value Taxation, 24 March 2009.

property taxes. The memory of how the poll tax helped bring Margaret Thatcher down in 1990 was no doubt a strong reminder of the risks involved.

Land policies since 2010 and options for reform

After 2010 there have been no new legislative approaches to the continuing problem of land hoarding, property speculation and the spiralling cost of housing and land. The price of land is now far in excess of the levels reached during the speculative booms of the 1960s and 1980s, with prices having increased by almost a 1,000% since 1945 and over 400% since 1995.[79] The Conservative government continued with a policy of privatisation. It also tried to further simplify the planning system in favour of private developers. However, despite promises to the contrary, the coalition government retained the Community Infrastructure Levy conscious of the need to mitigate the worse effects of property speculation. It introduced a number of relatively small changes through the Localism Act 2012, allowing some of the levy collected by local authorities to be passed to neighbourhood groups for local development schemes. The levy has been gradually taken up by number of local authorities seeking to fund infrastructure, most notably in London where it contributed to the Crossrail project. It is a charge payable after planning permission has been obtained and when development commences and is based on a financial viability assessment similar to those carried out for development control purposes. In 2010, it was anticipated that the levy would raise between £564 and £831 million a year and that it would be adopted by over two-thirds of local authorities.[80]

But its effectiveness in influencing the market for land has been questioned by radical housing reformers.[81] It has certainly not prevented the housing crisis, especially in London and the South East from deteriorating even further and now spreading to other areas of the country experiencing rising land costs and speculative redevelopment. Student housing, for example, had become a new source of profits for hedge funds and other institutional investors, following the introduction of student loans. This housing crisis not only affects low-income groups concentrated in a declining and deregulated social housing sector, where up to a third of tenants are dependent on housing benefit and where subletting is creating slum conditions and an environment where the human trafficking of migrant labour flourishes. It is also leading to unprecedented levels of poverty amongst sections of the middle classes

79 Ryan-Collins et al., *Rethinking the Economics of Land and Housing*, pp. 9–10; Hilber, 'UK Housing and Planning Policies'; Knoll, Schularick and Steger, 'No Price Like Home: Global House Prices, 1870–2012'; ONS, *The UK National Balance Sheet: 2017 Estimates*.

80 Dobson, 'Community Infrastructure Levy: Will It Deliver', p. 126; Bentley, *The Land Question*, pp. 57–9.

81 Bowie, 'Revisiting the Land Issue', p. 117; Bowie, *Radical Solutions to the Housing Supply Crisis*, p. 73; Minton, *Big Capital*, pp. 34–47.

unable to become owner-occupiers, giving rise to campaigning groups like 'Generation Rent'. 'Today, 11 million people in Britain rent privately in an overlapping series of submarkets ranging from the poor conditions and slum housing at the bottom end to student accommodation, micro "pocket living" flats, apartments for professionals and luxury housing at the top.'[82]

Despite these conditions, the scope for change remains limited. Contemporary mainstream land reform now encompasses a range of options covering taxation policy, and in particular attempts to speed up development control in order to release more land for housing. But there is little consensus about the way forward. Nor is there any new funding being made available in a period of austerity. There was no serious attempt to recover the 'unearned increment' for the community, apart from the relatively limited Community Infrastructure Levy which in practice favours private developers. Where reforms have been proposed, especially ones recommending changes to the tax system, but this has given rise to political inertia and problems of implementation given the scale of potential winners and losers involved in any change. Those arguing for the introduction of a land value tax have had to acknowledge that the issue has all the hallmarks of a political minefield: 'large numbers of people would be affected by any change; the status quo is seen to be unsatisfactory but there is little consensus about the appropriate response; and public understanding is low.'[83]

In opposition, the Labour Party promised to introduce a 'mansions tax', which it argued would be banded like the community charge, with individuals on low incomes able to defer payment until the property changed hands. It was calculated that this could raise £1.2 billion, and that homes worth between £2 or £3 million would each pay about £3,000 a year.[84] The party also commissioned a further housing review, chaired by Sir Michael Lyons, a former local authority chief executive and chairman of the BBC.[85] Like the earlier Barker Report, its main recommendation was to speed up the planning process to achieve an annual housebuilding target of 200,000. It was therefore strongly welcomed by the British Property Federation. But it avoided addressing the difficult financial issue of whether councils should be allowed to borrow more for direct housebuilding and how this might be funded. This was a time when housing benefit continued to subsidise landlords to over £20 billion a year and rising.

The Lyons Report also supported the call for a new generation of garden cities. After 2010 and largely in response to the housing crisis, there was a revival of academic and political interest in the idea, although there was disagreement about how they should be delivered and whether they should

82 Minton, *Big Capital*, pp. 102–3.
83 Brooks, 'Commentary', p. 54, in Maxwell and Vigor (eds.), *Time for Land Value Tax*.
84 *Land Value Taxation*, House of Commons Library (17 November 2014), p. 1.
85 *The Lyons Housing Review: Mobilising across the Nation to Build the Houses Our Children Need* (October 2014).

be funded by the public sector or by private investment.[86] The *Centre for Policy Studies* recommended that the private sector should be responsible for designing, funding and building new garden cities as part of a simplified planning process.[87] In contrast, the Town and Country Planning Association recommended the establishment of development corporations with strong delivery powers, funded by a mixture of public and private funds.[88] Other academic opinion argued that it was not within the skill set of the private market to deliver such new settlements and that the public sector should be given responsibility with government funding.[89] A group of economists put forward a case for sharing the uplift in the value of land more equitably to fund and make new garden cities happen.[90] In response to this pressure, the Deputy Prime Minister, Nick Clegg, announced in 2014, the government's intention to initiate three new garden cities of 15,000 houses each, starting with Ebbsfleet in Kent.[91] But it provoked a response from the Campaign to Protect Rural England, which maintained that new housing should be built on brownfield sites and that the countryside and the green belt should be protected from 'anonymous, soul-less, land-hungry housing estates'.[92] In 2017, the Conservative government published a White Paper on housing which recommended the introduction of legislation to allow for locally accountable New Town Development Corporations to help bring forward large-scale *private* developments, approved by streamlined planning procedures.[93] There was no mention of public housing, a concept rendered almost redundant.

After losing the general election in 2015, the Labour Party commissioned yet another report into the decline of home ownership, this time chaired by the property developer Peter Redfern, the CEO of the builder Taylor Wimpey. Published in November 2016, the report confirmed the party as a long-term champion of home ownership. It again identified a need to speed up planning in order to release more land for housing.[94] In the same year and pursuing broadly the same agenda, the new Conservative government, ruling without the constraining influence of the Liberal Democrats, enacted the Housing and Planning Act 2016. This extended the 'Right to Buy' to housing associations tenants and weakened town and country planning by allowing private companies to compete with local authority planning departments to deliver development control, amongst other changes to support private developers.

86 *Garden Cities, Towns and Villages*, House of Commons Briefing Paper, July 2017.
87 Centre for Policy Studies, *Simplified Planning*, May 2013.
88 Town and Country Planning Association, *The Art of Building a Garden City*, July 2014.
89 GVA Research Bulletin, *Unlocking Garden Cities*, March 2014.
90 *The Independent*, 24 January 2014.
91 *The Guardian*, 14 April 2014.
92 Campaign to Protect Rural England, *Planting the Seeds for Real Garden Cities* (May 2015).
93 Fixing Our Broken Housing Market, February 2017 (White Paper).
94 Redfern Review into the Decline of Homeownership (November 2016).

This legislation has been described by one radical housing reformer as the final abandonment of the fundamental principles of the post-war consensus established by the Town and Country Planning Act of 1947.[95]

As we have seen, the financial crash of 2008 was the catalyst for a revival of interest in the taxation of land values. Following the seminar organised by the Coalition for Economic Justice in 2009, the Institute of Fiscal Studies published in 2011 the influential *Mirrlees Review* into the tax system, which in terms of land reform, recommended the abolition of stamp duty and the reform of council tax based on up-to-date values on domestic property. It also proposed a land tax for business and agricultural land to replace business rates and stamp duty on non-domestic property.[96] Housing reformers have made similar taxation recommendations, including increasing inheritance tax, reintroducing Schedule A income tax on income from land, or reforming council tax into 'a national land and property tax' similar to the new land tax introduced in Ireland.[97] Other commentators addressing the dysfunction at the root of the housing crisis have advocated repealing the Land Compensation Act of 1961, a Conservative Party measure which enshrined the right of land-owners – in the case of compulsory purchase by the state – 'to be reimbursed not only for the value of their site in its current use but for any prospective use to which it might be put in the future (Hope value)'. Such a reform would allow the state to purchase land at existing use value and would 'loosen up the land market, prevent hoarding and douse speculation' while 'protecting private property'.[98]

Both the Labour Party and the Liberal Democrats advocated a Mansions Tax while in opposition. But as we have seen any tax reform relating to property is fraught with difficulties in terms of implementation, especially if it involves valuing land separately from the property built on it. In 2011, the Institute of Fiscal Studies usefully summarised the case for and against land value taxation, and concluded that

> There are significant difficulties to implementing the tax in practice – principally the need to value land separately from buildings, when most market transactions are for plots of land and the property situated on it. There are also concerns that a tax of this nature would penalise home owners on low incomes, particularly if trends in house prices have meant the value of someone's home has grown significantly faster than their income.[99]

---

95 Bowie, *Radical Solutions to the Housing Supply Crisis*, p. 12; Minton, *Big Capital*, pp. 46–7.
96 Institute of Fiscal Studies, *Tax by Design.*
97 Bowie, *Radical Solutions to the Housing Supply Crisis*, p. 165; Dorling, *All That Is Solid*, pp. 305–17.
98 Bentley, *The Land Question*, p. 2 and pp. 94–5.
99 Adam, *Land and Property Taxation*; see also *Land Value Taxation*, House of Commons Library (17 November 2014).

Summary

This pessimistic conclusion demonstrates quite clearly that throughout the history of land reform outlined in this book, the scale and complexity of the workload implications of administrative attempts to value land separately from the buildings on it, had always been underestimated by reformers and presented particular difficulties to valuation staff in central or local government departments. It has been a major constraint on policies seeking to tax land values, especially any levy on the unimproved value of land. It proved to be the Achilles heel of Lloyd George's attempt to undertake an evaluation of all land in order to implement his People's Budget in 1909.[100] Furthermore, the original idea of Henry George's single tax replacing all other types of taxation, has been progressively undermined during the twentieth century as public expenditure has grown way beyond nineteenth-century expectations. Land taxation has remained one of many possible new sources of potential state revenue. But other forms of taxation have proved to be more attractive alternatives when compared to the complexity involved in introducing the rating of site values, especially in the absence of a central register of land identifying ownership as a first and necessary step to aid collection of any land-based tax. Moreover, the growth of owner-occupation and the extraordinary ideological influence of home ownership make any attempt to radically change systems for taxing property, especially council tax, stamp duty or taxation of land values, fraught with electoral complexities leading to political inertia. The failure since 1991 to update the valuation of property for council tax purposes to reflect current values is a telling example of this inertia in practice.

The one area where there appears to be some degree of political consensus is the proposal for a central register of landownership, although private property interests are largely opposed. This has been a long-standing demand of land reformers since the nineteenth century if not before. The Conservative Party manifesto in 2017 promised to 'digitise planning processes and compile an open database of land ownership, forming "the largest repository of open land data in the world"'.[101] Lord Hailsham, who as Lord Chancellor under Thatcher, regarded the failure to create a transparent system of land registration, a task imposed by the 1925 Law of Property Act, as a 'recurring public scandal'.[102] But large-scale landowning interests had always sought to block a compulsory public register which could be used for planning or taxation purposes. The CLA had advised its members in 1991 that if they did not want the public to discover ownership they 'could vest the land in nominees to hold on their behalf'.[103] The *Guardian* doubted whether the 2017 manifesto promise would get past the landed interests within the Conservative Party.[104]

100 Offer, *Property and Politics*, pp. 363–9.
101 Conservative Party Manifesto, 2017.
102 Lewis, *Lord Hailsham: A Life*, p. 287.
103 Country Landowners' Association, *Registration of Title of Land*.
104 *The Guardian*, 31 May 2017.

The scope for land reform through mainstream politics in twenty-first century England is therefore limited. It is not only constrained by the ideological influence of home ownership (the triumph of private property), a belief shared across the political spectrum underpinning the concept of a property-owning democracy, but by the economic policy of austerity, which prevents any major public investment in social housing. The search for new sources of funding, such as a tax on the windfall profits of property developers, is unlikely to be realised in the near future. The Community Infrastructure Levy is an effective mechanism for private property developers to control the market for land. But it is a pale imitation of previous attempts by post-war Labour governments to recover the unearned increment for the community. Although neoliberalism as a body of economic belief is now under ideological attack following the crash of 2008, the interests of private property remains secure if a little less triumphant, protected by mainstream political opinion which sees home ownership as a defence against economic insecurity and as a natural right in a democratic society.

10 Conclusion

Before 1914 land reform occupied a central place in the political programmes of mainstream party politics to an extent that public opinion would find difficult to understand today. One important radical strand of such reform was the aim to recover the 'unearned increment' to pay for increasing government spending, as a possible substitute for other forms of taxation, and as an answer to a wide range of economic and social problems affecting both rural and urban areas. It did not threaten the principle of private ownership. The foundations of this policy were based on a long-standing tradition of radical agrarianism, influenced by theories of natural rights, and laissez-faire political economy with deep roots in English history. The demand for the taxation of site values on unimproved land, together with the policy of creating rural smallholdings, reached its climax with Lloyd George's Peoples Budget of 1909 and his land campaign of 1912 to 1914.

But the impact of the First World War, together with the mass sale of aristocratic land-holdings and the spread of owner-occupation after the war, downplayed the question of concentrated aristocratic landownership as a focus of radical political opposition. The extension of the franchise to all adult males and women over 30 in 1918 broke, to a large extent, the link between property and voting rights. The strength of this connection had been a major feature of radical land reform in the nineteenth century. The land question also dropped out of history after 1918 as the landed aristocracy withdrew from political involvement on various levels. Despite their political defeat, many of these aristocratic families have in fact survived through state support and diversification. They continue to exercise significant economic power through their ownership of land, alongside the role of land developers and property speculators. For contemporary critics of neoliberalism 'this landed developer interest takes an active role in making and remaking capitalism's geography as a means to enhance its income and its power'.[1]

1 Harvey, *The Enigma of Capital and the Crises of Capitalism*, p. 181.

By the outbreak of the Second World War, the policy of taxing the unimproved value of land no longer attracted political support as a panacea for a range of economic and social problems, including unemployment, agricultural depression and the general health and well-being of the nation. It had been largely replaced by growing support for town and country planning and the taxation of rising land values in urban areas as a means of generating additional income for local authorities. Land reform had moved in the direction of compensation to landowners and the collection of betterment, and away from taxing the landed aristocracy to extinction. Moreover, by 1939 taxation of land values had become identified with the failed policies of a diminished Liberal Party remaining loyal to an earlier tradition of radical agrarianism. For the Labour Party, more centralised solutions based on state planning were now necessary to address the problem of economic depression and distressed agricultural and industrial areas.

It took the impact of the Second World War to resurrect the question of land reform and move it in new directions. The impact of the Blitz saw the rebirth of interest in compensation and betterment as a way of controlling property speculation in bombed sites. The war ensured that town and country planning would become one of the planks of post-war reconstruction. It also demonstrated the effectiveness of state intervention in the control and management of land in support of the war effort. But this did not extend as far as nationalising all land. By the end of its participation in the wartime coalition, the Labour Party had retreated from this policy which had always remained a long-term objective stated clearly in its constitution. The experience of wartime administration had proved to its leadership that it was not politically necessary to threaten owner-occupation (in either town or country), nor economically efficient to take over all land to achieve agricultural efficiency. Nor was general state ownership a requirement of effective town and country planning nor a means of preventing speculation in land for reconstruction. Although the cost the state would have to pay for land for post-war reconstruction proved to be extremely controversial and nearly brought the coalition to a premature end in 1944, it also demonstrated the complexity involved in the state intervening in the market for land, where an increasingly large proportion of the population were owner-occupiers in both rural and urban areas.

The programme of legislation which the Labour government introduced after 1945 was built on the experience of their leaders during the wartime coalition. It was also a response to the economic and social conditions prevailing after the war. In terms of land reform, it was influenced by the recommendations of the Uthwatt Report on compensation and betterment. This report linked the question of taxing the unearned increment to the granting of permission for town and country planning purposes. The government therefore married the traditional policy of land taxation to a system of land-use control, rather than seek to tax the unimproved value of land itself through the traditional policy of site value rating. It rejected land nationalisation in favour of the nationalisation of development rights through a betterment levy of 100%. But, unfortunately, it did not anticipate the effect such a policy would have on the private market for land. It also ran out of time to carry through with the reforms, which some commentators said were beginning to work. But the failure of the financial clauses of the 1947 Town and Country Planning Act highlighted, in more general terms, the contradiction contained within a 'mixed economy' where land remained in private ownership, but where the state was not powerful enough to control the market in the public interest.

The Conservatives were ideologically opposed to the compensation and betterment aspects of the Town and Country Planning Act of 1947. This opposition was based on a general defence of private property rights, linked to ideas of personal freedom. They were not necessarily opposed to taxing development land at a level that did not hinder the market in a mixed economy. They eventually acceded to the interests of unfettered private property by returning to a free market in land by the end of the 1950s. However, this ideological support for a free market in land helped to create the circumstances for an unforeseen and unprecedented boom in property and land prices during the late 1950s and early 1960s. It was the widespread scandal of property speculation and the unprecedented rise in the price of land for housing and other developments, combined with the extraordinary political animosity it generated for the Conservative Party in the early 1960s and then again in the mid-1970s, that revived Labour Party enthusiasm in making two further attempts to recover the 'unearned increment' for the community. The party remained loyal to the idea of taxing land values based on a tradition of reform that could be traced back to the influence of John Stuart Mill and Henry George.

But the perennial problem of how to value land in the absence of a central register of ownership made this policy unworkable in practice, as did other practical administrative and largely unforeseen difficulties involved in trying to implement positive planning in a mixed economy. The Labour Party's attempt to solve the problem of compensation and betterment during the 1960s and 1970s failed for a combination of ideological and administrative reasons. It underestimated the workload implications at a central and local level. The idea of positive planning was not clearly enough defined or resourced to prove effective. Also, the general economic circumstances and crises of this period contributed to their failure. It was, however, the spread of owner-occupation, and changing patterns of land tenure after 1950 that made any attempts to control land use in the wider public interest a complex issue of policy, generating too many winners and losers for governments to take the risk of embarking on radical land reform, either via taxation or physical planning.

This book has argued that the primary cause of this failure was the ideological difference between the two main governing parties on the question of rights to land and wider issues relating to the role of property and the meaning of freedom in a democratic society. The direction of land reform after 1979 supports this thesis. Strong private property rights became a defining feature of neoliberal ideology in the last quarter of the twentieth century. But the strength of this ideology together with the way housing was financialised as an investment in a globalised economy contributed to uncontrolled speculation in land and led to the financial crash of 2008 and the current housing crisis. It remains to be seen how far these developments give rise to renewed demands for land reform. In terms of mainstream politics, the scope for reform is limited, although the Labour Party under the new leadership of Jeremy Corbyn might raise expectations. It is not clear how far the property speculator has now replaced the landed aristocrat as a focus of radical political opposition at the beginning of the twenty-first century. Finance capitalism has certainly taken the place of the aristocratic landowner as the enemy of progressive politics. Given the important changes in the pattern of landownership and tenure since the 1980s, and especially the decline of owner-occupation and the growth of the private rented sector in the first decade of this century, the Conservative Party may need to reinvent itself as more than the party of landlords and free enterprise. In the light of the growth of the private rented sector, progressive politics may be rejuvenated by championing the private tenant in reclaiming some control over land and housing as a natural right. The undermining of leasehold rights (highlighted by recent scandals of increasing charges made by freeholders) can only add to the pressure for reform.

In terms of the future, it is more likely that opposition to the triumph of private property will come from outside mainstream politics, although recent changes in the Labour Party opposing austerity and neoliberalism could provide the foundation for renewed attempts at land reform. Extra-parliamentary opposition can be described as falling within the scope of 'The Right to the City' movement, encompassing various attempts to combat the way urban areas in particular are being redeveloped by corporate financial interests, including the way public spaces are being privatised. The extent of major redevelopment schemes in London has emerged as a controversial political issue, now spreading to other built-up areas. The 'Right to the City' has been usefully described by Anna Minton in her critique of the role of 'Big Capital' in London; by the anthropologist David Harvey in his analysis of the growth of oppositional movements to neoliberalism; and by Alexander Vasudevan in his account of contemporary urban squatting.[2] For Minton,

> The politics of space is replacing traditional politics of class. The old hierarchy of upper, middle and working class, … no longer holds up in the face of a property-based economy where the income from rent far

---

2 Minton, *Big Capital*; Harvey, *A Brief History of Neoliberalism*; see also his *Rebel Cities* and *Spaces of Hope*; Vasudevan, *The Autonomous City*; A Verso Report, *The Right to the City* (London: Verso, 2017).

exceeds economic growth and wages.... But as spatial injustice sweeps the city, there is growing support for an alternative approach, based on the idea of the 'Right to the City', which is able to point towards a way out of the housing crisis, bring down prices and strengthen communities. A profoundly inclusive vision, its great strength is that it provides a framework for alternatives to the extreme emphasis on market conditions. It is based on widespread democratic participation and the reinvigoration of a culture of local politics that includes rather than excludes local people and communities.[3]

It remains to be seen how far this plea for democratic renewal in the face of powerful financial and property interests will succeed and on what scale. In current political terms, it is not likely that support for taxation of land values will be translated into effective legislative change. It would need to overcome some of the significant historical problems of implementation described in this book. But will other non-mainstream developments be able bring about a democratic revival strong enough to withstand the economic power of 'Big Capital'? For example, will community land trusts based on public ownership of land start to provide an alternative model to private ownership? Will local communities be able to exercise democratic control over the use of land in the way that land reformers in Scotland are hoping for – land still largely owned by aristocratic landed interests? Will local authorities be able to support self-build schemes as a radically different model of urban development to that offered by property developers? Will squatting movements, which have been largely hidden from history, survive in the face of legal and political hostility? Will a Labour government committed to radical land reform in the future be able to withstand the economic power of landed interests and their control over the market for land?

The depth of the current housing crisis has pushed the question of taxation of land up the political agenda. It may overcome the obstacles to radical land reform outlined in this book. Certainly, the extent of homelessness and rough sleeping, the lack of affordable housing, the remarkable inflation of land and property values and the undermining of the rights of leaseholders, has galvanised a range of different academic and political opinions into supporting the general principle of land taxation, although there are very few voices in favour of the more radical policy of land nationalisation. It remains to be seen if the demand for land reform will attract the same level of political interest today as it did in the late Victorian and Edwardian period, when concern about inequality and the concentration of wealth reached similar levels.

3 Minton, *Big Capital*, p. 111.

Bibliography

Primary sources

Manuscript collections

Public records (1940–1945)

CAB 65 – War Cabinet Minutes
CAB 66 – War Cabinet Memoranda
CAB 87 – War Cabinet Committees on Reconstruction
CAB 117 – War Cabinet Reconstruction Secretariat Files
HLG 43 – Local Government
HLG 80 – Committee on Land Utilisation in Rural Areas (Scott Committee)
HLG 81 – Expert Committee on Compensation and Betterment (Uthwatt Committee)
HLG 82 – Nuffield College Social Reconstruction Survey
PREM 4 – Confidential Papers Prime Minister's Office

Private papers

Lord Addison, Bodleian Library, Oxford
Attlee Papers, Bodleian Library, Oxford and Churchill College, Cambridge
Ernest Bevin MP, Churchill College, Cambridge
Hugh Dalton MP, British Library of Political and Economic Science, London
Michael Foot MP, People's History Museum, Manchester
Lord Hailsham, Churchill College, Cambridge
Philip Noel-Baker, Churchill College, Cambridge
William Piercy, British Library of Political and Economic Science, London
Lord Scott, Modern Records Centre, University of Warwick
John Silkin MP, Churchill College, Cambridge
Richard Stokes MP, Bodleian Library, Oxford

Other collections

Association of Municipal Corporations, University of Birmingham
BBC Written Archives, Caversham Park, Reading

Conservative Party Archives, Bodleian Library, Oxford
County Councils Association, University of Birmingham
Country Landowners' Association, Museum of English Rural Life, Reading
Labour Party Archives, People's History Museum, Manchester
Mass Observation, Harvester Microfiche, 1983
National Union of Agricultural Labourers, Museum of English Rural Life,
    Reading
Nuffield College Social Reconstruction Papers, Nuffield College, Oxford

Newspapers and periodicals

Country Life
Daily Herald
Estates Gazette
Land and Liberty
Property Owners' Gazette
Property Owners' Journal
The Chartered Surveyor
The Economist
The Guardian
The Independent
The Land Worker
The Political Quarterly
The Spectator
The Times
Town and Country Planning
Tribune

Secondary sources

Official papers and other reports (in chronological order)

Hansard, *Parliamentary Debates*
Hansard, *House of Lords Debates*
(1916) *The Settlement or Employment on the Land in England and Wales of Discharged
    Sailors and Soldiers (Verney Committee)*, Cd. 8182.
(1918) *First Report of the Committee of the Ministry of Reconstruction Dealing with
    Law and Practice Relating to the Acquisition and Valuation of Land for Public
    Purposes*, Cd. 8998.
(1918) *Report of the Work of the Ministry of Reconstruction*, Cd. 9231.
(1918) *Second Part of the Report of the Agricultural Policy Committee*, Cd. 9079.
(1940) *Royal Commission on the Distribution of the Industrial Population*, Cmd. 6153.
(1941) *Report of the Expert Committee on Compensation and Betterment (Uthwatt
    Report) – Interim*, Cmd. 6291.
(1942) *Committee on Land Utilisation in Rural Areas (Scott Report)*, Cmd. 6378.
(1942) *Report of the Expert Committee on Compensation and Betterment (Uthwatt
    Report) – Final*, Cmd. 6386.

(1944) *The Control of Land Use*, Cmd. 6537.

(1944) *Statistics Relating to the War Effort of the United Kingdom*, Cmd. 6564.

(1945) *Third Report from the Select Committee on National Expenditure (1944–45). Release of Requisitioned Land and Building.*

(1945) *National Parks in England and Wales (Report by John Dower)*, Cmd. 6628.

(1946) *Interim Report of the New Towns Committee*, Cmd. 6759; *Second Interim Report*, Cmd. 6794; *Final Report*, Cmd. 6876.

(1947) *Explanatory Memorandum on the Town and Country Planning Bill*, Cmd. 7006.

(1947) *Report of the National Parks Committee*, Cmd. 7121.

(1947) *Footpaths and Access to the Countryside: Report of the Special Committee*, Cmd. 7207.

(1947) *Post-War Contribution of British Agriculture to the Saving of Foreign Exchange*, Cmd. 7072.

(1949) *First Report of the Advisory Council on Smallholdings (Ministry of Agriculture and Fisheries).*

(1950) *Advisory Committee on Allotments and Report of the Committee on Domestic Food Production (Ministry of Agriculture and Fisheries).*

(1951) *Town and Country Planning: A Progress Report*, Cmd. 8204.

(1965) *The Land Commission*, Cmnd. 2771.

(1966) *Leasehold Reform in England and Wales*, Cmnd. 2916.

(1969) *Departmental Committee of Inquiry into Allotments (Thorpe Report)*, Cmnd. 4166.

(1973) *Defence Lands, Report of the Defence Lands Committee, 1971–73 (Nugent Report).*

(1974) *Land*, Cmnd. 5730.

(1977) *Policy for the Inner Cities*, Cmnd. 6845.

(1979) *Report of the Committee of Inquiry into Agricultural Land Acquisition and Occupancy (Northfield Report)*, Cmnd. 7599.

(1981) *Planning Gain, Report by the Property Advisory Group.*

(1996) *Household Growth: Where Shall We Live*, Cm. 3471.

(1999) *The Right to Buy*, Wilson, Research Paper 99.36.

(2003) Kate Barker, *Review of Housing Supply Interim Report.*

(2004) Kate Barker, *Housing Supply: Delivering Stability: Securing Our Future Housing Needs – Final Report.*

(2005) *Planning Gain Supplement: A Consultation*, HM Treasury and ODPM.

(2005) *The Government's Response to Kate Barker's Review of Housing Supply.*

(2007) Callcutt, *Review of Housebuilding Delivery.*

(2009) *Seminar on Land Value Taxation*, House of Commons Library.

(2011) Institute of Fiscal Studies, *Tax by Design: The Mirrlees Review.*

(2013) Office of National Statistics (ONS), *A Century of Home Ownership and Renting in England and Wales.*

(2014) *Land Value Taxation*, House of Commons Library.

(2014) *The Lyons Housing Review: Mobilising across the Nation to Build the Houses Our Children Need.*

(2016) *Redfern Review into the Decline of Homeownership.*

(2017) *Garden Cities, Towns and Villages*, House of Commons Briefing Paper.

(2017) Office for National Statistics, *The UK National Balance Sheet: 2017 Estimates.*

Contemporary books, articles and pamphlets

Stuart Adam, *Land and Property Taxation* (London: Institute of Fiscal Studies, 2011).

Lord Christopher Addison, *A Policy for British Agriculture* (London: Victor Gollancz, 1939).

Viscount Astor and B. Seebohm Rowntree, *The Agricultural Dilemma* (London: P. S. King & Son, Ltd, 1935).

Viscount Astor and B. Seebohm Rowntree, *British Agriculture: The Principles of Future Policy* (London: Penguin Books, 1939).

Kate Barker, 'The Political and Economic Case for a Planning Gain Supplement' in Peter Bill (ed.), *Building Sustainable Communities: Capturing Land Development Value for the Public Realm* (London: Smith Institute, 2004).

Kate Barker, *Housing: Where's the Plan?* (London: London Publishing Partnership, 2014).

John Bateman, *The Great Landowners of Great Britain and Ireland* (Cambridge: Cambridge University Press, 2014 [1876]).

F. W. Bateson, *Towards a Socialist Agriculture* (London: Victor Gollancz, 1946).

Tony Benn, *The End of an Era: Diaries 1980–90* (London: Hutchinson, 1992).

Tony Benn, *Free at Last: Diaries 1991–2001* (London: Hutchinson, 2002).

Daniel Bentley, *The Land Question: Fixing the Dysfunction at the Root of the Housing Crisis* (London: Civitas, 2017).

Lord Beveridge, *New Towns and the Case for Them* (London: University of London Press, 1952).

Peter Bill (ed.), *Building Sustainable Communities: Capturing Land Development Value for the Public Realm* (London: Smith Institute, 2004).

Robert Blatchford, *Britain for the British* (London: Clarion Press, 1908).

Geoffrey Boumphrey, *Town and Country Tomorrow* (London: Thomas Nelson & Sons, Ltd, 1940).

Bow Group, *Let Our Cities Live – A Pamphlet on Town Planning* (December 1961).

British Property Federation, *Policy for Land* (London, 1976).

British Property Federation, *Don't Kill the Goose! The Case for Tariffs Not Tax* (London, 2005).

Gerald W. Butcher, *Allotments for All: The Story of a Great Movement* (London: Allen & Unwin, 1918).

Lord Butler, *The Art of the Possible* (London: Penguin Books, 1973).

Campaign to Protect Rural England, *Planting the Seeds for Real Garden Cities* (London: CPRE's *Countryside Voice* magazine, 2015).

Edward Carpenter, *England's Ideal* (London: Swan Sonnenschein, 1895).

Barbara Castle, *Castle Diaries, 1964–70* (London: Weidenfeld & Nicolson, 1984).

Barbara Castle, *Fighting All the Way* (London: Pan, 1994).

Centre for Policy Studies, *Simplified Planning* (London, May 2013).

W. S. Churchill, *War Speeches, Vol. 2* (London: Cassell, 1945).

G. D. H. Cole, *The Post-War Condition of Britain* (London: Routledge, 1956).

Jesse Collings, *Land Reform: Occupying Ownership, Peasant Proprietary and Rural Education* (London: Longmans, 1906).

Country Landowners' Association, *Registration of Title of Land* (London: CLA, 1991).

Richard Crossman, *Diaries of a Cabinet Minister, Vol. 1* (London: Henry Holt, 1976).

Hugh Dalton, *The Capital Levy Explained* (London: Labour Publishing, 1923).

Hugh Dalton, *Practical Socialism for Britain* (London: G. Routledge, 1935).

D. R. Denman, *Land in a Free Society* (London: Centre for Policy Studies, 1980).

Directorate of Army Education, *The British Way and Purpose. BWP Booklets 1–18* (London: The Directorate of Army Education, 1944).

John Dower et al., 'Positive Planning in Great Britain'. Paper submitted to the Royal Institute of British Architects, *Journal of the Royal Institute of British Architects* (13 July 1935).

A. C. Duff, *Britain's New Towns: An Experiment in Living* (London: Pall Mall Press, 1961).

John Gummer, 'The Moral Argument against a Development Levy' in Peter Bill (ed.), *Building Sustainable Communities: Capturing Land Development Value for the Public Realm* (London: Smith Institute, 2004).

GVA Research Bulletin, *Unlocking Garden Cities* (London: GVA, 2014).

E. R. C. Hadfield and J. E. MacColl, *Pilot Guide to Political London* (London: Pilot Press, Ltd, 1945).

A. D. Hall, *Reconstruction and the Land: An Approach to Farming in the National Interest* (London: Macmillan, 1941).

Peter Hetherington, *Whose Land Is Our Land? The Use and Abuse of Britain's Forgotten Acres* (Bristol: Policy Press, 2015).

J. L. Hodson, *Home Front: Being Some Account of the Journeys, Meetings and What Was Said to Me in and about England during 1942–1943* (London: Victor Gollancz, 1943).

Ebenezer Howard, *Garden Cities of Tomorrow* (London: Faber & Faber, 1970 [1902]).

Ebenezer Howard, *Tomorrow: A Peaceful Path to Real Reform* (London: Routledge, 2003 [1898]).

Anthony Hurd, *A Farmer in Whitehall: Britain's Farming Revolution, 1939–1950* (London: Country Life, Ltd, 1951).

Tudor Jones, *The Case for Land Value Taxation* (London: The Liberal Party, 1973).

Labour Research Department, *Land and Landowners: A Study of the Social Basis and Immediate Policies and Proposals Relating to Land and Reconstruction* (London: Labour Research Dept., 1944).

George Lansbury, *My Life* (London: Constable, 1928).

George Lansbury, *My England* (London: Constable, 1934).

David Lipsey, *Labour and the Land* (London: Fabian Society; Fabian Tract 442, 1973).

John Locke, *The Second Treatise of Government* (London: Awnsham & Churchill, 1690).

Mass Observation, *The Journey Home* (London: Advertising Service Guild, 1944).

H. J. Massingham, *The English Countryman: A Study of the English Tradition* (London: Batsford, 1942).

John Stuart Mill, *The Principles of Political Economy* (London: John W. Parker, 1848).

James Mirrlees et al., *Tax by Design* (Oxford: Oxford University Press, 2011).

H. V. Morton, *In Search of England* (London: Methuen, 1927).

C. S. Orwin, *Speed the Plough* (London: Penguin, 1942).

C. S. Orwin, 'Rural Land Ownership and Planning' in Harry Bryant Newbold (ed.), *Industry and Rural Life* (London: Faber & Faber, 1942).

C. S. Orwin, *The Problems of the Countryside* (Cambridge: Cambridge University Press, 1945).

C. S. Orwin and W. F. Drake, *Back to the Land* (London: P. S. King & Son, Ltd, 1935).

F. J. Osborn (ed.), *Planning and Reconstruction, 1944–45* (London and New York: Todd Publishing, 1945).

Thomas Paine, *Agrarian Justice* (London: T. G. Ballard, 1840 [1797]).

W. A. Robson, *The War and the Planning Outlook*, Rebuilding Britain Series No. 4 (London: Faber & Faber, 1941).

Dorothy L. Sayers, *Unnatural Death* (London: Ernest Benn, 1927).

Evelyn Sharp, *The Ministry of Housing and Local Government* (London: Allen & Unwin, 1969).

Thomas Sharp, *Towns and Countryside* (London: Oxford University Press, 1932).

Thomas Sharp, *English Panorama* (London: J. M. Dent & Sons, 1936).

George Bernard Shaw (ed.), *Fabian Essays in Socialism* (London: Fabian Society, 1889).

Marion Shoard, *The Theft of the Countryside* (London: Temple Smith, 1980).

Marion Shoard, *This Land Is Our Land* (London: Gaia Books, 1997).

Lewis Silkin, 'Town and Country Planning' in Herbert Tracey (ed.), *The British Labour Party, Vol. 11* (London: Caxton, 1948).

Adam Smith, *Wealth of Nations* (London: W. Strahan & T. Cadell, 1776).

Philip Snowden, *An Autobiography, Vol. 2, 1919–1934* (London: Nicholson & Watson, 1934).

Reginald George Stapledon, *Make Fruitful the Land: A Policy for Agriculture* (London: K. Paul, Trench, Trubner & Co., 1941).

A. G. Street, *Farmer's Glory* (London: Faber & Faber, 1932).

A. G. Street, *Farm Cottages and Post-War Farming* (London: J. M. Dent & Sons, 1943).

Margaret Thatcher, *The Path to Power* (London: Harper Collins, 1995).

Wyndham Thomas, 'A Review of Development Land Taxes in Britain since 1947' in Peter Bill (ed.), *Building Sustainable Communities: Capturing Land Development Value for the Public Realm* (London: Smith Institute, 2004).

Town and Country Planning Association, *The Art of Building a Garden City* (London: TCPA, July 2014).

Verso Report, *Right to the City* (London: Verso, 2017).

B. S. Vesey-Fitzgerald (ed.), *Programme for Agriculture* (London: Michael Joseph, 1941).

Josiah C. Wedgwood, *The Land Question: Taxation and Rating of Land Values* (London: Labour Party, 1925).

Josiah C. Wedgwood, *Memoirs of a Fighting Life* (London: Hutchinson, 1941).

Tom Williams, *Labour's Way to Use the Land* (London: Methuen, 1935).

Tom Williams, *Digging for Britain* (London: Hutchinson, 1965).

Clough Williams-Ellis, *England and the Octopus* (Portmeirion: Golden Dragon Books, 1928).

Clough Williams-Ellis, *Britain and the Beast* (London: J. M. Dent & Sons, 1938).

Patrick Wright, *The Village that Died for England* (London: Cape, 1995).

G. M. Young, *Country and Town: A Summary of the Scott and Uthwatt Reports* (London: Penguin, 1943).

Scholarly books

Paul Addison, *Road to 1945: British Politics and the Second World War* (London: Pimlico, 1994).

Paul Addison, *Now the War Is Over: A Social History of Britain* (London: Pimlico, 1995).

Peter Ambrose, *Whatever Happened to Planning* (London: Methuen, 1986).

Peter Ambrose and Bob Colenutt, *The Property Machine* (Harmondsworth: Penguin, 1975).

Robert V. Andelson (ed.), *Land Taxation around the World, Vol. 1* (London: Wiley-Blackwell, 2001).

J. Stuart Anderson, *Lawyers and the Making of English Land Law, 1832–1940* (Oxford: Clarendon Press, 1992).

Alan Armstrong, *Farmworkers: A Social and Economic History, 1770–1980* (London: Batsford, 1988).

Paul Balchin, Jeffery Kieve and Gregory Bull, *Urban Land Economics and Public Policy* (London: Macmillan, 1988).

Michael Ball, *Housing Policy and Economic Power: The Political Economy of Owner Occupation* (London: Methuen, 1983).

Susan Barrett and Patsy Healey, *Land Policy: Problems and Alternatives* (Aldershot: Gower, 1985).

Susan Barrett, Martin Boddy and Murray Stewart, *Implementation of the Community Land Scheme: Interim Report April 1978* (Bristol: University of Bristol, 1979).

Max Beer, *The Pioneers of Land Reform* (London: Forgotten Books, 2015).

John Benson, *The Working Class in Britain, 1850–1939* (London: Longman, 1989).

John Bew, *Citizen Clem: A Biography of Attlee* (London: Riverrun, 2016).

Martin Blinkhorn and Ralph Gibson (eds.), *Landownership and Power in Modern Europe* (London: Harper Collins, 1991).

Vic H. Blundell, *Labour's Flawed Land Acts, 1947–1976* (London: Economic and Social Science Research Council, 1993).

Alastair Bonnett and Keith Armstrong (eds.), *Thomas Spence: The Poor Man's Revolutionary* (London: Breviary Stuff Publications, 2014).

Duncan Bowie, *Radical Solutions to the Housing Supply Crisis* (Bristol: Policy Press, 2017).

Duncan Bowie, *The Radical and Socialist Tradition in British Planning: From Puritan Colonies to Garden Cities* (London: Routledge, 2017).

Jamie L. Bronstein, *Land Reform and Working-Class Experience in Britain and the United States, 1800–1862* (Stanford, CA: Stanford University Press, 1999).

Stephen Brook, *Labour's War: The Labour Party during the Second World War* (Oxford: Clarendon Press, 1992).

Jonathan Brown, *Agriculture in England: A Survey of Farming, 1870–1947* (Manchester: Manchester University Press, 1987).

Jeremy Burchardt, *Paradise Lost: Rural Idyll and Social Change since 1800* (London: I. B. Tauris, 2002).

Kevin Cahill, *Who Owns Britain? The Hidden Facts behind Landownership in the UK and Ireland* (Edinburgh: Cannongate, 2002).

Angus Calder, *The Myth of the Blitz* (London: Pimlico, 1992).

Angus Calder, *The People's War: Britain 1939–1945* (London: Pimlico, 1992).

John Campbell, *Lloyd George: The Goat in the Wilderness 1922–1931* (London: Faber & Faber, 1977).

David Cannadine, *The Decline and Fall of the British Aristocracy* (London: Picador, 1992).

David Cannadine, *G. M. Trevelyan: A Life in History* (London: Penguin, 1997).

Malcolm Chase, *The People's Farm: English Radical Agrarianism, 1775–1840* (Oxford: Clarendon Press, 1988).

Gordon E. Cherry, *Environmental Planning, 1939–1969, Vol. 2: National Parks and Recreation in the Countryside* (London: HMSO, 1975).

Gordon E. Cherry, *Birmingham: A Study in Geography, History and Planning* (Chichester: John Wiley & Sons, 1994).

Gordon E. Cherry, *Town Planning in Britain since 1900* (London: Wiley-Blackwell, 1996).

Gordon E. Cherry and Alan Rogers, *Rural Change and Planning* (London: E. & F. N. Spon, 1996).

Thomas Clarke and Christos Pitelis (eds.), *The Political Economy of Privatisation* (London: Routledge, 1993).

Catherine Ann Cline, *Recruits to Labour: The British Labour Party, 1914–1931* (New York: Syracuse University Press, 1963).

Andrew Fenton Cooper, *British Agricultural Policy, 1912–1936* (Manchester: Manchester University Press, 1989).

Andrew Cox, *Adversary Politics and Land: The Conflict Over Land and Property Policy in Post-War Britain* (Cambridge: Cambridge University Press, 1984).

Graham Cox, Philip Lowe and Michael Winter (eds.), *Agriculture: People and Policies* (London: Allen & Unwin, 1986).

Matthew Cragoe and Paul Readman (eds.), *The Land Question in Britain, 1750–1950* (Basingstoke: Palgrave Macmillan, 2010).

David Crouch and Colin Ward, *The Allotment: Its Landscape and Culture* (Nottingham: Five Leaves Publication, 1997).

J. B. Cullingworth, *Environmental Planning 1939–1969, Vol. 1: Reconstruction and Land Use Planning 1939–1947* (London: HMSO, 1975).

J. B. Cullingworth, *Environmental Planning 1939–1969, Vol. 3: New Towns Policy* (London: HMSO, 1979).

J. B. Cullingworth, *Environmental Planning 1939–1969, Vol 4: Land Values, Compensation and Betterment* (London: HMSO, 1980).

J. B. Cullingworth and V. Nadin, *Town and Country Planning in the UK*, 13th Edition (London: Routledge, 2002).

J. B. Cullingworth (ed.), *British Planning: 50 Years of Urban and Regional Policy* (London: Athlone Press, 1999).

Caroline Dakers, *Forever England: The Countryside at War* (London: I. B. Tauris, 2016).

Martin Daunton, *House and Home in the Victorian City* (London: Arnold, 1983).

Martin Daunton, *Just Taxes: The Politics of Taxation in Britain, 1914–1979* (Cambridge: Cambridge University Press, 2002).

Martin Daunton (ed.), *The Cambridge Urban History of Britain, Vol. 3, 1840–1950* (Cambridge: Cambridge University Press, 2000).

Peter E. Dewey, *British Agriculture in the First World War* (London: Routledge, 1989).

Peter E. Dewey, *War and Progress: Britain 1914–1945* (London: Longman, 1997).

Jeffry M. Diefendorf (ed.), *Rebuilding Europe's Bombed Cities* (London: Macmillan, 1990).

Bernard Donoughue and G. W. Jones, *Herbert Morrison: Portrait of a Politician* (London: Littlehampton Book Services, 1983).

Danny Dorling, *All That Is Solid: How the Great Housing Disaster Defines Our Times* (London: Penguin, 2014).

Roy Douglas, *Land, People and Politics* (London: Allison and Busby, 1976).

James W. Ely, Jr., *The Guardian of Every Other Right: A Constitutional History of Property Rights* (Oxford: Oxford University Press, 2008).

Martin Francis, *Ideas and Policies under Labour, 1945–1951: Building a New Britain* (Manchester: Manchester University Press, 1997).

Michael Freeden, *The New Liberalism: An Ideology of Social Reform* (Oxford: Clarendon Press, 1978).

George H. Gallup (ed.), *The Gallup International Opinion Polls: Great Britain, 1937–1975, Vol. 1, 1937–1964* (New York: Random House, 1976).

Patricia Garside, *Town Planning in London, 1930–1960* (London: University of London, 1980).

Howard Glennerster, *British Social Policy since 1945* (Oxford: Blackwell, 1995).

Robin Goodchild and Richard Munton, *Development and the Landowner: An Analysis of the British Experience* (London: Allen & Unwin, 1985).

Alexander Gray, *The Socialist Tradition: Moses to Lennon* (London: Longmans, 1946).

Clare Griffiths, *Labour and the Countryside: The Politics of Rural Britain* (Oxford: Oxford University Press, 2007).

David Grigg, *The Transformation of Agriculture in the West* (Oxford: Blackwell, 1992).

Reg Groves, *Sharpen the Sickle: A History of the Farm Workers Union* (London: Porcupine Press, 1949).

Peter Hall, *Urban and Regional Planning*, 3rd Edition (London: Routledge, 1992)

Peter Hall et al., *The Containment of Urban England, Vol. 2: The Planning System* (London: Allen & Unwin, 1973).

Peter Hall (ed.), *Land Values* (London: Sweet & Maxwell, 1965).

Graham Hallett (ed.), *Land and Housing Policies in Europe and the USA: A Comparative Analysis* (London: Routledge, 1988).

R. J. Hammond, *Food and Agriculture in Britain 1939–45: Aspects of Wartime Control* (Stanford, CA: Stanford University Press, 1954).

Dennis Hardy, *From Garden Cities to New Towns: Campaigning for Town and Country Planning, 1899–1946* (London: Routledge, 1991).

Dennis Hardy and Colin Ward, *Arcadia for All: The Legacy of a Makeshift Landscape* (London: Mansell, 1984).

Kenneth Harris, *Attlee* (London: Weidenfeld & Nicolson, 1982).

Royden Harrison, *Before the Socialists: Studies in Labour Politics, 1861–1881* (London: Routledge and Kegan Paul, 1965).

David Harvey, *Spaces of Hope* (Berkeley, CA: University of California Press, 2000).

David Harvey, *A Brief History of Neoliberalism* (Oxford: Oxford University Press, 2007).

David Harvey, *The Enigma of Capital and the Crises of Capitalism* (London: Profile Books, 2011).

David Harvey, *Rebel Cities: From the Right to the City to the Urban Revolution* (London: Verso, 2013).

David Harvey, *The Ways of the World* (London: Profile Books, 2017).

Junichi Hasegawa, *Replanning the Blitzed City Centre: A Comparative Study of Bristol, Coventry and Southampton, 1941–50* (Buckingham: Open University Press, 1992).

Christopher Hill, *The Experience of Defeat* (London: Bookmarks, 1984).

Christopher Hill, *The World Turned Upside Down* (London: Penguin, 1984).

Christopher Hill (ed.), *Winstanley: The Law of Freedom and Other Writings* (Harmondsworth: Pelican Books, 1973).

B. A. Holderness, *British Agriculture since 1945* (Manchester: Manchester University Press, 1985).

Alun Howkins, *Reshaping Rural England: A Social History* (London: Harper Collins, 1991).

Stephen E. Hunt, *Yesterday's Tomorrow: Bristol's Garden Suburbs*, 2nd Edition (Bristol: Bristol Radical History Group, 2015).

Stephen Inwood, *A History of London* (London: Macmillan, 1998).

Kevin Jefferys, *The Churchill Coalition and Wartime Politics* (Manchester: Manchester University Press, 1991).

Kevin Jefferys, *Anthony Crosland: A New Biography* (London: Richard Cohen Books, 1999).

Kevin Jefferys (ed.), *Labour and the Wartime Coalition: From the Diary of James Chuter Ede, 1941–1945* (London: Historian's Press, 1987).

Gareth Steadman Jones, *Languages of Class: Studies in English Working Class History, 1832–1982* (Cambridge: Cambridge University Press, 1983).

Gareth Steadman Jones, *Karl Marx: Greatness and Illusion* (London: Allen Lane, 2016).

David Kynaston, *Austerity Britain, 1945–1951* (London: Bloomsbury, 2007).

Land Registry, *A Short History of Land Registration in England and Wales* (London: HMLR, n.d.).

Simon Lee, *Boom and Bust: The Politics and Legacy of Gordon Brown* (Oxford: Oneworld, 2009).

Geoffrey Lewis, *Lord Hailsham: A Life* (London: Jonathan Cape, 1997).

Hok Lin Leung, *Redistribution of Land Values. A Re-Examination of the 1947 Scheme* (Cambridge: University of Cambridge Department of Land Economy, 1979).

Nathaniel Lichfield and Haim Darin-Drabkin, *Land Policy in Planning* (London: Allen & Unwin, 1980).

Andro Linklater, *Owning the Earth: The Transforming History of Land Ownership* (London: Bloomsbury, 2014).

Patrick McAuslan, *The Ideologies of Planning Law* (Oxford: Pergamon Press, 1980).

A. M. McBriar, *Fabian Socialism and English Politics, 1884–1918* (Cambridge: Cambridge University Press, 1962).

Alan Macfarlane, *The Origins of English Individualism: The Family, Property and Social Transition* (Oxford: Blackwell, 1978).

David H. McKay and Andrew W. Cox, *The Politics of Urban Change* (London: Croom Helm, 1979).

Ian McLaine, *Ministry of Morale: Home Front Morale and the Ministry of Information in World War II* (London: Allen & Unwin, 1979).

C. B. Macpherson, *The Political Theory of Possessive Individualism: Hobbes to Locke* (Oxford: Oxford University Press, 1962).

C. B. Macpherson, *Property: Mainstream and Critical Positions* (Oxford: Blackwell, 1978).

Charles Madge and Tom Harrison, *Britain by Mass Observation* (London: Penguin, 1939).

Peter Mandler, *The Fall and Rise of the Stately Home* (New Haven, CT: Yale University Press, 1997).

David Marquand, *Ramsay MacDonald* (London: Cape, 1997).

Oliver Marriott, *The Property Boom* (London: Hamish Hamilton, 1967).

Doreen Massey and Alejandrina Catalano, *Capital and Land: Landownership by Capital in Great Britain* (London: Edward Arnold, 1978).

Carin Martiin, Juan Pan-Montojo and Paul Brassley, *Agriculture in Capitalist Europe, 1945–1960: From Food Shortages to Food Surpluses* (London: Routledge, 2017).

David Matless, *Landscape and Englishness* (London: Reaktion Books, 1998).

R. J. Middleton, *The Formulation and Implementation of British Agricultural Policy, 1945–1951* (Bristol: University of Bristol, 1992).

J. L. Milne (ed.), *The National Trust: A Record of Fifty Years' Achievement* (London: Batsford, 1945).

Alan S. Milward, *War, Economy and Society, 1939–1945* (Berkeley, CA: University of California Press, 1979).

Anna Minton, *Big Capital: Who is London For?* (London: Penguin, 2017).

David Mitrany, *Marx against the Peasant: A Study in Social Dogmatism* (London: Weidenfeld & Nicolson, 1951).

Charles Moore, *Margaret Thatcher: Authorised Biography, Vol. 1* (London: Allen Lane, 2005).

Kenneth O. Morgan, *Labour in Power, 1945–1951* (Oxford: Oxford University Press, 1984).

Kenneth O. Morgan and Jane Morgan, *Portrait of a Progressive* (New York: Oxford University Press, 1980).

Alan Murie, *The Right to Buy: Selling Off Public and Social Housing* (Bristol: Policy Press, 2016).

Bruce K. Murray, *The People's Budget 1909/10. Lloyd George and Liberal Politics* (Oxford: Oxford University Press, 1980).

K. A. H. Murray, *Agriculture: History of the Second World War* (London: HMSO, 1955).

J. M. Neeson, *Commoners: Common Right, Enclosure and Social Change in England, 1700–1820* (Cambridge: Cambridge University Press, 1993).

Howard Newby, *Country Life: A Social History of Rural England* (London: Penguin, 1988).

Howard Newby, Colin Bell, David Rose and Peter Saunders, *Property, Paternalism and Power: Class Control in Rural England* (London: Hutchinson, 1978).

Sian Nicholas, *The Echo of War: Home Front Propaganda and the BBC, 1939–45* (Manchester: Manchester University Press, 1996).

Micheline Nilsen, *The Working Man's Green Space: Allotment Gardens in England, France and Germany, 1870–1919* (Charlottesville, VA: University of Virginia Press, 2014).

R. Norton-Taylor, *Whose Land Is It Anyway? How Urban Greed Exploits the Land* (Wellingborough: Turnstone, 1982).

Edward T. O'Donnell, *Henry George and the Crisis of Inequality: Progress and Poverty in the Gilded Age* (New York: Columbia University Press, 2015).

Avner Offer, *Property and Politics, 1870–1914* (Cambridge: Cambridge University Press, 1981).

Glen O'Hara, *Governing Post-War Britain: The Paradoxes of Progress, 1951–1973* (Basingstoke: Palgrave Macmillan, 2012).

Ian Packer, *Lloyd George, Liberalism and the Land: The Land Issue and Party Politics in England, 1906–1914* (Suffolk: Royal Historical Society, 2001).

Harold Perkin, *The Rise of Professional Society* (London: Routledge, 2002).

Richard Perren, *Agriculture in Depression, 1870–1940* (Cambridge: Cambridge University Press, 1995).

Thomas Piketty, *Capital in the Twenty-First Century* (Cambridge and London: Harvard University Press, 2014).

Ben Pimlott, *Hugh Dalton: A Life* (London: Harper Collins, 1995).

Richard Pipes, *Property and Freedom* (New York: Alfred Knopf, 1999).

Sidney Pollard, *The Development of the British Economy, 1914–1967* (London: Arnold, 1969).

A. R. Prest, *The Taxation of Urban Land* (Manchester: Manchester University Press, 1981).

John Ratcliffe, *Land Policy: An Exploration of the Nature of Land in Society* (London: Hutchinson, 1976).

Alison Ravetz, *Remaking Cities: Contradictions of the Recent Urban Environment* (London: Croom Helm, 1980).

Eric Reade, *British Town and Country Planning* (Milton Keynes: Open University Press, 1987).

Paul Readman, *Land and Nation in England: Patriotism, National Identity and the Politics of Land, 1880–1914* (London: Royal Historical Society, 2008).

Richard Ronald, *The Ideology of Home Ownership* (Hampshire: Palgrave Macmillan, 2008).

W. D. Rubenstein, *Men of Property: The Very Wealthy in Britain since the Industrial Revolution* (London: Social Affairs Unit, 2006).

Josh Ryan-Collins, Toby Lloyd and Laurie Macfarlane, *Rethinking the Economics of Land and Housing* (London: Zed Books Ltd, 2017).

Peter Scott, *The Property Masters: A History of the British Commercial Property Sector* (London: Routledge, 2015).

John Sheail, *Nature in Trust: The History of Nature Conservation in Britain* (London: Blackie, 1976).

Robert Skidelsky, *Politicians and the Slump* (London: Macmillan, 1967).

Tom Stephenson, *Forbidden Land: The Struggle for Access to Mountains and Moorland* (Manchester: Manchester University Press, 1988).

John Stevenson, *British Society, 1914–45* (London: Penguin, 1984).

John Stevenson, *Popular Disturbance in England, 1700–1832* (London: Routledge, 2014).

Nigel Taylor, *Urban Planning Theory since 1945* (London: Sage Publications, 1998).

Joan Thirsk, *Alternative Agriculture: A History* (Oxford: Oxford University Press, 1997).

E. P. Thompson, *Customs in Common* (London: Penguin, 1993).

E. P. Thompson, *The Making of the English Working Class* (London: Penguin, 2013).

F. M. L. Thompson, *English Landed Society in the Nineteenth Century* (London: Routledge and Kegan Paul, 1963).

Andy Thornley, *Urban Planning under Thatcherism: The Challenge of the Market* (London: Routledge, 1991).

Nick Tiratsoo, *Reconstruction, Affluence and Labour Politics: Coventry, 1945–60* (London: Routledge, 1990).

David Torrance, *Noel Skelton and the Property-Owning Democracy* (London: Biteback, 2010).

Alexander Vasudevan, *The Autonomous City: A History of Urban Squatting* (London: Verso, 2017).

Nicola Verdon, *Working the Land: A History of the Farmworkers in England from 1850 to the Present Day* (London: Palgrave, 2017).

Colin Ward, *Cotters and Squatters: Housing's Hidden History* (Nottingham: Five Leaves Publications, 2002).

Martin J. Weiner, *English Culture and the Decline of the Industrial Spirit, 1850–1980* (Cambridge: Cambridge University Press, 2004).

E. H. Whetham, *British Farming, 1939–1949* (London: Nelson & Sons, 1952).

Andy Wightman, *Scotland: Land and Power. The Agenda for Land Reform* (Edinburgh: Luath Press, 1999).

Andy Wightman, *The Poor Had No Lawyers: Who Owns Scotland* (Edinburgh: Birlinn, 2013).

Margaret Willes, *The Gardens of the British Working Class* (New Haven, CT: Yale University Press, 2015).

Raymond Williams, *The Country and the City* (London: Spokesman Books, 2011).

J. A. Yelling, *Slums and Redevelopment: Policy and Practice in England, 1918–1945, with Particular Reference to London* (New York: St. Martin's Press, 1992).

Ken Young and Patricia Garside, *Metropolitan London: Politics and Urban Change, 1837–1981* (London: Arnold, 1982).

Ken Young and Nirmala Rao, *Local Government since 1945* (Oxford: Oxford University Press, 1997).

Scholarly articles and book chapters

Patrick Abercrombie, 'The Preservation of Rural England', *Town Planning Review*, 12, 1 (1926).

Robert V. Andelson, 'Land Taxation around the World', *American Journal of Economics and Sociology*, 59, 5, Supplement (2000).

Richard Barras, Doreen Massey and Thomas Andrew Broadbent, 'Planning and Public Ownership', *New Society*, 748–9 (28 June 1973).

Abigail Beach and Nick Tiratsoo, 'The Planners and the Public' in Martin Daunton (ed.), *The Cambridge Urban History of Britain, Vol. 3, 1840–1950* (Cambridge: Cambridge University Press, 2000).

John Beckett and Michael Turner, 'End of the Old Order? F. M. L. Thompson, the Land Question, and the Burden of Ownership in England, c.1880–c.1925', *Agricultural History Review*, 55, 2 (2007).

Mark Blaug, 'Henry George: Rebel with a Cause', *European Journal of the History of Economic Thought*, 7, 2 (Summer, 2000).

Quentin Bone, 'Legislation to Revive Small Farming in England, 1887–1914', *Agricultural History Review*, 49, 4 (October 1975).

Duncan Bowie, 'Revisiting the Land Issue', *Journal of Urban Regeneration and Renewal*, 9, 2 (2016).

D. K. Britton, 'Agriculture' in G. D. N. Worswick and P. H. Ady (eds.), *The British Economy, 1945–1950* (Oxford: Clarendon Press, 1952).

Richard Brooks, 'Commentary' in Dominic Maxwell and Anthony Vigor (eds.), *Time for Land Value Tax* (London: Institute for Public Policy Research, 2005).

Malcolm Chase, 'Out of Radicalism: The Mid-Victorian Land Movement', *English Historical Review*, 106 (1991).

Malcolm Chase, 'Nothing Less Than a Revolution? Labour's Agricultural Policy' in Jim Fryth (ed.), *Labour's High Noon: The Government and the Economy, 1945–51* (London: Lawrence & Wishart, 1993).

Malcolm Chase, '"Wholesome Object Lessons": The Chartist Land Plan in Retrospect', *English Historical Review*, 118, 475 (February 2003).

Gordon E. Cherry, 'The Town Planning Act, 1919', *The Planner*, 60, 5 (May 1974).

Gregory Claeys, 'Paine's Agrarian Justice (1796) and the Secularisation of Natural Jurisprudence', *Bulletin of the Society for the Study of Labour History*, 52, 3 (November 1987).

Graham Cox, Philip Lowe and Michael Winter, 'From State Direction to State Regulation: The Historical Development of Corporatism in British Agriculture', *Policy and Politics*, 14, 4 (1986).

Aled Davies, '"Right to Buy": The Development of a Conservative Housing Policy, 1945–1980', *Contemporary British History*, 27, 4 (2013).

H. W. E. Davies, 'The Planning System and the Development Plan', in J. B. Cullingworth (ed.), *British Planning: 50 Years of Urban and Regional Policy* (London: Athlone Press, 1999).

John Davis, 'Macmillan's Martyr: The Pilgrim Case, the "Land Grab" and the Tory Housing Drive, 1951–59', *Planning Perspectives*, 23, 2 (2008).

Michael Dawson, 'The Liberal Land Policy, 1924–1929: Electoral Strategy and Internal Division', *Twentieth Century British History*, 2, 3 (1991).

Alan Day, 'The Case for Betterment Charges' in Peter Hall (ed.), *Land Values* (London: Sweet & Maxwell, 1965).

Tim Dixon, 'Urban Land and Property Ownership Patterns in the UK: Trends and Forces for Change', *Land Use Policy*, 26 (2009).

Tom Dobson, 'Community Infrastructure Levy: Will It Deliver?', *Journal of Planning and Environmental Law*, 13 (2012).

John Emms, 'The Community Land Act – A Requiem', *Journal of Planning and Environmental Law* (1980).

Steven Fielding, 'New Labour and the Past' in Duncan Tanner, Pat Thane and Nick Tiratsoo (eds.), *Labour's First Century* (Cambridge: Cambridge University Press, 2000).

Andrew Flynn, 'Agricultural Policy and Party Politics in Post-War Britain' in Graham Cox, Philip Lowe and Michael Winter (eds.), *Agriculture: People and Policies* (London: Allen & Unwin, 1986).

Patricia Garside, 'The Failure of Regionalism in 1940s Britain: A Re-Examination of Regional Plans, the Regional Idea and the Structure of Government' in Patricia Garside and Michael Hebbert (eds.), *British Regionalism, 1900–2000* (London: Mansell, 1989).

Bentley B. Gilbert, 'David Lloyd George: The Reform of British Landholding and the Budget of 1914', *Historical Journal*, 21 (1978).

Malcolm Grant, 'Britain's Community Land Act: A Post-Mortem', *Urban Law and Policy*, 2 (1979).

Malcolm Grant, 'Compensation and Betterment' in J. B. Cullingworth (ed.), *British Planning: 50 Years of Urban and Regional Policy* (London: Athlone Press, 1999).

David Grigg, 'Farm Size in England and Wales from Early Victorian Times to the Present', *Agricultural History Review*, 35, 2 (1987).

Graham Hallett and Richard Williams, 'Great Britain' in Graham Hallett (ed.), *Land and Housing Policies in Europe and the USA* (London: Routledge, 1988).

Jose Harris, 'Labour's Political and Social Thought' in Duncan Tanner, Pat Thane and Nick Tiratsoo (eds.), *Labour's First Century* (Cambridge: Cambridge University Press, 2000).

C. Lowell Harriss, 'Land Value Increment Taxation: Demise of the British Betterment Levy', *National Tax Journal*, 25, 4 (December 1972).

Junichi Hasegawa, 'The Rise and Fall of Radical Reconstruction in 1940s Britain', *Twentieth Century British History*, 10, 2 (1999).

Douglas Hay, 'Property, Authority and the Criminal Law' in Douglas Hay, Peter Linebaugh, John Rule and Cal Winslow (eds.), *Albion's Fatal Tree: Crime and Society in Eighteenth-Century England* (London: Allen Lane, 1975).

Stephen Heathorn, 'An English Paradise to Regain? Ebenezer Howard, the Town and Country Planning Association and English Ruralism', *Rural History*, 11, 1 (2000).

Michael Hebbert, 'Frederick Osborn, 1885–1978' in Gordon E. Cherry (ed.), *Pioneers in British Planning* (London: Architectural Press, 1981).

Christian Hilber, 'UK Housing and Planning Policies: The Evidence from Economic Research', *Centre for Economic Performance* (London: LSE, 2014).

Christopher Hill, 'The Norman Yoke' in Christopher Hill (ed.), *Puritanism and Revolution* (London: Panther, 1958).

Robert Home, 'Land Ownership in the United Kingdom: Trends, Preferences and Future Challenges', *Land Use Policy*, 26 (2009).

Alun Howkins, 'The Discovery of Rural England' in Robert Colls and Philip Dodd (eds.), *Englishness: Politics and Culture, 1880–1920* (Beckenham: Croom Helm, 1986).

Alun Howkins, 'A Country at War: Mass Observation and Rural England, 1939–45', *Rural History*, 9, 1 (1998).

Alun Howkins, 'From Diggers to Dongas: The Land in English Radicalism, 1649–2000', *History Workshop Journal*, 54 (Autumn, 2002).

Dennis Norman Jeans, 'Planning and the Myth of the English Countryside in the Interwar Period', *Rural History*, 1, 2 (1990).

Geoffrey Keogh, 'The Economics of Planning Gain' in Susan Barrett and Patsy Healey (eds.), *Land Policy: Problems and Alternatives* (Aldershot: Gower, 1985).

Philip T. Kivell and Ian McKay, 'Public Ownership of Urban Land', *Transactions of the Institute of British Geographers*, 14, 2 (1988).

Katharina Knoll, Moritz Schularick and Thomas Steger, 'No Price Like Home: Global House Prices, 1870–2012', *Centre for Economic Policy Research* (September 2014).

Rodney Lowe, 'The Second World War, Consensus and the Foundation of the Welfare State', *Twentieth Century British History*, 1 (1990).

John Lowerson, 'Battles for the Countryside' in Frank Gloversmith (ed.), *Class Culture and Social Change: A New View of the 1930s* (Brighton: Harvester Press, 1980).

Ethel Mannin, 'Town Planning and the Common Man', *Town and Country Planning*, X, 40 (Winter, 1942–43).

Terry Marsden, 'Property-State Relations in the 1980s: An Examination of Landlord–Tenant Legislation in British Agriculture' in Graham Cox, Philip Lowe and Michael Winter (eds.), *Agriculture: People and Politics* (London: Allen & Unwin, 1986).

David Martin, 'Land Reform', in Patricia Hollis (ed.), *Pressure from Without in Early Victorian England* (London: Edward Arnold, 1974).

David Matless, 'Visual Culture and Geographical Citizenship: England in the 1940s', *Journal of Historical Geography*, 22, 4 (1996).

Simon Miller, 'Urban Dreams and Rural Reality: Land and Landscape in English Culture, 1920–45', *Rural History* 6, 1 (1995).

Nigel Moor, 'Inner-City Areas and the Private Sector' in Susan Barrett and Patsy Healey (eds.), *Land Policy: Problems and Alternatives* (Aldershot: Gower, 1985).

Kenneth O. Morgan, 'The Planners' in Kenneth O. Morgan (ed.), *Labour People* (Oxford: Oxford University Press, 1987).

R. J. Moore-Colyer, 'From Great Wren to Toad Hall: Aspects of the Urban-Rural Divide in Interwar Britain', *Rural History*, 10, 1 (April 1999).

R. J. Moore-Colyer, 'A Voice Clamouring in the Wilderness: H. J. Massingham (1888–1952) and Rural England', *Rural History*, 13, 2 (2002).

J. M. Neeson, The Opponents of Enclosure in Eighteenth-Century Northamptonshire', *Past and Present*, 105, 1 (1984).

Avner Offer, 'The Origins of the Law of Property Acts, 1910–25', *The Modern Law Review*, 40, 5 (September 1977).

Avner Offer, 'Farm Tenure and Land Values in England, 1750–1950', *Economic History Review*, 44, 1 (1991).

H. R. Parker, 'Land Values, Compensation and Betterment: A Review Article', *Town Planning Review*, 53, 2 (July 1982).

Harold Perkin, 'Land Reform and Class Conflict in Victorian Britain' in John Butt and Ignatius Frederick Clarke (eds.), *The Victorians and Social Protest* (Newton Abbot: Archon Books, 1973).

Nicholas Pronay, 'The Land of Promise: The Projection of Peace Aims in Britain' in Kenneth R. M. Short (ed.), *Film and Radio Propaganda in World War Two* (London: Croom Helm, 1983).

Alison Ravetz, 'Housing the People' in Jim Fryth (ed.), *Labour's Promised Land: Culture and Society in Labour Britain, 1945–51* (London: Lawrence & Wishart, 1995).

P. C. Rickwood, 'The National Land Fund, 1946–80: The Failure of a Policy Initiative', *Leisure Studies*, 6 (1978).

Ellen Rosenman, 'On the Enclosure Acts and the Commons', *BRANCH: Britain, Representation, and Nineteenth-Century History*, Dino Franco Felluga (ed.), *Web*, 20 (2014).

Simon Rycroft and Denis Cosgrove, 'Mapping the Modern Nation: Dudley Stamp and the Land Utilisation Survey', *History Workshop Journal*, 40, 1 (1995).

Bill Schwarz, 'The Language of Constitutionalism: Baldwinite Conservatism' in Editorial Collective, *Formations of Nation and People* (London: Routledge, 1984).

Peter Scott, 'British Regional Policy, 1945–52: A Lost Opportunity', *Twentieth Century British History*, 8, 3 (1997).

John Sheail, 'The Concept of National Parks in Great Britain, 1900–1950', *Transactions of the Institute of British Geographers*, 66 (November 1975).

John Sheail, 'The Restriction of Ribbon Development Act: The Character and Perception of Land-Use Control in Inter-War Britain', *Regional Studies*, 13, 6 (1979).

John Sheail, 'Interwar Planning in Britain: The Wider Context', *Journal of Urban History*, 11, 3 (May 1985).

John Sheail, 'John Dower, National Parks and Town and Country Planning in Britain', *Planning Perspectives*, 10 (1995).

S. G. Sturmey, 'Owner-Farming in England and Wales, 1900–1950' in Walter E. Minchinton (ed.), *Essays in Agrarian History, Vol. 2* (Newton Abbot: David & Charles, 1968).

Mark Swenarton and Sandra Taylor, 'The Scale and Nature of the Growth of Owner-Occupation in Britain between the Wars', *Economic History Review*, 38, 3 (1985).

Pat Thane, 'Labour and Welfare' in Duncan Tanner, Pat Thane and Nick Tiratsoo (eds.), *Labour's First Century* (Cambridge: Cambridge University Press, 2000).

E. P. Thompson, 'The Grid of Inheritance' in E. P. Thompson (ed.), *Persons and Polemics* (London: Merlin Press, 1994).

F. M. L. Thompson, 'English Landed Society in the Twentieth Century, 1, Property: Collapse and Survival', *Transactions of the Royal Historical Society*, 40 (1990).

F. M. L. Thompson; 'English Landed Society in the Twentieth Century, 2, New Poor and New Rich', *Transactions of the Royal Historical Society*, 1 (1991).

F. M. L. Thompson; 'English Landed Society in the Twentieth Century, 3, Self-Help and Outdoor Relief', *Transactions of the Royal Historical Society*, 2 (1992).

F. M. L. Thompson; 'English Landed Society in the Twentieth Century, 4, Prestige without Power?', *Transactions of the Royal Historical Society*, 3 (1993).

F. M. L. Thompson, 'The Land Market, 1880–1925: A Reappraisal Reappraised', *Agricultural History Review*, 55, 2 (2007).

F. M. L. Thompson, 'The Strange Death of the English Land Question' in Matthew Cragoe and Paul Readman (eds.), *The Land Question in Britain, 1750–1950* (Basingstoke: Palgrave Macmillan, 2010).

Michael Tichelar, 'Socialists, Labour and the Land: The Response of the Labour Party to the Land Campaign of Lloyd George before the First World War', *Twentieth Century British History*, 8, 2 (1997).

Michael Tichelar, 'Central-Local Tensions: The Case of the Labour Party, Regional Government and Land-Use Reform during the Second World War', *Labour History Review*, 66, 2 (2001).

Michael Tichelar, 'The Labour Party and Land Reform in the Inter-War Period', *Rural History*, 13, 1 (2002).

Michael Tichelar, 'The Conflict over Property Rights during the Second World War: The Labour Party's Abandonment of Land Nationalisation', *Twentieth Century British History*, 15, 3 (2003).

Michael Tichelar, 'The Labour Party, Agricultural Policy, and the Retreat from Rural Land Nationalisation during the Second World War', *Agricultural History Review*, 51, 2 (2003).

Michael Tichelar, 'The Scott Report and the Labour Party: The Protection of the Countryside during the Second World War', *Rural History*, 15, 2 (2004).

Ursula Vogel, 'The Land Question: A Liberal Theory of Communal Property', *History Workshop Journal*, 27 (1989).

Helen Walker, 'The Popularisation of the Outdoor Movement, 1900–1940', *British Journal of Sports History*, 2 (1985).

Urlan Wannop, 'New Towns' in J. B. Cullingworth (ed.), *British Planning: 50 Years of Urban and Regional Policy* (London: Athlone Press, 1999).

J. T. Ward, 'Measuring Changes in Farm Sale Prices', *Chartered Surveyor* (December 1957).

S. Ward, 'The Town and Country Planning Act, 1932', *The Planner*, 60, 5 (May 1974).

Peter Weiler, 'The Rise and Fall of the Conservatives' Grand Design for Housing', 1951–64', *Contemporary British History*, 14, 1 (Spring, 2000).

Peter Weiler, 'Labour and the Land: From Municipalisation to the Land Commission, 1951–1971', *Twentieth Century British History*, 19, 3 (2008).

Peter Weiler, 'Labour and the Land: The Making of the Community Land Act, 1976', *Contemporary British History*, 27, 4 (2013).

Michael Winter, 'Land Use Policy in the UK: The Politics of Control', *Land Development Studies*, 7 (1990).

Michael Winter, 'Revisiting Landownership and Property Rights' in Hugh Clout (ed.), *Contemporary Rural Geographies* (London: Routledge, 2007).

Unpublished theses

J. S. Rowett, 'Labour Party and Local Government: Theory and Practice in the Inter-War Years' (Oxford: University of Oxford, DPhil, 1979).

Michael Tichelar, 'The Labour Party and Land Reform, 1900–1945' (Bristol: University of the West of England, PhD, 2000).

Tatsuya Tsubaki, 'Post-War Reconstruction and the Questions of Popular Housing Provision, 1939–1951' (Warwick: University of Warwick, PhD, 1993).

Helen Walker, 'The Outdoor Movement in England and Wales, 1900–1939' (Sussex: University of Sussex, PhD, 1988).

Index

Commonwealth Land Party
Graham Pearce.

Printed in Great Britain
by Amazon